QUEER CHRISTIANITIES

Queer Christianities

Lived Religion in Transgressive Forms

Edited by

Kathleen T. Talvacchia, Michael F. Pettinger,
and Mark Larrimore

NEW YORK UNIVERSITY PRESS
New York and London

NEW YORK UNIVERSITY PRESS
New York and London
www.nyupress.org

References to Internet websites (URLs) were accurate at the time of writing.
Neither the author nor New York University Press is responsible for URLs that
may have expired or changed since the manuscript was prepared.

LIBRARY OF CONGRESS CATALOGING-IN-PUBLICATION DATA
Queer Christianities : lived religion in transgressive forms / edited by Kathleen T.
Talvacchia, Michael F. Pettinger, and Mark Larrimore.
pages cm
Includes bibliographical references and index.
ISBN 978-1-4798-2618-6 (cl : alk. paper) -- ISBN 978-1-4798-9602-8 (pb : alk. paper)
1. Homosexuality--Religious aspects--Christianity. 2. Church work with gays. 3. Queer
theology. 4. Christianity. I. Talvacchia, Kathleen T., editor.
BR115.H6Q435 2014
  270.086'64--dc23
2014025201

New York University Press books are printed on acid-free paper,
and their binding materials are chosen for strength and durability.
We strive to use environmentally responsible suppliers and materials
to the greatest extent possible in publishing our books.

Manufactured in the United States of America

10 9 8 7 6 5 4 3 2 1

Also available as an ebook

CONTENTS

ACKNOWLEDGMENTS

Bringing this volume together has been a joy and a privilege. Working together across disciplinary boundaries, at first in our planning trio and then with our wonderfully generous contributors, has been an experience not only satisfying but uplifting. The responses and support of many interlocutors along the way have added to our sense that this project meets a need, addresses a moment, and gives voice to something important.

Our thanks go out to those who made possible the conference that inspired this volume and those who helped restructure and reimagine it as a book for a wider audience: the Provost's Office of The New School, Mark Hostetter, Karen Noyes, and Jennifer Hammer from NYU Press.

It is in that spirit of gratitude that Kathy would like to acknowledge Lauren Benton, Dean of the NYU Graduate School of Arts and Science, for supporting her scholarly work in the midst of the demands of being an Associate Dean. She would also like to extend her love and gratitude to the many members of the Talvacchia and Pak families who have given her the courage to take risks both personal and professional; to her children, Jocelyn and Chloe, who keep her honest and make her laugh with joy; and to Su Yon Pak, whose unfailing belief pushes and sustains her as a life partner and an intellectual colleague.

Michael's joy and gratitude extend to the Church of Saint Francis Xavier in Manhattan, and particularly to the men and women of the gay and lesbian ministries, as well as the students in his "Sex and Theology" seminar at Eugene Lang College, who offered enthusiastic and valuable insights in the wake of the conference. He wishes to express his appreciation for the work and support of his research assistants, Sebastian Morales-Bermudes, Aaron Pope, and Claire Codner. And last but certainly not least, Fran Snyder and Stuart Siegel listened to him collect his thoughts and scatter them again more times than he can remember or thank them for.

Mark would like to thank the endlessly resourceful students and staff of Eugene Lang College, Karen Bray, Trixie Cane, Peter Carey, Barbara DiPietro, Georgina Drew, Michael Gilligan, Tim Marshall, Elizabeth Maxwell, and Winnie Varghese, and the enduring inspiration of Victor Preller.

We dedicate the book to all queer Christians—those with the freedom to be out and those who remain hidden.

Introduction

MARK LARRIMORE

Christianity is a queer thing.
—Elizabeth Stuart, *Gay and Lesbian Theologies: Repetitions
with Critical Difference*

This book explores the living worlds of queer Christianities.

The title may disconcert. Like other traditions, Christianity has often oppressed sexually nonconforming people. The harm it has done is vast and ongoing, and yet queer people have also thrived in Christian contexts. They have made and continue to make homes for themselves within Christian traditions. But more disconcerting still, for many who believe that the terms are mutually exclusive, is the growing number of theologians and practitioners who find Christianity itself to be at heart queer. Queer folk have found Christian traditions not only hospitable to queer lives but in deep ways congruent with them. Theory and theology are only just catching up with the fact that queer Christians have for a long time been quietly constructing new identities, articulating new understandings of faith, and creating new religious communities.

Queer Christianities

The point of "queer Christianities" goes beyond noticing that there are, and always have been, "queers" in the church. This is undoubtedly the case—we are everywhere, and have long gravitated to institutions and sectors of society that work at a perpendicular to the business of pro-creative sexuality. The point is stronger, too, than the claim that Christianity can offer a place for queer folk and would be transformed in wonderful ways by explicit inclusion of gender-nonconforming people and practices. As theologian Patrick S. Cheng has shown us, this, too, is true.[1] But there is more to say.

This book's focus on "queer Christianities" rejects the premise that some relationship has yet to be established between queerness and queers on the one hand and Christianity on the other. Queer people are not outsiders to the church. Christianity has not only always had queer members, has not only always had the potential to be queered, but has from the start been a site of radical queerness. Has it also provided support and language for soul-destroying normativities, including heteronormativities? Without question. At its truest, however, Christianity challenges human idols of "nature," "morality," "family," and "identity" in queer ways. It can do this even in practices and doctrines that might seem most normalizing, like marriage and sin.

The "Christian family values" used to persecute sexual minorities in our time are themselves of recent vintage and unrepresentative of Christian tradition and promise.[2] The ideal of a society in which everyone is happily (or unhappily) married to a member of the opposite sex and all intercourse open to the possibility of procreation would strike many in the long history of Christianity as aberrant. Christianity from its origins was leery of sex, even procreative sex, though not necessarily of eros. Like every other institution of the Greco-Roman world, marriage was questioned by the earliest Christians. In his First Letter to the Corinthians, Paul had to answer the question should the followers of Jesus marry at all? By the fifth century, bishops were sometimes involved in negotiating marriage contracts and were often asked to give formal blessings at weddings.[3] How were such blessings to be differentiated from the medieval custom of blessing same-sex friendships described by historian John Boswell?[4] And when a newly established consensus that marriage was one of seven sacraments made the blessing ceremony obligatory for all licit marriages in the twelfth century, it was on a kind of analogy with the nuptials long celebrated by celibate religious with Christ.[5]

"Queering" Christianity may be necessary today not because Christianity is unqueer but because it has forgotten its own radical queerness. The sexual nonconformists' experience is the one that forces all Christians to acknowledge the parlous gift that is sexuality itself.[6] Liberation theologies have taught us a "preferential option for the poor" and excluded, teaching us to find truer Christian living among the disadvantaged. Respectable theology is shot through with ideology and domination. Women's and gay liberation theologies have shown this to be true also in questions of gender and sexuality. Marginalized people's experience is a truer framework for understanding the meaning of the gospel, and that includes the experience of sexual minorities. Theologian Marcella Althaus-Reid calls us to be thoroughly "indecent," to theologize "without underwear."[7]

Some of the most exciting work at seminaries today links queerness with postmodern and postcolonial perspectives.[8] Christianity is a religion of liberation and a celebration of the richness of human experience, but it shares with queer thinking concerns about the inclusivist logic of most theologies and politics of liberation—necessary though they are in making a more just and more human world. We all hope and strive for a future in which there is no oppression, no marginalization. Yet the totalizing tendencies of conceptions of the natural or normal, even the best-intentioned, require constant vigilance and, indeed, challenge. As Christians are called to be in the world but not of it, Christian identities are ultimately all provisional.

The word "queer" is used promiscuously in the chapters that follow. Sometimes it names an acronym that starts with the letters "LGBT," the umbrella term for the unfolding richness of sexual identities and expressions. Sometimes "queer" is something more specific—the "Q" in the acronym, the self-identification of people for whom "straight" and "gay" identities, and perhaps any fixed identities, are experienced as constraining. Sometimes "queer" understands itself to be an open frontier, a radical hospitality, a hope and even expectation that whatever we take for granted as a map of human experience will need to be redrawn again and again. Sometimes "queer" is used to articulate marginalized experience, and the margins' challenge to the norms of putative centers, even outside the context of same-sex desire. Queerness has taught us to expect surprise, even from ourselves.

We have not in this book sought uniformity in usage of the term, but this does not quite mean that anything goes. We can say that "queer" is more verb than noun or adjective, that it involves bodies but distrusts restrictive rhetorics of "nature" and "identity," that it seeks and finds boundaries and plays with them, that it challenges judgments of the pious and the licit in general and in particular. It deals with questions of great moment in experiences often deeply painful, but queering is fundamentally about the discovery of new pleasures and relationships. It expects and encourages fluidity, risk, and play. Christian queerness experiences the paradoxical workings of divine grace and love in all this. The Christian mystery is, after all, a scandal to law, foolishness to thought.[9] Its appetite for disruption is prophetic.

Transgressive Forms: Celibacies, Matrimonies, Promiscuities

We speak of "queer Christian*ities*" to emphasize the diversity within Christianity and to resist temptations to uniformity, to what several of our authors call "normalization." Queer Christians experience their lives as sacred work—a work at whose heart is a kind of disrupting clarifying transforming play. "Queerness" is not an identity but a playing with identity and identities in the great and small moments and relationships of actual lives. And yet at the heart of these queer Christian lives we find what might at first seem a paradox: people *committed* to living in unsettled and unsettling ways. Queer Christians do not just transgress against the forms of an oppressive and heteronormative Christianity, but find specific Christian practices themselves—sometimes the most orthodox!—to be forms of and for transgression.

This book is structured around a trinity of states of queer Christian life: *celibacies*, *matrimonies*, and *promiscuities*. "States of life" is an old Roman Catholic name for settled Christian commitments, something we intend not to dismiss but to honor by our queering. We've chosen fusty old names because they allow us to be more playful in appraising, appropriating and reimagining the forms of Christian lives, and for good measure we've pluralized them. The plurals force us to see generative, restless multiplicity even in those institutions that seem most defined, and patterns and choices in what otherwise might seem shapeless and undefinable. Queer Christian lives are wildly, deliciously varied and can be expected to keep pushing the limits of normalizing structures of all kinds, but they are themselves lived out in forms of Christian life. Here we find answers not only to *why* one might find queer good news in Christianity but to *how* one might actually live out a queerly Christian life.

"Celibacy" and "matrimony" are traditional (at least in the singular): they are recognized and sanctioned states of Christian sexual life. "Promiscuity" decidedly is not. It's not a nice term, not a common self-identifier, and it is often used in prejudicial ways. It's a troubling term, but for all these reasons the unsettled plural "promiscuities" is helpful for engaging the many other forms of queer Christian life as forms of transgression, and indeed transgressive forms. Promiscuities embraces all the things celibate and married folk are not supposed to be—so much so that we must wonder if the terms are not defined by mutual exclusion. Too much of Christian life is based on unacknowledged and even mutual structures of shaming and exclusion.[10]

Yet this structure of inclusion and exclusion has been anything but stable. The Protestant Reformation universalized heterosexual marriage, even while demoting its status as a sacrament. To modern understandings of sexual identity and expression, too, celibacy seems the queerest thing of all—as it seemed already to the world around early Christianities. Marriage, meanwhile, continues to change its meaning and scope. The extension to all adult citizens of "marriage equality" banks on a stability of definition and purpose it never had (which may be good news for the marrying kind, too!). Promiscuities, for most of tradition relegated to an outer darkness called sexual sin, contains multitudes—including, perhaps, the key to what makes a celibacy or matrimony Christian.

The triad celibacies-matrimonies-promiscuities, like triangles and trinities of all kinds, is designed for tension. Aligning these words in this way—plural, parallel, and unranked—*should* be upsetting. A text that did not produce discomfort through its testing of status and contrast would not deserve the name queer—or Christian. Nobody *really* thinks that all or even most of celibacies, matrimonies, and promiscuities are equally legitimate forms of life, let alone Christian life. Three-legged stools may be stable, but every human triangle has been explosive, thank God. A book like this could not be written by one person, or even three. To maximize its punch, its contributions challenge us and each other in content, discipline, method, and voice. Some of the chapters are more traditionally scholarly, others more reflective and even sermonic, many engage personal experience. Queer religious experience demands an openness to methodologies beyond any theory-practice divide.

Exploring these states of life together, traditional understandings of the good of sexuality are revealed as more internally varied, fluid, and indeed mutually interdefined than many traditional theologians have imagined. Many committed celibates—women and men—were married to Christ, even as their humanly unpartnered state was thought to make them open to a promiscuous hospitality. Early heterosexual marriages and contemporary "ex-gay" marriages aspire to a kind of celibate matrimony, while all good marriages explode the human dyad in a fruitfulness shortchanged by merely biological understandings of fecundity.[11] And queer Christian promiscuities ranging from the structured scenes of BDSM to erotic friendship invite us to richer and more complex understandings of the potentially transgressive queerness of relationships and experiences in all their forms.

Lived Religion

What unites all the chapters in this book is a commitment to understanding queer Christianities through the forms of experience. This is more radical than it may seem. Recent work in the academic study of religion has drawn attention to the importance of "lived religion" not only in individual experiences but also in the articulation and unfolding of traditions.[12] The way religion actually lives is distorted by the tendency to think of religions quintessentially as systems of beliefs and practices, anchored in sacred texts, maintained by trained elites and conducted in official houses of structured worship. As sociologist Meredith B. McGuire has argued, this focus on "upper body religion" emerged in Western culture only in recent centuries.[13]

Religious studies here meets theology, which has in recent decades reframed itself in "contextual" terms. As theologian Stephen B. Bevans explains, contextual theologies bring together "the faith experience of the *past* . . . recorded in scriptures and kept alive, preserved, defended— and perhaps even neglected and suppressed—in tradition" with the "experience of the present, the *context* . . . [of] individual and contemporary-collective experience."[14] Theology has always been contextual, of course, but only in our time have theologians fully acknowledged this and factored it into their self-understanding. Bevans continues: "As Filipino theologian Leonardo N. Mercado puts it, 'The people are the best contextualizers'; and the role of the theologian is to function as a mid-wife to the people as they give birth to a theology that is truly rooted in a culture and moment in history."[15] This realization redefines the relationship between the theologian and believers at large in a manner congruent with that being explored by scholars of lived religion.

Only to outsiders do religious communities seem uniform, their authorities unified, and their laities docile. So many religious texts preach devotion, obedience, and orthodoxy precisely because so many religious people, including perhaps the most serious, are doing religion on their own terms. As historian Robert A. Orsi has put it, "There is . . . no religion that people have not taken up in their hands"[16]—an insight we would want only to amplify by bringing in whole bodies and their desires. Many queer religious people find their bodily and their spiritual experience to be the twin lodestars of their lives.[17] The nonnormative character of their desires and relationships makes them unusually aware of their own agency as religious people, but what they do is in many ways no different from what all people do. The study of lived religion turns received notions of religious inspiration, competence, and purity on their heads by seeing ordinary people as creatively forming their own religious worlds, with or without the resources and authorities of religious traditions, if not indeed against them. (Ecclesiastical authorities did and do not always look kindly on these processes, needless to say.)

If it is in the crucible of actual lives that religious practices and ideas thrive or wither, it is also in this crucible that religion is recast and reinvented. The creative religious agency of ordinary people is a challenge to and for traditional scholars of religion no less than for theologians, and not only for those who think of religion in terms of systems and wholes. A reexamination of everyday lived experience means seeing the potential for religious creativity and complexity not only in nonspecialist and nonauthorized lives but in everyday experience—an experience that generations of prophets and theorists have seen as at best inert, and more likely destructive of religious ideas. Lived experience challenges views that implicitly or explicitly pathologize this-worldly, embodied experiences of all kinds.

"Experience" is more complicated and conflicted than it seems. The idea of private experience may seem the last refuge of nonconforming individuals and communities fighting hegemonic domination and explanation, but experience is not reliably self-interpreting.[18] Experience is always comprehended socially, intersubjectively, if not necessarily uncontentiously. Experiences are both individual and shared, shaped by and in turn shaping practices and discourses shot through with power relations. Experience is not passive, any more than malleable bodily, social, and spiritual desires are. In exploring queer Christianities, experience is in need of both critique and trust. A hermeneutics bringing together suspicion, retrieval, and action is called for. The chapters in this book share queer Christians' never completed work of owning bodily, social, and spiritual experiences and shaping them into lives through forms old and new.

Queer people are especially clear-eyed about these processes. No queer Christian ever had an easy time defining and inhabiting her form of life. (Two of this volume's three editors left the church at one point, one of them returning to a different denomination.) The pain and the privilege of lives structured by nonconforming desires is a greater intentionality—one from which all Christians might well learn. Attention to lived experience shows how religion itself lives, how ideas and practices spread and change. Agency and imagination can be found throughout Christian communities. There are rich resources for reflection to be found at each level, and in the relations—not always conflictual—between levels.

Nobody is a Christian in a bubble. Every Christian has an understanding of the Christian past, of its moments of glory and of shame, and of the ways to recognize and avoid the latter. Every Christian is aware, if not always appreciative, of the variety of Christian lives in and beyond the circumstances of her own life—perhaps never more so than today. Every Christian finds ways of understanding the deepest, most exalting, and most troubling parts of their selves in terms of Christian categories, rituals, or relationships. Lived religion is not "fixed, unitary, or even particularly coherent"; the religions we live out offer at best a "practical coherence."[19] Queer Christian lives have more to make sense of and may find this predicament itself a gift.

Christian life cannot be understood only in terms of individuals and their relationships, however, much though one may sometimes wish it could be. Church communities play a crucial role in Christianity's queer work, even as they have done much harm in blessing and enforcing unjust social orders. The shared life of worshipping communities, an indispensable part of any picture of Christianity, is more varied than most people both within and outside Christian institutions appreciate. As reminders of the queer work church can do, this book includes two "Church Interludes," placed between the larger parts, exploring states of life. One describes the way an established church has responded to the call of its queer members. The second explores the creation of a new church community whose decolonizing Christian response to "oppression sickness" requires the recovery of old and even non-Christian practices.

*   *   *

Our offer of a variety of uses of "queer" and a deliberately destabilizing triangle of states of life—we seek no hierarchy, closure, or synthesis!— is not merely arbitrary. The chapters that follow have been commissioned and arranged to provide a stimulating colloquy, by turns pleasing and upsetting but never, we hope, dull or irrelevant. Within each of the three parts readers will encounter ideas to deepen or unsettle their understanding of Christian pasts, to amplify or challenge their sense of the range of contemporary forms of queer Christian living, and to inspire reflection—theoretical or theological. Read together, they not only complement but also complicate each other in the queer ways just described. The disturbance patterns created by the chapters within each of the three parts, and those generated between the parts, offer a rich portrait of the paradox and promise of queer Christianities.

NOTES

1. Patrick S. Cheng, *Radical Love: An Introduction to Queer Theology* (New York: Seabury, 2011).
2. Jane Shaw, "Reformed and Enlightened Church," in *Queer Theology: Rethinking the Western Body*, ed. Gerard Loughlin (Oxford: Blackwell, 2007), 215–29.
3. See Philip Lyndon Reynolds, *Marriage in the Western Church: The Christianization of Marriage during the Patristic and Early Medieval Periods* (Leiden: E. J. Brill, 2001). For the complications that negotiating and blessing a marriage could pose for an individual bishop, see David G. Hunter, "Augustine and the Making of Marriage in Roman North Africa," *Journal of Early Christian Studies* 11 (2003): 63–85.

4. John Boswell, *Same-Sex Unions in Premodern Europe* (New York: Villard, 1994).

5. Gerard Loughlin, "Introduction: The End of Sex," in *Queer Theology: Rethinking the Western Body*, ed. Gerard Loughlin (Oxford: Blackwell, 2007), 1–34.

6. Rowan Williams, "The Body's Grace," in *Sexuality and Theology: Classic and Contemporary Readings*, ed. Eugene F. Rogers (Oxford: Blackwell, 2002), 309–21.

7. Marcella Althaus-Reid, *Indecent Theology: Theological Perversions in Sex, Gender and Politics* (London: Routledge, 2000).

8. Susannah Cornwall has remarked that queer theology seems much more capacious a category than queer theory. Cornwall, *Controversies in Queer Theology* (Louisville, KY: Westminster John Knox Press, 2011).

9. 1 Corinthians 1:23.

10. James Alison, *Faith beyond Resentment: Fragments Catholic and Gay* (New York: Crossroad, 2001).

11. Margaret A. Farley, *Just Love: A Framework for Christian Sexual Ethics* (New York: Continuum, 2006), 226.

12. See Robert A. Orsi, *Between Heaven and Earth: The Religious Worlds People Make and the Scholars Who Study Them* (Princeton, NJ: Princeton University Press, 2006); and more generally Robert A. Orsi, ed., *The Cambridge Companion to Religious Studies* (Cambridge: Cambridge University Press, 2012).

13. Meredith B. McGuire, *Lived Religion: Faith and Practice in Everyday Life* (New York: Oxford University Press, 2008), 39, drawing on Peter Burke, *Popular Culture in Early Modern Europe* (London: Temple Smith, 1978).

14. Stephen B. Bevans, *Models of Contextual Theology*, rev. ed. (Maryknoll, NY: Orbis, 2002), 5. See also Stephen B. Bevans and Katalina Tahaafe-Williams, eds., *Contextual Theology for the Twenty-First Century* (Eugene, OR: Wipf and Stock, 2011).

15. Bevans, *Models of Contextual Theology*, 18, citing Leonardo N. Mercado, "Notes on Christ and Local Community in the Philippine Context," *Verbum SVD* 21 (1980): 303; and Mercado, *Elements of Filipino Theology* (Tacloban, Philippines: Divine Word University, 1975), 13.

16. Robert A. Orsi, "Is the Study of Lived Religion Irrelevant to the World We Live In?," *Journal for the Scientific Study of Religion* 42 (2003): 172.

17. Melissa M. Wilcox, *Queer Women and Religious Individualism* (Bloomington: Indiana University Press, 2009).

18. Robert Sharf, "Experience," in *Critical Terms for Religious Studies*, ed. Mark C. Taylor (Chicago: University of Chicago Press, 1998), 94–116.

19. McGuire, *Lived Religion*, 185, 15.

PART I

Celibacies

Celibacy was long the most prized among Christian "states of life"—indeed, the paradigmatic state of Christian life, distinguished from pagan and Jewish practices. It may seem today no more than an anachronism, a pathology haunting the Christian traditions, but as the chapters in this part suggest, such a judgment would be premature.

Like "Matrimonies" and "Promiscuities," the title of this part invokes a traditional term ripe for queering. "Celibacy" abuts other terms and forms of living, including chastity, abstinence, asceticism, and asexuality, and raises questions of nonsexual eros and mystical sex. It is the only form of sexual life many churches permit their queer members. All these people might be bothered by our pluralizing insistence—not "celibacy" but "celibac*ies*"—that the meaning is neither obvious, unitary, nor stable.

The chapters in this part set out to complicate received understandings of celibacies from historical and contemporary experience. David G. Hunter traces the unlikely emergence of celibacy as the ideal of religious life in the earliest Christian centuries and marks its queer potential. Lynne Gerber explores the equally unlikely emergence of celibacy as an ideal in our own time, in communities of Evangelical "ex-gays," and finds these new forms of life destabilizing modern Protestant ideals of hetcrosexual marriage. Anthony M. Petro assesses the possibility and significance of "queer Christian celibacy" for a secular queer politics, finding it to have a far more transgressive potential than may at first appear. Finally, Sister Carol Bernice speaks *as* a contemporary queer Christian celibate, the quiet eloquence of her reflections on her life demonstrating the inspiring power of consummated experience.

In our time no less than in times past, what sounds most orthodox in theory can prove the queerest in practice.

1

Celibacy Was Queer

Rethinking Early Christianity

DAVID G. HUNTER

Sometime early in the fifth century in the Egyptian desert near Sce-
tis (modern Wadi El Natrun), a prominent spiritual teacher known as
Amma Sara was approached by two desert monks. In an effort to test
the old woman, they warned her not to become conceited because male
ascetics came to her for spiritual advice and counseling. Amma Sara
remained undaunted. "According to nature I am a woman," she replied,
"but not according to my thoughts." On another occasion Amma Sara
spoke to her male disciples even more pointedly about her female spiritual authority: "I am the man; you are the women."[1]

This anecdote helps to illustrate the central argument of this chapter: that the practice of celibacy among the early Christians can properly be considered a form of "queer Christianity." "Queer" is used here
in one of the senses delineated by Patrick S. Cheng, that is, to refer to
a transgressive form of religious life, especially one that is "transgressive or opposed to societal norms, particularly with respect to sexuality
and gender identity."[2] Amma Sara, by virtue of her ascetic behavior—
the renunciation of sex, marriage, property, and all the other features
of "normal" human life—attained a level of spiritual discernment that
enabled her to adopt a "male" role in ancient monastic society. This
inversion of gender roles was just one of several ways in which the
early Christian practice and theology of celibacy "queered" traditional
social norms. The early Christian exaltation of celibacy as the ideal of
human behavior profoundly devalued marriage and procreation and

subverted the traditional patriarchal household as the bedrock of civic and political life. In the course of rationalizing and defending celibacy, early Christian writers developed new notions of human "nature" that decentered binary categories such as "male" and "female" and relegated all sexual activity (heterosexual as well as homosexual) to an ancillary, even "unnatural," aspect of the human person.[3] Such transgressive practices and discourse deserve to be called "queer."

The Origins of Christian Celibacy

Celibacy in one form or another has been practiced in most of the world's religions. If we want to understand its specifically Christian meanings and functions, we must take a closer look at its historical emergence within the web of beliefs and practices that constitutes ancient Christianity. A good place to begin is the following statement from a prominent bishop of the early fourth century, Eusebius of Caesarea, a noted historian, apologist, and biographer of the first Christian emperor Constantine. Writing in his apology, *The Proof of the Gospel*, Eusebius characterized the two modes of life prevalent in the Christianity of his day:

> Two ways of life were thus given by the law of Christ to His Church. The one is above nature and beyond common human living; it admits not marriage, child-bearing, property nor the possession of wealth, but wholly and permanently separated from the common customary life of mankind, it devotes itself to the service of God alone in its wealth of heavenly love! And they who enter on this course, appear to die to the life of mortals, to bear with them nothing earthly but their body, and in mind and spirit to have passed to heaven . . . . Such then is the perfect form of the Christian life.

After thus characterizing the "perfect" life of the celibate Christian, Eusebius turned to "the other more humble, more human" way:

> [This] prompts human beings to join in pure nuptials and to produce children, to undertake government, to give orders to soldiers fighting for right; it allows them to have minds for farming, for trade, and the other

more worldly interests as well as for religion . . . . And a kind of second-ary grade of piety is attributed to them . . . so that all people . . . have their part in the coming of salvation, and profit by the teaching of the Gospel.[4]

Eusebius's statement was virtual orthodoxy in the early fourth cen-tury: celibacy was a heavenly way of life, as vastly superior to marriage as heaven was to earth. Celibate Christians find themselves embraced in a "heavenly *eros*," as Eusebius put it; by dying to earthly life, they anticipate the life of the resurrection. In contrast to married Christians, whose hearts and minds were fixed resolutely on earth, the celibate enjoyed a foretaste of heaven, where, as Jesus said, they would neither marry nor be given in marriage (e.g., Matthew 22:30). This "virtual orthodoxy" of Eusebius became actual orthodoxy by the end of the fourth century, when a monk named Jovinian was condemned as a her-etic for rejecting this hierarchy of "states of life."[5] Only in the Protestant Reformation of the sixteenth century do we find Christians once again seriously challenging the idea that celibacy was the ideal form of Chris-tian life.

It seems odd that Christianity should have developed such a positive emphasis on celibacy. Jewish tradition, out of which early Christian-ity emerged, was not, by and large, sympathetic to celibacy. The Jew-ish scriptures affirmed the goodness (even the necessity) of procreation, and early rabbinic tradition interpreted Genesis 1:28 (the injunction to "increase and multiply") as the first of the commandments. Sayings attributed to Jesus in the New Testament affirmed the permanence of marriage and rejected traditional Jewish allowance of divorce and remarriage. Citing passages from Genesis, such as "God made them male and female" (Genesis 1:27) and "the two shall become one flesh" (Genesis 2:24), Jesus is said to have declared: "What God has joined together, let not man put asunder" (Mark 10:6–9). Jesus's prohibition of remarriage after divorce, which was echoed in Paul's teaching as well (cf. 1 Corinthians 7:10), eventually became the basis of the traditional Christian notion of a sacramental bond of marriage that persists until the death of one of the spouses.

Despite this affirmation of the permanence of marriage, other ten-dencies emerged in early Christianity that favored celibacy. Most nota-ble of these was the apostle Paul's discussion of the topic in his First

Letter to the Corinthians, a passage that became fundamental to all later Christian reflection on marriage and celibacy. Paul was no extremist. He argued that Christians who were married should continue to have sexual relations with each other, although the reason for this permission was rather grudging: "lest Satan tempt you because of your lack of self-control" (1 Corinthians 7:5). He also allowed that unmarried Christians might marry, although, again, his rationale was essentially a negative one. If the unmarried and widows cannot exercise self-control, they should marry, Paul writes, "for it is better to marry than to be aflame with passion" (1 Corinthians 7:9). The reason for Paul's preference for celibacy, it seems, was his expectation that Jesus would return shortly, that the dead would be raised, and that the entire cosmos would be transformed into the kingdom of God. In view of this impending crisis, it was best for all Christians to remain in the state of celibacy or marriage in which they found themselves (1 Corinthians 7:26). Even those who had wives, Paul urged, "should be as though they had none" (1 Corinthians 7:29).

Paul's teaching had an enormous impact on subsequent Christian tradition. In later times, when the expectation of an imminent end of time had faded, Christians looked back on his words as a paradigm for all time and not just for an interim. Paul's view that a lack of self-control was the only real reason to marry suggested to many later Christians that marriage was only for the weak and self-indulgent. Moreover, neither Paul nor Jesus said anything about procreation as a legitimate purpose of sex or marriage. Removed from their original context, Paul's words sounded like a simple declaration of the superiority of celibacy over marriage, rather than a provisional ethic in place until Jesus returned in the Second Coming.

Given this ambivalent legacy, it is not surprising that Christians in the second century displayed divergent views on the matter of celibacy. The mainstream or "orthodox" position seems to have been that marriage was permissible, though usually only once and only for procreation. Christian apologists, such as Justin Martyr, Minucius Felix, and Athenagoras of Athens, articulated this strict moral position in the hope that non-Christian critics would stop believing rumors about Christian orgies and would accept Christians as exemplars of a self-controlled way of life.[6] But a number of Christians took a more radical view and repudiated sexual activity altogether. The view that celibacy was required of all Christians was held by some Gnostic Christians, as well as by the followers of Marcion and a Greek writer from Syria named Tatian. Marcion believed that an inferior and immoral Creator-God had produced the world, not the loving almighty Father of Jesus. In Marcion's view, Christians were forbidden to marry or to procreate, lest they perpetuate the corrupt creation of this wicked god.[7]

A slightly more moderate position was taken by Tatian, a man often credited with founding the "Encratite" heresy (from the Greek *enkrateia*, meaning "self-control" or, in this case, "celibacy"). According to Tatian, humans were originally created as a harmonious union of body, soul, and spirit. Having rejected their union with God's Spirit, the first human beings lost their immortal nature and became involved in the bestial activities of sex, birth, and death.[8] Tatian admitted that sexual relations had been necessary near the beginning of time when the population needed to grow, but now that Christ has come and inaugurated a new age, sex is no longer to be tolerated. Although Tatian's views were labeled "heresy" by the earliest Christian heresy hunters (e.g., Irenaeus, Hippolytus, and Clement of Alexandria), they remained congenial to many second-century Christians. Various writings known as "apocryphal" gospels and acts of apostles appeared in the second and third centuries espousing the central tenets of Encratite theology. Works such as the *Acts of Judas Thomas* and the *Acts of Paul and Thecla* circulated for centuries, and well beyond the so-called heretical groups that originally produced them.

In the third century it seems that enthusiasm for celibacy became an even more pronounced feature of ancient Christianity. Two writers exerted a profound influence on the subsequent shape of Christian theology: Tertullian and Origen. Tertullian, a native of North Africa, was an antiheretical writer who had attacked Marcion for rejecting the created world. But Tertullian himself came under the influence of a charismatic movement, the "New Prophecy," that proclaimed the imminent end of the world. Tertullian came to see sex, even within marriage, as a kind of "sin." Commenting on Paul's statement in 1 Corinthians 7:9 that it was better to marry than to burn with passion, Tertullian argued that if marriage is "good" only by comparison with something worse, then "it is not so much a good as it is a kind of lesser evil."[9] Although he came to be regarded as a heretic himself, Tertullian's views exerted significant influence on later writers. In the fourth century, for example, the church father Jerome frequently borrowed from Tertullian's writings (usually without acknowledgment) in his own enthusiastic pronouncements for celibacy.

Another influential third-century author, Origen of Alexandria, likewise bequeathed to posterity a vision of celibacy that resembled in some ways the rigorist views of Tatian. Origen believed that humans were originally created to be purely spiritual creatures. But after these first spirits fell from their original condition, God decided to make a physical world in which they might learn to turn back to God.[10] Because the goal of these creatures is to return to their original state of spiritual contemplation, Origen regarded sexual activity as a dangerous distraction, a regrettable necessity caused by the primal sin. Commenting on Paul's First Letter to the Corinthians, for example, Origen wrote:

> Do not think that the body is meant for sexual intercourse, just because "the stomach is meant for food and food for the stomach" (1 Cor 6:13). If you want to know the chief reason for the existence of the body, take note: it is meant to be a temple for the Lord, and the soul is meant to be holy and blameless, to serve as a handmaid to the Holy Spirit and to become a priest to the Holy Spirit that is within you. For Adam had a body in paradise, and yet it was not in paradise that "Adam knew his wife Eve" (Gen 4:1), but when he had been expelled after the disobedience.[11]

Here Origen presents a theme that was dear to the Encratite tradition, but one that eventually found its way even into the writings of the most "orthodox" Christians. Observing that Genesis 4:1 ("Now Adam knew his wife Eve, and she conceived and bore Cain") stated that sexual relations occurred only after their expulsion from paradise, most Christians in the early church concluded that sexual activity and procreation were strictly "postlapsarian" phenomena, that is, they occurred only after the "fall" (*lapsus*) of Adam and Eve. Thus it was the "original sin" of the first humans and their subsequent mortality that made sexual reproduction necessary to create the human race.

The upshot of this early Christian viewpoint was that human sexuality was no longer considered part of the original (or final) constitution of human beings. All sexual activity—even heterosexual intercourse for the purpose of procreation—was a departure from nature as originally created and, therefore, in a sense "unnatural." This position is found in the work of a number of the Greek and Latin fathers, even some of those who did not share Origen's idea of the preexistence of souls. One of the more moderate Greek fathers, John Chrysostom, argued in an early treatise on virginity that in paradise the first human beings lived in a wholly nonsexual state: "Desire for sexual intercourse, conception, labor, childbirth and every form of corruption had been banished from their souls. As a clear river shooting forth from a pure source, so were they in that place adorned by virginity." Marriage, by contrast, according to Chrysostom, "springs from disobedience, from a curse, from death."[12]

In the early fifth century Augustine of Hippo gave his own unique take on what was now widely regarded as the "problem" of sex, marriage, and procreation. Unlike many of his contemporaries, Augustine rejected the Encratite/Origenist assumption that the body and sexuality were inherently postlapsarian phenomena. He insisted that God had originally created humans as physical and sexual persons. Prior to their fall from grace in the Garden of Eden, Adam and Eve *could* have engaged in sex and produced children without sin, if they had remained obedient to God's command not to eat from the forbidden tree. Had they not sinned, they would eventually have chosen the proper time to procreate, and their bodies would have worked in harmonious union with their minds and wills.

But something went wrong with this ideal scenario. Before actually engaging in intercourse, the first humans disobeyed God and suffered the penalty of sin and death. Although Augustine believed in the original bodily and (hetero-) sexual nature of Adam and Eve, he came to believe that human nature had been profoundly damaged by the "original sin," specifically in its sexual functioning. Besides mortality and bodily weakness, Augustine argued, Adam and Eve (and all their subsequent offspring) suffered a distortion of their sexual nature that led to disordered desires, "concupiscence (or lust) of the flesh." Because of this disruption in their original nature, human beings now experience sexual desire as something beyond the full control of reason and will, directed randomly to licit and illicit objects alike. While it can be harnessed and directed toward procreation, sexual desire remains a troublesome and distracting dimension of human experience.

For the purposes of this chapter, the significance of Augustine's teaching is that it placed all human sexual activity—heterosexual as well as homosexual—under the shadow of sin. There is no longer any "natural" use of sex, that is, any sexual activity free of the pernicious influence of lust. Even when married couples engage in heterosexual intercourse with the sole intention of producing children—something that rarely or never happened, Augustine candidly admitted—an element of unrestrained, irrational (and, therefore, evil) desire is present. Although Augustine accepted that procreation in itself was something good, it was the good use of something evil, namely, the "lust of the flesh." Moreover, because Augustine believed that the original purpose of procreation was to produce the line of the Jewish people that would lead to Christ, he thought that there was no longer any positive reason to procreate children after the coming of Christ. As a result, Augustine believed, it was best to pray for the help of God to avoid sexual activity altogether and to embrace celibacy.[13]

Much of the early Christian idealization of celibacy flowed directly from a tendency to view sex, marriage, and procreation as a result of the primal sin. This, however, was not the only rationale given for celibacy. In a number of ascetic writings one finds the notion that the celibate man or woman has entered into a spiritual marriage with Christ. For example, we find the erotic imagery of the Song of Songs transformed into an ascetic romance between Christ (the royal Bridegroom) and the individual celibate Christian (the bride). By the late fourth century, this biblical motif found liturgical expression in a ritual of virginal consecration in which young women were "married" to Christ in a ceremony modeled on a Roman wedding.[14] Augustine, for one, hoped that the virgin's spousal union with Christ might result in a more intense love of Christ.[15] More often than not, however, the elevation of celibacy was posited on the depreciation of all sexual activity and, specifically, on its association with original sin.

Despite the differences between the extreme asceticism of Marcion and Tatian and the more moderate views of John Chrysostom and Augustine, they all share the assumption that heterosexual intercourse and procreation, as practiced in this life, do not belong to human nature in its original or ideal state. Traditional marriage is part of the "fallen" state, not the original creation. The dominant Christian tradition came to view marriage and procreation as the choice of an inferior life, a third-best option after virginity and permanent widowhood. Echoing the apostle Paul, much of the subsequent Christian tradition, at least until the Reformation, insisted that marriage and procreation were options for the weak, that is, for those without the power (or gift) of celibacy.

Conclusion: Those "Queer" Early Christians

In what sense, then, can the early Christian practice and discourse of celibacy be regarded as "queer"? First, as the foregoing discussion has shown, much of early Christian thought "denaturalized" traditional cultural assumptions about the necessity and divine origins of sex, marriage, and procreation. By separating all sexual activity from the nature originally created by God, early Christian discourse also "decentered" social institutions, such as the family and household, which Greeks, Romans, and Jews considered the foundation of social and political life. Early Christian enthusiasm for celibacy placed a profound question mark over what might be called traditional "family values." It had been axiomatic in Greco-Roman culture that the marital union of the couple was the foundation of the household, the city, and the state. As the Roman statesman and philosopher Marcus Tullius Cicero wrote: "The origin of society is in the joining of men and women, next in children, then in the household, all things held in common; this is the foundation of the city and, so to speak, the seed-bed of the state."[16] If, as Cheng has suggested, "queer" refers to "a self-conscious embrace of all that is transgressive of societal norms, particularly in the context of sexuality and gender identity," then the early Christian doctrine of celibacy could be said to have "queered" the traditional commitment to marriage and procreation that was the foundation of both Jewish and Greco-Roman cultures.[17]

Second, scholars of early Christianity have increasingly recognized that the ascetic life, and celibacy in particular, contributed to a kind of destabilization of gender relations and even gender categories, at least as represented in the extant literature. We have already seen the example of Amma Sara. Similar examples of "gender-bending" can be found throughout the ascetic texts of ancient Christianity, such as, for example, the stories of the apostle Thecla in the *Acts of Paul and Thecla* composed sometime in the second century. In this imaginative narrative the maiden Thecla, captivated by the preaching of Paul regarding sexual continence, rejects her suitor Thamyris to adopt the virginal life. In the course of her adventures Thecla escapes from execution by burning and exposure to wild beasts, baptizes herself in a pool of ravenous seals, and follows the apostle, even to the point of clothing herself as a man.

While the story of Thecla is almost certainly a fiction, it captured the imagination of Christians for centuries. Tertullian, for example, says that women appealed to the example of Thecla to defend their right to preach and baptize.[18] Sites associated with Thecla remained the locus of pilgrimage for centuries. The fourth-century pilgrim Egeria speaks of her visit to the shrine of Saint Thecla in Isauria, where the *Acts of Paul and Thecla* were read in their entirety in a liturgical context.[19] It is difficult to find an ascetic text in late antiquity that does *not* make reference to Thecla as the model of a female virgin who transcended (and transgressed) the accepted norms of gendered behavior.[20] The notion of the female ascetic as a "manly woman" or as a woman who had attained "manly virtue" became a rhetorical commonplace in ancient ascetic literature. It was a potent reminder of the manner in which celibate Christians, especially women, transgressed cultural norms and redefined (one might say "queered") traditional definitions of virtue.[21]

Finally, Christian celibacy led to the creation of new forms of human community that offered new modes of life to men and women in the ancient world. Same-sex communities—monasteries of male and female ascetics—sprang up throughout the Mediterranean beginning in the third century. Female monasteries offered a viable alternative to life in a patriarchal household and new opportunities for the education of women and the exercise of female leadership. Male communities offered new scope for advancement and the exercise of talent outside of the military or traditional civic *cursus honorum*. Celibacy made possible a concentration of resources that led, in Christian monasticism, to the creation of hospitals, schools, and other institutions on which civilization has come to depend. If it is "queer" to question the hegemony of traditional ideals of marriage, to destabilize gender distinctions, and to create alternative lifestyles and new forms of community, then early Christian celibacy was decidedly "queer."

NOTES

1. Trans. in Benedicta Ward, *The Sayings of the Desert Fathers: The Alphabetical Collection* (Kalamazoo, MI: Cistercian Publications, 1975), 230.
2. Patrick S. Cheng, *Radical Love: An Introduction to Queer Theology* (New York: Seabury, 2011), 5.
3. According to Cheng, another common meaning of "queer" is "the erasing or deconstructing of boundaries, particularly with respect to the essentialist or fixed binary categories of sexuality and gender" (ibid., 8).
4. Eusebius of Caesarea, *Demonstratio evangelica* 1.8 (PG 22.76), trans. W. J. Ferrar, *Eusebius: The Proof of the Gospel*, vol. 1 (London: SPCK, 1920), 48–50, slightly altered.
5. On the Jovinianist controversy, see David G. Hunter, *Marriage, Celibacy, and Heresy in Ancient Christianity: The Jovinianist Controversy* (Oxford: Oxford University Press, 2007).
6. Justin, *Apologia 1*, 15, 29; Minucius Felix, *Octavius* 31.5; Athenagoras, *Legatio pro Christianis* 33.6.
7. The most extensive source for the thought of Marcion is the *Adversus Marcionem* of Tertullian.
8. Tatian, *Oratio ad Graecos* 11.1.
9. Tertullian, *De exhortatione ad castitatem* 3.
10. Origen, *De principiis* 1.4–5.
11. Origen, fr. 29 in *Fragmenta ex commentariis in 1 Cor.*, ed. C. Jenkins, *Journal of Theological Studies* 8–9 (1908): 370–71.
12. John Chrysostom, *De virginitate* 14.3 and 14.6, trans. in Elizabeth A. Clark and Sally R. Shore, *John Chrysostom: On Virginity, against Remarriage* (New York: Edwin Mellen Press, 1983), 21–22. In some of his later, more mature writings, John Chrysostom softened the ascetic rhetoric of his youth and came to speak of sex and marriage in more positive terms.
13. Augustine's fully developed theory of creation, fall, and sexual concupiscence appeared only around the year 410 in his treatise *De Genesi ad litteram*. After that, it was repeated frequently, e.g., in *De nuptiis et concupiscentia, Contra Julianum, Opus imperfectum contra Julianum*, and *De civitate dei*.
14. This ritual, however, is found only in the Western church. Ambrose of Milan was an especially vocal proponent of it. See his treatises *De virginibus, De virginitate, De institutione virginis*, and *Exhortatio virginitatis*.
15. Augustine, *De sancta virginitate* 40.41.
16. Cicero, *De officiis* 1.17.54.
17. Cheng, *Radical Love*, 6.
18. Tertullian, *De baptismo* 17.

19. Egeria, *Peregrinatio ad loca sancta* 22–23.

20. One can find a thorough overview of the development of Thecla-centered piety in Stephen J. Davis, *The Cult of Saint Thecla: A Tradition of Women's Piety in Late Antiquity* (Oxford: Oxford University Press, 2001). One sees this social subversion in the example of other women in the apocryphal acts who spurn their husbands, rejecting patriarchal authority in pursuit of higher loyalties, e.g., the story of Mygdonia, wife of Charisius, in the *Acts of Thomas.*

21. Many of the relevant sources are treated in Gillian Cloke, *This Female Man of God: Women and Spiritual Power in the Patristic Age, 350–450 AD* (London: Routledge, 1995).

2

"Queerish" Celibacy

Reorienting Marriage in the Ex-Gay Movement

LYNNE GERBER

The theology of Christian marriage has been the effort to
promote sex without eroticism.
—Mark D. Jordan, *The Ethics of Sex*

I love this all-knowing God. And I love my wife more than
ever. After 25 years of marriage, I still find her to be the best
thing going, sexually and emotionally. And I am still as
capable as ever of violating the boundaries that have become
my truth and cause. Maybe that's why on a recent trip without [her] I insisted on a roommate at every stop, was in daily
contact with two accountability partners at home, and had
another two praying for me continually while I was gone.
Andy Comiskey, "Telling the Haggard Truth"

Homosexually oriented Christians in the ex-gay movement commit
themselves to a certain celibacy.[1] Convinced that homosexual sex is a sin
and committed to sinlessness (insofar as they are able), they choose to
not express homosexual desire in erotic, genital acts. But this restraint
is not necessarily accompanied by restraint from all sexual expression.
Ex-gays are free to marry in heterosexual unions and once they do so
are permitted, in fact expected, to engage in heterosexual erotic, genital
acts. Their celibacy is thus a queerish one, requiring abstention from
sex strongly desired and permitting sex tepidly desired. Within the
movement, what this abstention should be called is a live issue. The distinctions different groups in the movement make between terms such

as "chastity" and "celibacy," the malleability of these terms, and what is at stake in such distinctions are useful to explore, as are the unexpected implications of this celibacy for Christian marriage. This chapter argues that queerish ex-gay celibacy can generate a traditional ideal of Christian marriage—union without eros—in both heterosexual unions and homosexual unions. It is based on qualitative research I conducted into the ex-gay movement, including participant observation at ex-gay conferences; interviews with ministry members, leaders, and supporters; and content analysis of ministry materials.[2]

First, a word on my use of "queerish." "Queer" as a term is used in a number of ways: to designate erotic desires outside of heterosexuality, to reclaim a spoiled identity, to point to that which is not "normal," to dissolve categories of identification by ever pointing toward something beyond them. So capacious a term is ripe for overapplication. David Halperin notes that "its lack of definitional content renders ["queer"] all too readily available for appropriation by those who do not experience the unique political disabilities and forms of social disqualification from which lesbians and gay men routinely suffer in virtue of our sexuality."[3] It is also all too readily available for application to people who may experience such political disabilities and social disqualifications but do not wish to align with others who do, as well as to those whose lives can be understood in queer terms but lack interest in, or oppose, the political possibilities of queerness. People in the ex-gay movement can be described in both ways. Rather than simply utilize a term that is not entirely accurate in relation to the politics of this queer-tinged project, I use "queerish" to designate the complicated position this movement, its rhetoric, and its people have in relation to queerness.[4]

Is It Celibacy?

In thinking about celibacy in the ex-gay movement, a useful place to start is to consider whether or not the kind of sexual abstention the movement requires is rightly considered celibacy. The dictionary definition of celibacy includes three elements—nonmarriage, sexual abstention, and religious commitment—which in combination constitute celibacy.[5] But celibacy is a fraught category in the Protestant tradition. Suspicion of celibacy as practiced in the Catholic Church precluded the development of a legitimized Protestant celibate identity. The reluctant Evangelical admission that marriage may not be available to everyone who desires it has led some to try to create just such an identity for people who do not marry.[6]

In the Evangelical world in general and in the ex-gay movement in particular, there is much slippage in the language used to indicate restraint from sexual activity. "Abstinence," "purity," "celibacy," "chastity," and "virginity" are all used without great attention paid to parsing distinctions. Some Evangelical theologians, by contrast, take pains to make such distinctions. In *Welcoming but Not Affirming*, Stanley J. Grenz argues that celibacy and abstinence should not be confused. "Unlike celibacy," he writes:

> abstinence in singleness is not a particular calling for certain persons, but an ethical ideal for all who are not married. And unlike celibacy, which is a chosen, permanent (or semi-permanent) response to a sensed call from God, the commitment to abstinence in singleness is a particular, and for many people temporary, outworking of the overarching call to a life of sexual chastity that comes to all.[7]

In this view, celibacy is best understood as an individual calling. Restraint from sexual activity in anticipation of eventual (heterosexual) marriage is seen as categorically distinct from a similar restraint that is deliberately chosen and not bound by the expectation of its eventual release.

In the ex-gay context, whether the ex-gay position is considered one of celibacy depends, in part, on one's location within that movement. The movement is made up of a diverse array of pastors, therapists, people struggling with their sexual identity, and parents, spouses, children, and other family members of these "strugglers."[8] People and organizations in this movement take differing positions regarding theology, therapeutic intervention into homosexuality, and gay politics, but until recently the movement has been largely united in the view that homosexual orientation is something that can change with faith, therapy, and obedience to God's will. Exodus International, the movement's defining organization, was able to maintain its diverse coalition for many years using the possibility of change as its binding assertion.

The consensus on change, however, has crumbled, and the field of the ex-gay movement has been realigning.[9] In 2012 Exodus International officially renounced its support of reparative therapy, the practice of attempting to change sexual orientation through therapeutic means, and has taken a significantly more moderate position on the question of change. "In the past," said Exodus president Alan Chambers in an interview in the *Atlantic,* "we've been aligned with organizations that believe feelings can completely change. . . . We now believe that's an unrealistic and unhealthy expectation that can cause a lot of damage."[10] Ministries that still affirm such a possibility are either going it alone or regrouping under the banner of a new organization, the Restored Hope Network, which "hold[s] up the power of God to redeem individuals and families from sin's control, even in the area of homosexuality."[11] These differing perspectives on whether or not orientation change is possible generate differing positions on whether ministry participants are celibate, abstinent, or something else entirely. Here I will compare the "change-is-possible" position with the "change-is-unlikely" position.

The change-is-possible camp is founded on the assumption that heterosexuality is God's created intention. Homosexuality as a physiological reality, in this view, does not exist. "There really is no such thing as a homosexual," writes Focus on the Family's Mike Haley. "As strange as this may sound, it's true. We are all biological heterosexuals."[12] Therapeutic intervention into homosexuality involves persuading the ex-gay person of this reality and encouraging him or her to identify not as gay or lesbian, nor as a struggler, but as heterosexual. Reparative therapist Joseph Nicolosi writes about changing identification as perhaps the most significant change his clients make: more significant (and, notably, more achievable) than eliminating same-sex desire:

> Growth through reparative therapy is an ongoing process. Usually some homosexual desires will recur during periods of stress or loneliness. Rather than *cure* therefore, I speak of the goal of *change,* in which there is shift in the identification of the self. . . . As one ex-gay man described it, "For many years I thought I was gay. I finally realized I was not a homosexual but a heterosexual man with a homosexual problem."[13]

For our purposes the most significant point here is the denial of any ontological difference between homosexuality and heterosexuality. All sexual desires and preferences are understood within the framework of foundational heterosexuality. That elision is carried over into the question of celibacy. Ex-gay people who are unmarried are depicted as single people subject to the same requirements of Christian sexual ethics as anyone else: abstinence in anticipation of heterosexual marriage. There is no acknowledgment that the struggler's abstinence is different in degree or in kind than that of any other single Christian. Like all believers, the single struggler is restrained from sexual activity until the release of that constraint via marital sanctioning.

Even when marriage is not on the horizon, people in this camp make a distinction between understanding the struggler's sexual restraint as a reflection of homosexuality versus as a reflection of heterosexual singleness. A post on New Hope Ministries' blog contrasts the two positions. "Celibate homosexuality" is "less than the best God offers us," whereas "victorious singleness" is "being in the center of God's will."[14] The practical difference seems to be the degree to which the struggler views him- or herself as a homosexual who has made a commitment to celibacy as a result of sexual orientation or a heterosexual single who awaits the sexual promise of heterosexual marriage. Jack, the director of a West Coast ministry, made a similar distinction when he explained how his self-description changed:

> I really don't say that I'm celibate anymore. I say that I'm chaste. Because when a person says they're celibate you're saying I'm going to remain single, this is it, ten-four, case closed, over and out. . . . But when a person says they're chaste they say ok I'm single and I'm not sexually active but I'm still very much open to the possibility of becoming married.

"Celibacy" is rejected as a way of describing abstention because of its categorical association with homosexuality.

The change-is-unlikely school has only recently emerged. There is not a lot of material available yet articulating how it will reconcile homosexual orientation with Christian orthodoxy. However, its recognition of the persistence of same-sex desire suggests that its logic will not be constrained by the insistence that homosexuality does not exist.

Holding that homosexuality is unlikely to change, that it is nevertheless sinful, and that heterosexual marriage between people of differing
sexual orientation is not necessarily advisable, this position may well
advocate something akin to traditional Christian celibacy. Seeds of that
possibility are already evident. In the Exodus newsletter, Chambers
writes, "The use of therapy and psychology to change orientation, and
its promise to cure, has eclipsed and devalued our calling as believers to
live a life of daily surrender that may include suffering as a part of our
experience as aliens of this world."[15] Recognizing the possibility of suffering may bolster a formulation of celibacy as a religious response to
homosexuality.

A Queerish Celibacy

In either case, the outcome is quite similar: ex-gays are expected to live
lives of sexual abstention out of religious commitment. They believe
Jesus calls them to renounce the possibility of expressing their deepest
erotic desires. And they are expected to abstain from same-sex marriages that would reflect and channel those desires. The cognitive dis-
sonances of the change-is-possible school notwithstanding, ex-gays
in both cases are expected to be celibate in relation to their queerer
desires. But in each case there's also a queer exemption: the possibility
of legitimized sexual activity within heterosexual marriage.

   In the change-is-possible school, this twist is encouraged and celebrated when it occurs. As we have seen, no distinction is made between
a homosexual struggler and a heterosexual single person in relation
to sexual activity outside of marriage. The obvious difference between
the two regarding the likelihood of eventual sexual satisfaction is not
explicitly recognized, and the struggler is frequently, if sometimes cau-
tiously, counseled to look forward to the sexual possibilities of heterosexual marriage. This anticipation is likely heightened by the recent
Evangelical trend toward depicting heterosexual Christian marriage
as the site of ultimate sexual satisfaction.[16] While ex-gay leaders in this
school are at times careful about constructing heterosexual marriage
as evidence of orientation change, when it occurs it is seen as a good
sign, especially when accompanied by children. By the logic of this system, the naturally heterosexual struggler should enjoy the same sexual

pleasures that await anyone else in marriage. The promise of abstinence is the same: "Sexual renunciation now . . . adds to sexual fulfillment later."[17]

But promise notwithstanding, there is also a recognition that the erotic desire felt by the struggler in heterosexual marriage will not be qualitatively comparable to homosexual desire. In the view of these ex-gay leaders, God does not replace same-sex desire with opposite-sex desire. Rather, he replaces it with desire that is more reflective of his will in relation to sexuality. "God never uses lust to change us," writes New Hope Ministries leader Frank Worthen, "so if the world demands lust as proof of change, we should not be caught up in such deception."[18] As we will see, the tepidity of ex-gay heterosexual desire can come to signify not the failure of sexual reorientation but the realization of ideal Christian love.

The change-is-unlikely school also recognizes the possibilities of sexual expression for strugglers in the context of heterosexual union. Some in this camp are starting to talk about "mixed-orientation marriage," where each partner in the marriage has a different sexual orientation. John Smid, the former director of Love Won Out, has publicly identified as a homosexual person in such a marriage.[19] The mere acknowledgment of the difference in orientation marks a major shift. It also recognizes that the position of a struggler in a heterosexual marriage and the tensions that emerge in such a marriage are different in kind than those in more conventional heterosexual marriages. For example, Wendy Gritter, director of New Dimension, a former ex-gay ministry that shifted its position regarding homosexuality, writes:

> The reality is those in long term mixed-orientation marriages often deeply love one another. They have shared a depth of experience and life that means something. At the same time, in the depth of that shared life, there can be a poignant awareness that something is absent—something that transcends the normal challenge of married life.[20]

And if Gritter's website is an example, heterosexual marriage when one partner is not heterosexually oriented is not recommended, although the possibilities in such marriages for those already committed are respected.[21] If the logic is followed, this school, again, is likely to move toward a model of ex-gay celibacy—or perhaps to an acceptance (however reluctant) of gay marriage.

Queerish Celibacies and Christian Marriages

The queerish twist of ex-gay celibacy can seem ironic at best, cruel at worst. It is a celibacy in which sexual abstinence is required in the face of one's most deeply felt erotic desires but sexual expression is encouraged and affirmed in relation to tepid desires. While the sexual act within marriage would technically violate a vow of celibacy, it is unclear whether it violates the spirit of chastity. And ironic or cruel as it may be, from another perspective this queerish ex-gay celibacy is not entirely unlike the ideal of Christian marriage.

The contemporary Evangelical emphasis on heterosexual marriage as the site of ultimate sexual fulfillment is a relatively new and relatively rare position within the history of Christian marriage. Christian marriage was developed as a reluctant if necessary alternative to deeper Christian ideals of celibacy and virginity. The designation of marriage as the only legitimated context for sexual expression did not mean that sexual expression was celebrated in that context. "Marriage," writes Mark Jordan, "shelters some sexual activity from an otherwise absolute critique of sexual pleasure."[22] It was intended to contain sex and to help spouses get beyond it. Marital theologies often maintained ideals of celibacy within marriage, arguing that married sex was not sinless and should thus be minimized, and "claiming that the best Christian marriages would tend as soon as possible to be marriages without sex."[23]

This sex without eroticism is one way of describing, or understanding, queerish ex-gay celibacy and its marital exception. Indeed, there are discursive tropes depicting marriages between ex-gay men and heterosexual women in ways that reflect these antierotic ideals. Heterosexual marriages with ex-gay men are described as built on holier, more enduring foundations than mere desire, such as deeper interpersonal knowledge and friendship. The lack of visceral heterosexual desire is legitimated by claiming that healed sexuality is not lustful sexuality. Rather, in the words of ex-gay leaders Bob Davies and Lori Rentzel, it is "godly sexuality."[24] Heterosexual marriages with ex-gay men are also depicted as advantageous, both spiritually and to the women in them, because the male partner is often attracted only to one person of the opposite sex, eliminating a source of jealousy and sexual sin. Ex-gay man Alan Medinger, for example, writes: "I love my wife, and we have had a wonderful and enjoyable sexual/romantic relationship since my healing. But she is the only woman with whom I wish to have sex. . . . It is only because of the Fall that men have problems lusting for women outside of that committed relationship."[25] Craig, also an ex-gay man, told me: "I desire my wife sexually and I'm very glad that I don't have a problem with lust for other women or men." From this perspective, heterosexual ex-gay marriage, with its queerish insistence on restraint in relation to visceral desire and expression in relation to muted desire, becomes a queer version of the ideal Christian marriage that has used the institution and its identities not to express desire but to move beyond it.

But there is an additional way in which queerish ex-gay celibacy can resemble Christian marriage: in the reinvention of homosexual part-nerships in celibate ex-gay contexts. There are a few documented exam-ples of homosexual lovers who continue their relationships in the ex-gay context, presumably with the added element of sexual abstinence. Ethnographer Tanya Erzen tells the story of Hank, a longtime member of New Hope Ministries, and his former partner Paul, who joined the ministry three years after Hank.[26] The two were no longer lovers, but the ministry provided a context for them to continue their union in a nonsexual but not altogether unchristian form.

A more visible case is that of former Exodus board member Elaine Sinnard and her once partner Penny Dalton. According to their testi-monies, the two lived together as lesbian lovers and converted to Chris-tianity at roughly the same time. They stopped sexual activity, moved into separate bedrooms, and started an ex-gay ministry in their home. "Penny and I continue to share a home," wrote Sinnard,

which has puzzled some people who ask, "How can you live with your former lover and claim to be free of homosexuality?" If I was still bat-tling homosexual attractions and unhealthy emotional entanglements, I definitely could not live with Penny and remain a strong, peaceful Chris-tian. But for the past 16 years, we have both been increasingly healed and now relate to each other as heterosexual women.[27]

Not everyone in the ex-gay movement had so sanguine a view of Dalton and Sinnard's testimony. L.I.F.E. Ministries directors Ron Highley and Joanne Highley criticized Exodus for allowing Sinnard to stay in leadership, arguing that ex-gays should not live with former partners and that those who do should not hold leadership positions. "The example of these two women," they wrote, "has encouraged other former homosexual couples to remain together and be endorsed by Exodus to minister from that situation."[28] The debate over whether this was a case of legitimate healing, false healing, emotional dependence, or simply bad PR was not addressed by Exodus publicly, and Sinnard maintained her leadership position.

Whatever else may be said about Hank and Paul or Elaine and Penny, they may be considered cases of queerish ex-gay celibacy and/ or queerish Christian marriage. In both cases, the partners moved past and indeed renounced the erotic aspects of their unions, but they maintained high degrees of intimacy, continued to share their lives, and developed what Dalton called, in describing her relationship with Sinnard, "godly friendship."[29] They have achieved what, in Jordan's view, Christian marriage was intended to achieve: the supplanting of erotic identities by anti-erotic ones. They also achieved levels of sacrifice and commitment that are elements of the Christian marital ideal, elements that are not often realized in unions heterosexual or homosexual.

*   *   *

In his introduction to *Queer Theology*, Gerard Loughlin writes that queer theology "finds—like queer theory—that gay sexuality is not marginal to Christian theology, but oddly central. . . . The most orthodox turns out to be the queerest of all."[30] In the case of queerish ex-gay celibacy, some of the queerest Christian marriages may turn out to be the most orthodox of all. Ex-gay celibacy and its Janus-faced expectation that strugglers abstain from the sex that is most desirous while affirming sex sustained by something other than desire may generate the most traditional of Christian unions: heterosexual unions unthreatened by eros and homosexual unions grounded in its sacrifice.

NOTES

1. My thanks to Sara Moslener, Kent Brintnall, Heather White, Sarah Quinn, and Shaina Hammerman for generous help in thinking through this chapter. Citations for the epigraphs are Mark D. Jordan, *The Ethics of Sex* (Oxford: Blackwell, 2002), 117; and Andrew Comiskey, "Telling the Haggard Truth," http://desert-stream.org/Groups/1000040183/Desert_Stream_Ministries/Looking_For_Help/Free_Resources/Articles_and_Newsletters/Articles_and_Newsletters.aspx, accessed February 15, 2013.

2. All names of interview subjects are pseudonymous.

3. David Halperin, *Saint Foucault: Towards a Gay Hagiography* (Oxford: Oxford University Press, 1997), 65.

4. For more, see Lynne Gerber, "The Opposite of Gay: Nature, Creation and Queerish Ex-Gay Experiments," *Nova Religio* 11, no. 4 (2008): 8–30.

5. *Merriam-Webster Dictionary*, www.merriam-webster.com/dictionary/celibacy, accessed February 15, 2013.

6. See, e.g., Marcy Hintz, "Choosing Celibacy: How to Stop Thinking of Singleness as a Problem," *Christianity Today*, September 12, 2008, www.christianitytoday.com/ct/2008/september/20.47.html, accessed February 15, 2013.

7. Stanley J. Grenz, *Welcoming but Not Affirming: An Evangelical Response to Homosexuality* (Louisville, KY: Westminster John Knox Press, 1998), 126–27.

8. Terminology is fraught in the ex-gay movement, and there is disagreement about what to call ministry participants. "Ex-gay" is widely recognized but internally unpopular. "Struggler" is used as shorthand for a person who struggles with same-sex desire.

9. Things have changed very quickly indeed in the ex-gay world. Between the time when this chapter was originally written and when it is being published, Exodus International made a public apology for its sexual reorientation practices, shut down its offices, and announced that the people involved would launch a new ministry that does not focus on reorientation. This chapter was written at a particular moment, when Exodus still existed and was charting a course away from its past. But while the organizational players have changed, I think the two logics described here will continue to shape the Evangelical approach to homosexuality and orthodox Christianity.

10. Jennie Rothenberg Gritz, "Sexual Healing: Evangelicals Update Their Message to Gays. Interview of Alan Chambers," *Atlantic*, June 20, 2012, www.theatlantic.com/national/archive/2012/06/sexual-healing-evangelicals-update-their-message-to-gays/258713/, accessed February 15, 2013.

11. "Welcome to Restored Hope Network," www.restoredhopenetwork.org/, accessed February 15, 2013.

12. Mike Haley, *101 Frequently Asked Questions about Homosexuality* (Eugene, OR: Harvest House, 2004), 22.

13. Joseph Nicolosi, *Healing Homosexuality: Case Stories of Reparative Therapy* (Lanham, MD: Rowman and Littlefield, 2004), 173.

14. "Celibate Homosexuality or Victorious Singleness?," New Hope blog, December 31, 2012, www.newhope123.org/new-hope-blog/, accessed February 15, 2013.

15. Exodus International newsletter, December 2012, http://exodusinternational.org/wp-content/uploads/2009/12/December-2012.pdf, accessed February 15, 2013.

16. Christine J. Gardiner, *Making Chastity Sexy: The Rhetoric of Evangelical Abstinence Campaigns* (Berkeley: University of California Press, 2011).

17. Heather R. White, "Virgin Pride: Born Again Faith and Sexual Identity in the Faith-Based Abstinence Movement," in *Ashgate Research Companion to Contemporary Religion and Sexuality*, ed. Stephen J. Hunt and Andrew Yip (London: Ashgate, 2012), 246.

18. New Hope newsletter, July 2006.

19. John Smid, *Ex'd Out: How I Fired the Shame Committee* (Charlotte, NC: Create Space Independent Publishing Platform, 2012), 225–32.

20. Wendy Gritter, "Mixed-Orientation Marriage: A Case Study for the Now and the Not Yet," Bridging the Gap blog, March 29, 2012, http://btgproject.blogspot.com/search/label/mixed%20orientation%20marriage, accessed February 15, 2013.

21. Ibid.

22. Jordan, *Ethics of Sex*, 107.

23. Ibid., 118.

24. Bob Davies and Lori Rentzel, *Coming Out of Homosexuality: New Freedom for Men and Women* (Downers Grove, IL: InterVarsity Press, 1993), 27.

25. Alan Medinger, "God Healed My Marriage," 1985, www.exodusglobalalliance.org/godhealedmymarriagep2.php, accessed February 15, 2013.

26. Tanya Erzen, *Straight to Jesus: Sexual and Christian Conversions in the Ex-Gay Movement* (Berkeley: University of California Press, 2006), 86–87, 123–25.

27. Elaine Sinnard, "Finding Joy as a Woman," http://exodus.to/content/view/255/148/, accessed November 8, 2008.

28. Ron Highley and Joanne Highley, "Our Objections to a Current Exodus Policy," in *The Best Words of L.I.F.E.: Celebrating 20 Years of L.I.F.E. Ministries* (New York: L.I.F.E., 2002), 229.

29. Penny Dalton, quoted in Bob Davies, *Portraits of Freedom: 14 People Who Came Out of Homosexuality* (Downers Grove, IL: InterVarsity Press, 2001), 164.

30. Gerard Loughlin, "Introduction: The End of Sex," in *Queer Theology: Rethinking the Western Body*, ed. Gerard Loughlin (Malden, MA: Blackwell, 2007), 9.

3

Celibate Politics

Queering the Limits

ANTHONY M. PETRO

"Why aren't you telling them, bluntly, stop!" chided Emma, a medical doctor during the first years of the AIDS crisis, who thought community leaders were not doing enough to tell gay men to stop having sex. "Every day you don't tell them, more people infect each other." These lines come from Larry Kramer's play *The Normal Heart* (1985), an autobiographical depiction of his early work with the Gay Men's Health Crisis, one of the first organizations founded to combat AIDS. *The Normal Heart* captured the panic and fear that many gay men in New York faced in the early years of the epidemic, but it also introduced one of the central debates dividing gay and lesbian activists in this period: the place of queer sex amid a life-threatening epidemic.

Kramer joined the choir of voices admonishing gay men to limit sexual encounters. In *The Normal Heart*, he recast this call in medical terms, when Emma faults Ned (Kramer's surrogate) for failing adequately to warn gay men about the dangers of sex. Some activists nonetheless saw the practical and political pitfalls of this position. After first calling for gay men to limit sexual partners, Michael Callen and Richard Berkowitz eventually authored one of the first safe sex pamphlets, *How to Have Sex in an Epidemic*, which they handed out in New York in 1983.[1] A year earlier in San Francisco, the Sisters of Perpetual Indulgence, a performance-based queer protest group drawing upon religious camp and gender drag, produced a safe-sex brochure called *Play Fair!* Both of these publications resisted the sexual moralism glimpsed in calls to limit sex partners or to stop having sex; they instead adopted sex-positive language to educate gay men about safer sexual practices.[2]

AIDS activist Douglas Crimp took these calls a step further. In "How to Have Promiscuity in an Epidemic," he criticized the sexual moralism and panic of those who called on men to limit sexual practices, including gay and AIDS activists and leaders of the newly formed Christian Right alike. Crimp espoused the political value of promiscuity itself.[3] The stakes for queer activists like Crimp were clear: sexual moralism and medical panic should not curb the political and social gains made by gay activists since the 1960s. AIDS was not a wake-up call, as some gay leaders have since framed it, for homosexuals to come of age, give up their promiscuity, and become responsible members of society.[4] Rather, as Crimp put it, "AIDS showed anyone willing to pay attention how genuinely ethical the invention of gay life had been," which included an ethics of responsibility that followed from queer sex itself.[5]

The centrality of sex to the history of queer politics makes clear the challenge in comprehending something like *queer Christian celibacy*. How could living a life without sex be queer? Should a religious call to give up sex be considered queer? These reservations presuppose a specific hermeneutics of queer analysis and a claim about queer politics and its limits, which this chapter takes up by offering two interventions. First, through a brief discussion of queer politics and the place of sex within queer history, it questions whether Christian celibacy, or any celibacy for that matter, ought to be called queer.[6] Yet, second, it insists that queer politics could nonetheless benefit from a dialogue with Christian celibacy. Indeed, to paraphrase anthropologist Claude Lévi-Strauss, it may be "good to think with" the idea of queer Christian celibacy, by examining how some strains—such as Evangelical ex-gay ministries and faith-based abstinence rhetoric—reveal the normative desires of secular queer and lesbian/gay politics. Modern Christian celibacy challenges two dogmas of mainstream queer and lesbian/gay politics: the normative, secular construction of sexual identity and the restrictive ways that sex, pleasure, and desire come together to define what sex actually is.

Delimiting Queer Politics

One of the very few references to celibacy in queer discussions of sex comes in Pat Califia's list titled "Forty-Two Things You Can Do to Make the Future Safe for Sex." Between recommendations to "cross dress" and to "masturbate, and don't hurry," Califia advises readers to "talk to a sex worker, a transgendered person, a celibate, a sadomasochist, a heterosexual—anybody whose sexual identity or practices are different from yours."[7] Califia's brief discussion highlights two points central to the politics of the word "queer." Quite often today, it is used as an umbrella term to account for the proliferation of sexual and gender identities beyond gay and lesbian (i.e., LGBTQI and so on) and is often seen in references to the "queer community." This way of using the term is tied to the political project of increasing possibilities for sexual and gender expression. We see an additional valence of "queer" in Califia's quotation, which is to celebrate difference. Here, "queer" normatively includes and *affirms* lesbian, gay, bisexual, transgender, questioning people, and so forth, to which, following Califia, we might add celibates, sadomasochists, sex workers, and even heterosexuals. Perhaps at some point we could see another addition: what Tanya Erzen has called a new sexual and religious identity in itself, the Christian "ex-gay."[8]

Including celibates and ex-gays demonstrates the commitment to diversity in this way of using "queer," but it also animates a set of concerns. For one, this approach translates the sexual projects initiated by queer activism into a tool of categorization and inclusion, and an increasingly vague and problematic one at that. All too often, "queer" actually signifies (secular white) gay and lesbian politics; it masquerades as inclusiveness at the expense of marginalized forms of expression, identity, and practice.[9] Perhaps most important, this diversity/encompassment model also obscures or even denies the very limits to queer inclusion. Labeling Christian celibacy as queer seems a welcome addition to the rainbow of sexual expression, but it raises the important question of how far we can push the political and analytic abilities of the term. Can anyone be queer? Where does one draw the line?

To be clear, my claim is not that we must limit in advance or police what should or should not be labeled "queer." But the term—both as a political and as an analytic tool—has limits. Ignoring those limits allows it to float about unmarked, as though "queer" could somehow magically include anyone. But in historical and contemporary practice it does not. And to ask the term to include everything would be unreasonable. To preserve some political and descriptive particularity, we must ask what the limits of "queer" might be and whether Christian celibacy, including figures like the ex-gay in particular, brushes against that limit. Lynne Gerber hits on this point in her essay in this volume, when she describes Evangelical ex-gays as "queerish." I want to suggest that Christian celibacy more generally—not just that among ex-gays, but even among self-identified members of the lesbian and gay community who decide to be celibate—presses against the political and descriptive limits of the term "queer." We should not lose sight of the particularities of queerness, including its historical emergence within the politics of sexuality surrounding the AIDS epidemic sketched earlier, nor the often-invisible limits to its politics of inclusion.

What, then, makes a project queer? Queer politics resists easy definition, both because of the diversity of queer activists themselves and because much of queer politics refuses the normative gestures of definition. Lauren Berlant and Michael Warner have suggested that queer politics should seek to create

> not just a safe zone for queer sex, but the changed possibilities of identity, intelligibility, publics, culture and sex that appear when the heterosexual couple is no longer the referent or privileged example of sexual culture. Queer social practices like sex and theory try to unsettle the garbled but powerful norms supporting that privilege—including the project of normalization that has made heterosexuality hegemonic—as well as those material practices that, though not explicitly sexual, are implicated in the hierarchies of property and propriety that we will describe as heteronormative.[10]

"Queer politics" is helpfully contrasted with "lesbian and gay politics." The latter issues from a "framework of individual identity, community representation, needs and rights discourses, and state provision."[11] This political project is premised not only upon the politics of identity but increasingly upon the supposition of gay identity as essentialist, even genetic. Identity becomes the basis for making rights claims at the level of state politics. This approach emphasizes being gay (or lesbian or bisexual or queer) over having sex, to the extent that these can be separated. Queer politics, in contrast, has balked at the need for state authorization, championed antiassimilationist and nonindividualist forms of politics, and advanced projects geared toward making queer sex public while also increasing the range of practices that people might find pleasurable.

Lesbian and gay politics finds its clearest expression today in the Human Rights Campaign, especially in its quest to legalize gay marriage. Queer activists may not oppose this project (though some certainly do) but are far more interested in undermining the institution of marriage altogether. Queer politics finds suspicious the normative assumptions that sex in most or all cases ought to be intimate, monogamous, loving, and legally sanctioned, and it resists efforts to render gay people in every way like heterosexuals, save for the same-sex spouse. Lesbian and gay politics is so popular today that even some Republican members of Congress support it. Queer politics often appears so distant that most college students, much less mainstream Americans, continually have trouble imagining viable alternatives to gay marriage, much less to the most "normal" ways of being gay, straight, or (maybe) bisexual. Who champions promiscuity today not merely as a phase that gay people ought to grow out of but as a way of life? As a politics? The search for "normal hearts" has outpaced the radical politics of the queer movement since the 1980s and 1990s.[12] Adding mainstream Christian support for gay rights to this picture would seem to be a final nail in the coffin of queer politics.

This is the background against which the queer potential of contemporary Christian celibacy must be considered. Queer politics has not been just about pushing against the grain or about having an identity; it has also been about *doing*, and much of that activity has had to do with sex. As Elizabeth Freeman reminds us, "'queer' cannot signal a purely deconstructive move," which would "risk evacuating the messiest thing about being queer: the actual meeting of bodies with other bodies and with objects."[13] But must queerness be founded in sex? Can we be queer without sex? What would we lose in moving away from these historically salient concerns and from grounding queer politics in sexual acts?

My point here is not that queer politics must be tethered to the concerns of its history—that it started off poised against arguments to stop having sex and thus must remain so. Rather, queer politics should remain in tension with normalizing social pressures regarding sex. I'm troubled by the supposed queerness of celibacy because, like in the 1980s, no one is telling queer people not to be celibate. Gay sex remains the primary threat to the heteronormative social order (one that has increasingly encompassed gay marriage, though notably on the common terms of romantic love). Perhaps one could imagine a social context in which celibacy were queer; I do not think we've reached such a point. Yet queer politics should not let go of Christian celibacy too quickly, either. Though I've argued that Christian celibacy falls outside the limits of queer politics, I propose that it nonetheless offers a useful tool for questioning those very parameters and perhaps even for queering the limits of queer and lesbian/gay politics themselves.

The Queer Extent of Christian Celibacy

The figure of the ex-gay presents a powerful challenge to the identity-based politics central to the umbrella version of queer and lesbian/gay politics. This identity politics treats sexual desire as natural or biological, a point poignantly captured in Lady Gaga's hit song "Born This Way." If one is born gay, then one cannot help it, and thus rights should be freely given. This view has come under attack by a number of queer activists, but it is also challenged by ex-gays.

Ex-gays are caught between their Christian (often Evangelical) view of homosexual behavior as sinful and a homosexual attraction experienced as unwilled but nonetheless alterable. For most secular Americans and mainline and progressive Protestants, the answer seems simple: you cannot change your sexual attraction, but you can change your religious affiliation, either by leaving the church altogether or by finding a gay-affirming church. But, as Gerber has shown, ex-gays refuse the secular assumption that religion is cultural and flexible, while sexual desire remains unyielding. According to Gerber, "Ex-gays who are most successful in their project resist the modern privileging of [homo]sexual identity over religious identity. . . . These are simply two different ways of organizing the self that, in the discursive context of Evangelical Christianity, are believed to be incompatible."[14]

Gerber builds upon the historicist projects of scholars like Michel Foucault, who have demonstrated the history of modern homosexual and heterosexual identities, the particular conjunctions of body, desire, and self that have come together in the modern period to make sex into an identity. Sexual identity comes to be read by moderns as a deep truth about the self just waiting to be revealed (or, worse, exposed). In contrast, Foucauldian interpretations posit another goal that has been taken up by queer activists and scholars. Rather than understand homosexual desire as a natural component of the self in need of liberation—whether from the law, the church, or elsewhere—these queer thinkers have called for the creation of novel pleasures, for reimagining configurations of desire, the body, and the self. This move does not fully disavow the politics of sexual identity. Identities are good to the extent that they might allow for new pleasures, but "we must not think of this identity as an ethical universal rule."[15] Sex is not fixed but rather becomes the possibility for creative life and for alternative formulations of politics. Foucault thus distinguishes between efforts to reassert ourselves "as gay" versus trying to "become gay."[16] To become gay is a project: it is less a starting point upon which to build identity than a trajectory for enacting continually new forms of life.

One site for this kind of becoming, this attempt to multiply desires and pleasures, can be found in sadomasochistic (S/M) communities, in which people take part in new practices that render the body a site of eroticization. Here Foucault sees a shift away from attaching sex to pleasure in the ways one would usually expect. One of the key features of S/M, he maintains, is "the desexualization of pleasure." "The idea that bodily pleasure should always come from sexual pleasure as the root of all our possible pleasure—I think that's something quite wrong," Foucault writes. "These practices are insisting that we can produce pleasure with very odd things, very strange parts of our bodies, in very unusual situations, and so on."[17] Foucault laments the "traditional construction of pleasure," which includes the pleasures of the flesh, "drinking, eating, and fucking." He calls not for alternatives but for additions.

The fact that sex is so "easy and numerous" for homosexuals today becomes a problem for Foucault. "In this type of casual encounter," he writes, "it is only after making love that one becomes curious about the other person." After the act, "you find yourself asking your partner, 'By

the way, what was your name?'"[18] All of the "energy and imagination"
that in heterosexual relationships are channeled into courtship "now
become devoted to intensifying the act of sex itself," and "it runs the risk
of quickly become boring."[19] Can taking a break from sex be a form of
queer celibacy? For Foucault, such innovation could come in the form
of asceticism—not in the renunciation of pleasure but in a move away
from our intensification of sex acts. "Can that be our problem today?"
asks Foucault. "It's up to us to advance into a homosexual ascesis that
would make us work on ourselves and invent—I do not say discover—a
manner of being that is still improbable."[20]

The consideration of new practices, possibly detached from sex acts
themselves, reveals the power of celibacy to challenge queer assumptions not only about particular conjunctions of body, desire, and pleasure but also about what constitutes sex itself. The consideration of
celibacy-as-queer might help us to refine what we mean by sex. It challenges the prevailing assumption that sex should be defined exclusively
as genital intercourse, a narrowing common in the aftermath of the
AIDS epidemic.

The tensions raised by the link between AIDS and sex in the 1980s
were combated through national sex education campaigns that heralded
what is sometimes called the ABC approach: abstinence, be faithful, use
a condom. This was the position taken by America's Evangelical Surgeon
General C. Everett Koop. The brochure Understanding AIDS (1988),
mailed to nearly every family in the United States, warned Americans
that if they were not going to stick to faithful marriages or abstinence,
then they should be sure to use a condom, "from start to finish."[21] The use
of condoms has since become HIV-prevention common sense not only
for Koop and mainstream America but for most gay men as well. Indeed,
our idea of safe sex has been reduced precisely to these options: no sex
or sex with a condom. But what kind of sex is imagined in this picture?
What does it mean to use a condom "from start to finish"? When exactly
does sex start? And what if there is no obvious appendage on which to
apply a condom? How do lesbians enact these recommendations?

By the late 1980s the gospel of condoms as both starting and end-
ing point for safe sex had narrowed sex to genital intercourse, even
within gay communities. What we have lost in this transition, however, is the variety of forms that sex could take, and the variety of other

constellations of desire, pleasure, and embodiment that might become not only a substitute for but even preferable to genital sex. As Cindy Patton has argued, earlier discussions of safe sex focused precisely on new forms of sexual pleasure that removed sex from its genital expressions. Education materials produced by AIDS collectives—including the pamphlets cited earlier in this chapter—described the plethora of activities in which people could engage without exchanging bodily fluids. These included holding jerk-off parties; engaging in less risky behaviors like petting, making out, or golden showers; or engaging in role-play, including many practices found within S/M activities. The focus here was less about what kinds of sex to avoid than about what kinds of practices people could engage in. It was about increasing sexual possibilities.[22]

Of course, in the wake of AIDS, some gay men avoided sex altogether. Celibacy became a practical option. We can see this reflected in new editions of *The Joy of Gay Sex*. While the original 1977 edition made no mention of celibacy, fifteen years later an entry was included that detailed the positive effects of sexual abstinence:

> What most discover when they become celibate is a surprising lack of pressure and stress in their lives. They feel relieved, relaxed, capable of being more objective about themselves and their relationships to others. Without the constant need to be sexually desirable, they begin to recognize abilities and values in themselves that may have been overlooked or underrated: charm, a sense of humor, psychological penetration, conversational ability, creativity. Work on these areas (free of sexual pressures) can lead to a fuller sense of yourself, providing a new confidence which ultimately makes you even more desirable should you decide to end your period of celibacy.[23]

Celibacy begins to be seen in a new light, one not all that different from what Foucault had in mind. We see celibacy not for what it leaves out (namely, sex) but for what it might add to one's life. We often think of celibacy as the restriction or repression of sexual desire, but we might ask instead: What kinds of desires could celibacy itself create? Can we imagine a sexually productive celibacy? What might celibate desire look like? What might celibate pleasure be?

Conservative Christians, in some ways, have been leading the way in developing the erotic potential of celibacy and abstinence. The popularity of Mormon author Stephenie Meyer's *Twilight* series is one case in point.[24] In these books and films, abstinence becomes charged with erotic excitement, offering not the denial or renunciation of sexual desire but its affirmation. In many ways, the genital sexual intercourse, once it happens—within the bounds of marriage, of course—is disappointing both for the readers and for the characters. The true joy comes not from liberating desire but from creating it, shaping it, and containing it. Of course, this is why sex comes only in the final book of the series. To paraphrase a little folk wisdom: it's not where you end up, but how you get there.

Christian forms of celibacy introduce novel ways of narrating the malleability of desire, often by connecting it to spiritual understandings of love and pleasure. In this sense, as Gerber has suggested, the goal of ex-gay ministries is not to turn homosexuals into heterosexuals, a feat many now think impossible, but rather to create Christians. The ex-gay program may be read as an attempt not to deny sexual desire but rather to reroute it into religious pleasure. This is not to say that these techniques are "queer" or beyond critical reproach. Yet queer politics must not counter these claims through an appeal to some ostensibly natural sexual desire, but rather through a new set of practices of pleasure, a new ethics of sexuality, responsibility, and politics.

If Christian celibacy lies outside the parameters of queer politics as I have elaborated it, it nonetheless pushes against those limits in challenging ways. Recent Christian approaches to celibacy unsettle some common assumptions within queer and lesbian/gay politics, especially in demonstrating the limitations of secular sexual identity politics and the reduction of sex to genital intercourse. Christian celibacy prompts us to ask, in other words, to what extent *not* having sex opens new ways for identifying erotic possibilities and novel pleasures. That's a sexless queer politics with which we might have to contend.

NOTES

1. The pamphlet, first published in 1983, is reprinted in Richard Berkowitz, *Stayin' Alive: The Invention of Safe Sex* (New York: Basic Books, 2003), 187–218.

2. See Jennifer Brier, *Infectious Ideas: U.S. Political Responses to the AIDS Crisis* (Chapel Hill: University of North Carolina Press, 2009), 11–44; and Cindy Patton, *Fatal Advice: How Safe-Sex Education Went Wrong* (Durham, NC: Duke University Press, 1996).

3. Douglas Crimp, "How to Have Promiscuity in an Epidemic," *October*, Winter 1987, 237–71.
4. Crimp attributes this narrative especially to Andrew Sullivan; see Crimp, "Melancholia and Moralism: An Introduction," in *Melancholia and Moralism: Essays on AIDS and Queer Politics* (Cambridge, MA: MIT Press, 2002), 3–6.
5. Ibid., 16.
6. This essay follows popular usage today, in which "celibacy" and "abstinence" refer generally, and often interchangeably, to the avoidance of physical sex, whether for a short period of time or for one's lifetime.
7. Pat Califia, *Public Sex: The Culture of Radical Sex* (San Francisco: Cleis, 1994), 155.
8. Tanya Erzen, *Straight to Jesus: Sexual and Christian Conversions in the Ex-Gay Movement* (Berkeley: University of California Press, 2006).
9. See Cathy Cohen, "Punks, Bulldaggers, and Welfare Queens: The Radical Potential of Queer Politics?," *GLQ* 3 (1997): 437–65.
10. Lauren Berlant and Michael Warner, "Sex in Public," in Michael Warner, *Publics and Counterpublics* (Brooklyn, NY: Zone Books, 2005), 187–88.
11. Warner, *Publics and Counterpublics*, 221.
12. Michael Warner, *The Trouble with Normal* (Cambridge, MA: Harvard University Press, 1999).
13. Elizabeth Freeman, *Time Binds: Queer Temporalities, Queer Histories* (Durham, NC: Duke University Press, 2010), xxi.
14. Lynne Gerber, *Seeking the Straight and Narrow: Weight Loss and Sexual Reorientation in Evangelical America* (Chicago: University of Chicago Press, 2011), 223.
15. Michel Foucault, "Sex, Power, and the Politics of Identity," in *Ethics: Subjectivity and Truth* (New York: New Press, 1998), 166.
16. Ibid., 163.
17. Ibid., 165.
18. Michel Foucault, "Sexual Choice, Sexual Act," in *Ethics: Subjectivity and Truth* (New York: New Press, 1998), 151.
19. Ibid.
20. Michel Foucault, "Friendship as a Way of Life," in *Ethics: Subjectivity and Truth* (New York: New Press, 1998), 137.
21. U.S. Department of Health and Human Services, *Understanding AIDS*, Publication No. (CDC) HHS-88-8404 (Washington, DC: U.S. Government Printing Office, 1988), 4.
22. Patton, *Fatal Advice*.
23. Charles Silverstein and Felice Picano, *The New Joy of Gay Sex* (San Francisco: HarperCollins, 1992), 25. Cf. Charles Silverstein and Edmund White, *The Joy of Gay Sex: An Intimate Guide for Gay Men to the Pleasures of a Gay Lifestyle* (San Francisco: Outlet, 1977).
24. Samira K. Mehta and Anthony M. Petro, "Big Vampire Love: What's So Mormon about *Twilight*?," *Religion Dispatches*, December 4, 2009, religiondispatches.org.

4

How Queer Is Celibacy?

A Queer Nun's Story

SISTER CAROL BERNICE, CHS

So far in this part, historians and theorists have raised serious questions about the queerness of Christian celibacy. The choice of many early Christians to embrace a life of celibacy challenged and subverted the sexual norms of Jewish and Greco-Roman society. But celibacy as a form of Christian life was generally rejected by Protestant reformers, starting with Luther, who saw vows of celibacy as an obstacle to God's first commandment to humans: go forth and multiply. Modern secular society inherited this Reformation skepticism of celibacy, though it is more likely to express it in terms of personal expression than as a matter of procreation. Our deepest passions are assumed to be sexual, and our personal fulfillment is thought to demand sexual relations. In retrospect we might call those early Christian celibates "queer," but what does that have to do with the liberating work that has come to be associated with the word "queer" in our own time? Can celibacy be queer now?

Queer history and queer theory can only answer that question when they encounter the lived experience of people who identify themselves as leading lives both celibate and queer. In trying to bring the reader as close as possible to the living voices of queer Christian celibates, the following contribution shares the transcript of a talk given at the Queer Christianities conference held at The New School in March 2012. The speaker was Sister Carol Bernice of the Community of the Holy Spirit, a monastic community for women in the Episcopal Church.

While there are a number of monastic rules, all Christian monastics profess a life of simplicity, chastity, and prayer. Most monastic

communities observe some form of the Divine Office (also called Liturgy
of the Hours), in which the members regularly gather several times a day
to listen to scripture and to sing the Psalms together. The earliest monastic
communities grew up in the deserts of Syria and Egypt. The desert is also
the setting for the lives of the prophets, and desert prophets like Elijah and
John the Baptist served as models for the mothers and fathers of monas-
ticism. To withdraw from the world can be a loving, urgent call for the
world to reform.

If monasticism poses a prophetic challenge to secular norms of power
and prestige, it has proved no less challenging to the clerical hierarchy.
The monk or nun has often provided alternative models of sanctity and
authority to those of the bishop, and the monastic community is at once a
part of the church and apart from the church. The narrative and reflection
that Sister Carol Bernice provides us confirm that there are individuals
who continue to find their deepest fulfillment in a celibacy that is Chris-
tian and queer. And that witness might prove prophetic, for Christians
and queers alike.

My name is Sister Carol Bernice, and I am queer and celibate, and I've
often been asked, by those whom I presume are well-meaning folks,
which of these states of life caused the other. The truth of the matter is that I became a lesbian and a Christian on the selfsame day—it
was in September—fifteen years ago, and from that point on they both
together led quite naturally and eventually to the consecrated celibate
life I lead today.

Let's do the math. Today I am sixty, so I was forty-five years old
before I stood up in the clear light of a new day and with joy announced
to the world, "Yes, I am what I am." I had spent a lifetime—adolescence,
young adulthood, and right up into middle age—ignoring and denying
the impulses of my heart. Much in my upbringing—at home, at school,
alas in church also, and in society at large—unconsciously propelled me
into beliefs and behaviors contrary to my deepest sense of self.

Though feeling isolated and afraid, I slowly began to nurture and
protect a hidden inner life while simultaneously striving for success and
accomplishment in the so-called normal, outer world that I defined as
straight and secular. A house divided against itself cannot stand, and
while the crash was many years in coming, it was, thanks be to God,

inevitable. Every day during the recitation of Psalm 51 at Lauds, I am reminded of this time.

> I was born in sin, conceived in sin, yet you want the truth to live in my innermost being, Teach me your wisdom!

What I was doing to help myself was reading every feminist and mystic author I could scout out. I did not know that, as naturally as night follows day, all this reading would lead to radical feminism and the nunnery. It all started innocently enough. I started with Gloria Steinem and ended up with Mary Daly and Adrienne Rich. I started with Maharishi Mahesh Yogi and ended up with Saint Teresa of Ávila and Hildegard.

So the inevitable day of reckoning came, and the demands of my inside and outside worlds could no longer both be met. From the collapse and chaos that ensued I came out and was reborn all at once. The person who rose from the ashes that day was a Woman Loving Woman and a Lover of The Way. Yet the person who rose up that day was still also a mother and is now a grandmother. I cherish these fruits of my former life just as I cherish the fruits of a religious tradition whose historic practices, doctrine, and language I can no longer abide.

For those of you, perhaps most of you hearing these words, who have had a similar, profound conversion experience, I need not tell you how exhilarating and liberating it is. Nevertheless, let me just say that on that day I felt like Dorothy as she steps out of black-and-white Kansas into the colorful world of Munchkin Land. Suddenly I myself was transparent, that is, the same on the outside as on the inside, and the world was rich in color, depth, and detail and was so affirming and inviting, not to mention musical!

Of course, this is the condensed, bare-bones version of my coming-out story cum spiritual autobiography, but I wanted to get us to the point in my life where I began to discern a vocation to the Religious Life and with it the implication that celibacy might just be the deeper yet desire of my heart. There was, however, first and most wonderfully, the reward of all my fumblings toward Lesbos—she whom I loved and who loved me. Her name was Evalyn, and though she never came out publicly as I have done, we were known as a couple among our friends and to anyone with ears to hear and eyes to see. She died after only seven years of our being together, but one of my sisters in community, who knew us both, said just the other day that she always senses Evalyn's presence among us here and now. Our life together and her death have provided me with a virtual treasure trove of formative experience and guiding principles upon which to base a life of poverty, chastity, and obedience. I learned from her that we live and die for each other.

You say to my heart, "Seek my face" and so it is your face I seek!

This is verse 8 from Psalm 27, and whenever it comes up in the round of the Divine Office, I am reminded of that time in my life. I was curiously at peace with the prospect of Evalyn's imminent death and totally, joyously alive in those moments of communion with her. I experienced a whole and holy sense of communion both with my beloved and dying partner and with the eternal Beloved with a capital "B." No one was more surprised than I by the depth of that joy. In some kind of reverse pride, I never thought I would be called. But in a grace-given humility, I knew I wanted more and more of that and opened myself to what I now recognize as the promptings of the Holy Spirit. Never had I been so open, and let me tell you that, in my experience, openness is the key to total happiness.

All of this was happening to me in Wyoming in my small hometown on the High Plains. One Sunday after church I happened to notice a flyer with the pictures of three nuns on it, announcing a silent retreat weekend at Thomas the Apostle Center in Cody. I decided on the spot to go. It started on Friday night, and by Saturday afternoon I was inquiring of the sisters if I, too, could become a sister. They did not say no. I look back now and think I had my vocation handed to me on a platter. There it was, clear and shining before me: a life of devotion in the company of women. That they were engaged and energetic, beautiful and intelligent, and on fire with the Holy Spirit was all the more cause for rejoicing.

I completely and unreservedly embraced the prospect and within two years found myself living in a convent in Manhattan. Not for one instant have I felt myself deprived of love. Never have I felt like I have given up something—only gained. I do not feel less whole as a person, that is to say, I do not feel less sexual. In my body I have a deeply rooted felt sense that my sexuality is simply flourishing. I don't know what surprises me more about this—that it is so even though I am celibate or that it is so even though I am over sixty! With the poets I can sing the body electric and rejoice in the dearest freshness deep down things. For me, celibacy affords the openness to each and all which makes for kindness.

I used to hear it said that our sexuality exists on a continuum, with this kind at one end and that kind at the other. One of my sisters once said she thinks sexuality travels in a more three-dimensional geography. I like that idea and see that in my own journey I have been all over that map and at sea a good bit of the time. But I am glad I did not persist in that early notion of trying for normal through straight and secular channels. We know that many of us founder in that horrible attempt. I'm glad I got through to queer; and if queer is queer because of its stance in relation to normal, then I am doubly glad I got through to celibate because celibate, for me, is mighty queer.

I would like to close with a little poem, titled "Off the Platte," that I wrote upon coming to the Religious Life:

> In January, February and March-a-berry*
> of one aponce a time
> in a wee little house
> lived a woman well, yes well, past the prime
> of life, or so was common thought.
> Yet she possessed, and does yet still,
> a dream of love, and love fulfilled.
> So down the wind swept prairies
> and across the Mandan plain,
> up the Ohio valley and out to the Eastern main—
> She came by grace to women—
> They opened their golden door.

*From my son, aged five, who proudly announced he could say the names of the months and also around that time asked for a story that began "one aponce a time."

Thank you.

A Congregation Embodies Queer Theology

JON M. WALTON

What does it look like when a congregation does queer theology? There is a tendency to think about queer Christianity in terms of individuals and intimate relationships on the one hand, or in terms of theory, dogma, and preaching on the other. But Christianity is also church, the meetings on Sundays and during the week, the life cycle events, and shared experiences of a community working together to live out the Christian message. At the First Presbyterian Church in the City of New York, the congregation I have pastored for over a dozen years, we have come to live out a congregational work that embodies the church's queerest doctrine of all, the doctrine of the Incarnation, that move that God makes toward us embodying in flesh and action love that crosses over all boundaries and breaks down all divisions.

First Presbyterian was founded in 1716 and has a long tradition of progressive leadership. It is known to historians of American religion as the site of the famous sermon "Shall the Fundamentalists Win?" in 1922, when our then preaching minister, the theological modernist Harry Emerson Fosdick, launched a challenge to biblical literalism, a literalism with which Christianity continues to struggle ninety years later. Today, First Presbyterian is known as one of the churches that distributes water to the marchers in New York's Gay Pride Parade each June. Our geographic location in Greenwich Village might seem the reason for our progressivism, but while First Presbyterian's incarnation of

God's love for us is counterintuitive, thus queer as can be, our concerns are shared with congregations across the land. We are queer because we are Christian. This is an expression of the queer grace of God.

Who Are We?

Some of our congregation's members would be surprised to hear our church described as "queer." Some would think it their worst nightmare. Others would say that we are still waiting for more queerness to be made manifest among us. But in a larger sense, many might agree that queer things, which is to say unusual, unexpected, and inspired things, have been going on here for a very long time. I am not the first pastor to welcome or discuss the issue of queerness in the life of this congregation, and given legalized same-gender marriage, parenting among gay couples, and an ongoing discussion of sexual ethics among single gays, I will not be the last.

Queer welcome starts with the pastor coming to understand that she or he is meant to help the congregation live out this assurance spoken by Jesus: "Anyone who comes to me, I will never drive away" (John 6:37). It is embodied by a congregation that takes seriously a radical commitment to open its doors to the street and let them swing widely outward. That church must be ready to embrace change because many who will be brave enough to walk through the doors of the church have been through other doors and have not received the welcome they needed or wanted. It is not always easy, but if a congregation is willing to accept that change, dramatic, good, and grace-filled things can happen.

I became very aware of the context into which I had arrived when we began to reach out in a positive and welcoming way to the surrounding queer community. I naively thought it would be a good idea that we start a "gay" group. This was almost twelve years ago. This church, like so many others during the 1980s and 1990s, had lived through the AIDS crisis, which became the occasion forcing us to deal with our internalized and externalized homophobia. There had always been a joke that the church would have to address that homophobia if suddenly one day everyone who was gay in the church turned purple. Little did we know that that purple would be the lesions of Kaposi's sarcoma and the weight loss of wasting disease.

ACT UP had queered our consciousness about AIDS and public policy, and Queer Nation had promoted the use of what Patrick S. Cheng calls "transgressive action"[1] to bring queer awareness to the forefront in people's thinking. Yet the full effect of those political, social, and confrontational movements was not as clear to me as it would be after I had reached out to our gay and lesbian members and invited the establishment of a gay group. In a word, I had not taken full cognizance of what a very complex and multilayered community we had become because of AIDS.

I found that many social factors were shaping the self-identities of our queer members. Some gay men did not want to be in a group with lesbians. Some lesbians did not want to be in a group with gay men, which is to say that both felt that their concerns and issues were important and distinctive enough that they should be addressed separately. We began to realize that we should have a men's group and a separate women's group, and that we were understaffed to support that ministry. Then we realized that three members of the group were transgendered, which made things even more challenging.

The most striking separation, however, was not gender identification but age difference. Men in their fifties and older, survivors of the AIDS epidemic, wanted to be together and tell stories about how hard it was to come out and how difficult to be a survivor whose cohort of friends had died. The younger members of the group were the complete opposite. Their attitude was, "We're here, we're queer, get over it." I needed a new model for ministering with the queer community.

But those were not the only strata of differentiation that I found. I discovered that there were people who were out at church but not at work and not with their families. Some people were out at work and at church but not with their families. Some were out to their families and out at church but not at their work.

Our transgendered members were particularly sensitive as to how out they wanted to be or not be known. While one person might not want to discuss the issues of being transgendered, another woman in the group who had reassigned from being male, I later learned had decided to reassign again after a few years and had gone back to identifying as a male. Learning about the fluidity of queer identities deepened our understanding of a God who breaks out of assigned roles and binary divisions.

Calling Each by Name

Not everyone in the congregation wholeheartedly embraced the diversity we were discovering. I remember one Sunday I had spoken, as I often do, with a reference to some aspect of the inclusion of gay members in our church. A longtime congregant, an older woman, approached me after the sermon and said that she appreciated what I had to say but that she hoped I would never say it again. "Please don't point out the fact that we have gay members again," she said.

When I asked her why, she answered, "We all know that there are gay and lesbian members of the church, we just don't need to talk about it. They're here, they're welcome, they know it, and we don't need to speak about it. We're past that." Perhaps she was staking out a position of postmodern enlightenment for our congregation, a paradisiacal Elysium in which the straight lions were lying down with the gay lambs. But as Woody Allen reminds us, "The lamb[s] won't get much sleep."[2]

"We're past that," she said. But I told her that nothing could be further from the truth. No one knows that they are welcome until you say and show that they are. A gay man in the church who is an actor said to me once how much he had appreciated my using an illustration in which I referred to "partners" rather than to "husband and wife." He said, "I don't need to be in every sermon, and I don't need to be the leading man, but it's important to be reminded from time to time that I am in the cast."

As the cast grows, as our awareness of the diversity of the cast grows, the congregation's understanding of itself and its dramatic possibilities grows too. Today, it's really the congregation that is preaching the *apologia*, living out the clearest message about the changing nature of our life together. Over the past ten years, there has been a significant change in congregational composition. Not only are ethnic, racial, and international diversity represented within our membership, but on Baptism Sundays if we have five couples who are baptizing their infants, it is not at all uncommon that one or two will be same-gender couples. We have come to expect that.

I would guess that among the families of the congregation there are probably twenty-five or more same-gender couples in the church with children. These parents are teaching Sunday school, nursing children in a discreet corner of the sanctuary, raising teenagers who are rebelling and asserting themselves; they are couples in their forties who are caring for their senior parents, and couples and singles who are facing all the same challenges of life together as a family that every other family faces. When we have a toddler play date for the church and serve bagels and coffee after worship, these same-gender parents mix it up with all the other couples in the church, and no one thinks a thing of it.

But that's the case not because we're past it. It is, I think, because we knowingly choose it. I am sure that people come here and join here because we have that sense of openness, because we make a point of visibly and knowingly affirming the uniqueness of everyone.

Our same-gender parents have worked hard to have their children. They have faced a complex legal system that may address the issues of surrogacy, adoption, and same-gender parenting but doesn't make it easy. If straight couples have problems getting pregnant, so do same-gender couples. And whether parents become parents by surrogacy, artificial insemination, adoption, or inventive means of other sorts, they have worked hard to have their children, every bit as hard as the straight parents in the congregation who have had difficulty with pregnancy. If anything, this becomes a bond uniting queer and straight parents because of the common experiences they have as survivors of parenting trials.

For each child being baptized on Baptism Sundays, there are twenty people to support the family—friends, grandparents, extended family. If there are five couples baptizing a child, there is a witness to a hundred people, reaching far beyond the life of this one congregation. The number of people also adds to the impact and impression of those who are a part of that service. Our God cared enough about us to put on flesh and know human life with all its beauty and pain.

Marriage

Probably no issue in the contemporary church is as controversial as is marriage. We know some of the issues on the table about this matter. Heterosexual marriage fails at a rate of nearly 50 percent. Queer folks are asking questions, as is everybody else, about whether marriage is the right way or the best way to make an enduring commitment. Is it a mimicking of a straight agenda? Is it adopting heterosexual values that are somehow different from queer values? Can we even talk about queer values as such, or can we only say that there are as many queer values as there are queer people, and that there will be points of convergence and points of divergence with other queer people as there will be with straight people. And what about monogamy in marriage?

For those of us in the church, there are some fundamental issues about marriage that we are only beginning to ask. In the Presbyterian Church, we have the Book of Common Worship somewhat like the Episcopal Book of Common Prayer. Within that Book of Common Worship there is no marriage ceremony for same-gender couples. The Presbyterian Directory for Worship says that marriage is defined as a covenant between a man and a woman.

When the first of the same-gender couples who asked to have a legal marriage ceremony requested that service to be performed, we found that our application forms and our marriage booklet describing the policies of the church were no longer appropriate. There was a place for the bride and a place for the groom to provide their information, but none for the bride and the bride. We quickly changed the forms to ask information about Spouse A and Spouse B. Likewise, we had no wording for same-gender marriage ceremonies.

All of our clergy staff had performed *commitment* ceremonies, but when the State of New York signed same-gender marriage into law, we began to ask in what ways were we now in a different position as pastors officiating on behalf of a state that issues same-gender marriage licenses but in a church that does not recognize same-gender marriages? Any of us who are pastors in the Presbyterian Church and perform same-gender marriage ceremonies remain subject to scrutiny by our denomination and may face disciplinary charges that can be brought against us by any Presbyterian who objects and wishes to challenge us.

The ecclesiastical gymnastics involved in this theological conundrum are absurd. One pastor in Massachusetts was tried on the basis that she married two women in a ceremony in that state. She did, of course, but the Presbyterian General Assembly Judicial Commission, which heard her case, acquitted her of doing so on the grounds that she could not have officiated at a marriage ceremony because the Presbyterian Church does not recognize same-gender marriage! This is a head-in-the sand-approach to ecclesiastical jurisprudence. If you say it doesn't exist, it doesn't exist even though it does.

I suppose that, as in many congregations, robust discussion continues among our queer members about marriage and whether people wish to be married or not. But we also have a large and growing number of queer couples who are raising children and finding that they are queering the idea of what is to be queer. They are finding and making communities of support and welcome that cross gender and matrimonial lines. They are sometimes finding more in common with other parents of children their own age, straight parents, other queer parents, and other family that are drawn into the circle of their lives. In that sense, what seems on the surface to be most orthodox is possibly queerest.

This is a good thing. Hillary Clinton's contention that it takes a village to raise a child is borne out in the experience of the church. In our Presbyterian baptismal service we do not have godparents who take responsibility for the spiritual welfare of the child. We ask the entire congregation in a formal question whether they will promise to support and encourage this family in their Christian journey and whether they will encourage the parents as well as the children who stand before them in their commitment to raise their child in the faith.

When we have a same-gender couple or family standing in front of the church making a promise, and a congregation promising to help them, a very queer and wonderful thing is happening. All kinds of walls are coming down, and the world is becoming a more holy and blessed place, a little more like the commonwealth of God, because we are enacting the fact that we are the body of Christ, to borrow a theological term, and individually members of that body. We treat all the members of that body with due honor, as Saint Paul so aptly described, and no member of the body can do as well without all the other members of the body working in concert.

Incarnation: The Queerest Act of All

This radical welcome, opening our doors and allowing those who come in to change us and deepen our understanding of God, is queer indeed. What inspires us to be so welcoming is the doctrine of the Incarnation, the theological assertion that God has queered the divide between heaven and earth and taken on human form and dwelled among us. It is the theological underpinning that defines what we are to be and to do in the church, because we are the body of Christ. God doing what is least expected, breaking out of an assigned role, breaking open the binary division, putting on flesh and blood and knowing human life, sensing pain, feeling fear, struggling in prayer, experiencing temptation, tasting death. Incarnation, the queerest act of all.

Patrick Cheng has recently argued that God is "radical love," a "love so extreme that it dissolves existing boundaries that might normally seem fixed."[3] Cheng summons Gerard Loughlin's argument that "God is radically unknowable . . . fundamentally an identity without essence."[4] But the very point of the Incarnation, it seems to me, is that God chooses to become known across substantial and real *difference*: the infinite being who chooses to take on finite existence in the life, death, and resurrection of Jesus Christ.

Queerness, it seems to me, responds to an opposition that would deny its existence, which would push it to the side and label it aberrant and therefore either irrelevant or heretical. Cheng argues that God's love is so radical that it "dissolves the dualism between matter and spirit."[5] "God" and "humanity" are no longer "mutually exclusive categories" but instead come together in Jesus Christ.[6] Yet that crossing the barrier between heaven and earth, matter and spirit, human and divine is a juxtaposition of being and reality that is God's work and not ours. It is an opposition and definition that cannot be given away.

Cheng argues that these differences are dissolved, and that this opens the door to an embodiment of radical love that crosses social boundaries, sexual boundaries, and gender boundaries. But the truth is that it is precisely the traversing of the real and definable *distance*, the bridging of the real and demonstrable difference, that is the point, not that there is no longer a distinction. In Jesus Christ real and substantial distinction is met and overcome. This is not an illusory difference between matter and spirit, the human and the divine, "a drag show," as Cheng playfully suggests.[7]

I guess I am too much of a Calvinist to throw that away. God is God, and we are human and therefore not-God. In Christ that boundary is traversed not because we become godlike but because God takes on humanity and dwells among us. It is God who takes that initiative, and we are the recipients of that grace. I see that not as a matter of patriarchy or dominance but as an act of grace. Grace, then, is an expression of love that knows no bounds, the distance the Divine Lover is willing to traverse to reach the beloved.

It seems to me that what the church is meant to be and do is to be the place of meeting, the bed of blessing, the table of invitation, the mikvah and bathing place of our preparation for sacred encounter. It is the place where The One who is not us meets the one who is us, and in that sense it is the place where our deepest longings are known, our truest self is celebrated, our fullest joy is realized.

Hospitality

We in the church are the body of Christ, the physical expression of Christ's presence in the world today. We can therefore be no less welcoming or hospitable than he was, when he said, "Anyone who comes to me I will never drive away" (John 6:37). In the church there must be hospitality—hospitality in the largest and most expansive sense of the Christian tradition, rising out of the desert communities where our ancestors in faith lived, and no one could long exist without the care and nurture of the other who might welcome the stranger. Hospitality reaches across the distance between us and welcomes relationship. It invites communion.

If hospitality is how we are welcomed into this meeting place, then what the church is called to do is to go even beyond its doors to the streets, to all the places where the Lover and the beloved meet. We must go there because the church has been in the past and in so many people's experience a place of inhospitality. I think today the church has to go out of its way to counteract that long history of rejection by proactively reaching out to the queer community in acts of welcome and deeds that demonstrate that the body of Christ includes even me, even you.

The queer theology of the First Presbyterian Church in the City of New York is perhaps most concretely expressed when this congregation goes to the streets and reaches beyond the gates of its fence on the last Sunday of June each year. Members of this church and others who come from the presbytery serve 5,000 cups of water to marchers in the Gay Pride Parade. The parade begins with Dykes on Bikes and winds its way through all the representative groups that reflect the vibrancy of the queer community, the drag queens and ethnic and nationality groups, the churches and the bars, the Renaissance Faire characters, the Rentboys dancing, the Harvey Milk School kids, the gay cheerleaders.

It is one of the highlights of the liturgical year for us, a kind of Pentecost of the queer spirit in our church calendar. Because it makes incarnate the love and hospitality of God, it is the church at its best and at its most faithful and at its queerest all at the same time.

V. Gene Robinson, Episcopal bishop of New Hampshire, preached the sermon in our worship service on Pride Sunday in 2009, the fortieth anniversary of Stonewall, and then joined me and members of this congregation in serving cups of water to the parade. From the pulpit where Fosdick called out the fundamentalists, the first openly gay bishop in Christian history enjoined us to imagine that God, who is everywhere, was in the midst of that parade, and in the church as well. But, he warned, the church must approach the parade in humility:

When you offer a cup of water bearing the name of Christ . . . you are the oppressor offering a cup of water to the oppressed. They get it. They get the act of compassion. My question is, "Do you get it?" Do you realize the important thing that you do by giving a cup of water to those people out there who have been hurt by us and continue to be hurt by us?[8]

There is work to do engaging the glorious diversity of humans created in the divine image, but also back home in our churches.

It's not enough to pull people out of a raging stream who are drowning, we have to walk back upstream and find out who's throwing them in the first place.

It's that tough systemic work both within our religious communities and in the culture that we must be committed to changing. And those of you who are heterosexual, we need you desperately. I think God is calling you to understand this as an issue of justice.

To a lot of people across this great nation what's happening out here [the Gay Pride march] this afternoon is a total nightmare. I'm here to tell you that it is no nightmare. It is God's dream coming true before your very eyes.[9]

The calling, then, is for my church and yours to be a faithful church, incarnating the queer love of a God who has traversed the greatest distance of all to be with us.

Addendum

Since the submission of this chapter, the 221st General Assembly of the Presbyterian Church (U.S.A.) approved an "Authoritative Interpretation" of the Constitution of the church which will allow ministers of the denomination in states which allow same gender marriages to perform such marriages without fear of ecclesiastical censure. A constitutional amendment was also sent to the 172 presbyteries which would redefine marriage as being "a civil contract between two persons, traditionally a man and a woman" rather than "a civil contract between a man and a woman." The amendment must be approved within one year (by June, 2015) by a majority of the presbyteries, each of which has one vote. There is no question that civil law is changing rapidly. The question is whether Presbyterians will embrace new and more inclusive theological and Biblical understandings of marriage which will allow them to respond to that social change. In the meantime, regardless of what changes occur in civil law, pastors will have to make a decision as to whether they will bless the commitments of their GLBTQ members.

NOTES

1. Patrick S. Cheng, *Radical Love: An Introduction to Queer Theology* (New York: Seabury, 2011), 5.
2. Woody Allen, *Without Feathers* (New York: Random House, 1972), 25.
3. Cheng, *Radical Love*, 50.
4. See Gerard Loughlin, "Introduction," in *Queer Theology: Rethinking the Western Body*, ed. Gerard Loughlin (Malden, MA: Blackwell, 2008), 7; cf. Cheng, *Radical Love*, 54.
5. Cheng, *Radical Love*, 67.
6. Ibid., 79.
7. Ibid., 54.
8. V. Gene Robinson, "Keep on Dancing," sermon preached at the First Presbyterian Church in the City of New York, June 28, 2009, privately published.
9. Ibid.

PART II

Matrimonies

Marriage is thought by many to be the unchanging norm of Christian sexuality. It is the other traditional "state of life." Even before recent efforts to extend marriage to same-sex unions, however, it has been anything but fixed. Elaborated in uneasy relationships with changing civil understandings of marriage and family, Christian matrimony was sacramentalized on analogy with celibates' unions with Christ. Its goods—"unitive" and "procreative"—were contested and varying in meaning long before the modern ideal of complementary heterosexual partnership and understandings of eros in biological terms. Decoupling "matrimonies" from these late and limiting developments raises fascinating queer questions about commitment, fruitfulness, friendship, reciprocity, family, and the relationship of religious and civil bonds.

The traditional word "matrimony" lends its name to this part because it affords critical distance from discussions of marriage, unions, partnerships, and the like that usually elide the question of the *religious* significance of the relationship at issue. The pluralized matrimon*ies* reminds us that even Christian marriage has meant and means many things.

William E. Smith III takes us into the lives of two twelfth-century women torn between two lovers—Christ, the bridegroom of consecrated *sponsae christi*, and a human husband; while each was drawn to a different husband, their predicaments show the uncertainty of human marriage at the very moment it was becoming sacramentalized.

Heather R. White analyzes the first same-sex marriages in New York in the early 1970s and how they complicate both widely held ideas about the place of religion in the gay rights movement and the tense relationship of religious and sexual rights. Teresa Delgado finds queer potential in the practice of contemporary married heterosexual Catholics as they live out a different, and more queer-friendly, understanding of the good of marriage than (currently) recognized by the Vatican. Finally, Jennifer Harvey offers scenes from the life of a contemporary queer family, reflecting on how the daily struggles and joys of partnership and parenthood provide sacred opportunities to disrupt sinful patterns of the "normal."

The fruitfulness of this form of Christian sexual life continues to surprise.

5

Two Medieval Brides of Christ

Complicating Monogamous Marriage

WILLIAM E. SMITH III

Women could marry Jesus in western medieval Europe. They could do this in a way men could not because gender altered a person's marital possibilities in the Middle Ages as it no longer does. For certain women, as Sarah McNamer explains, "if the standard rituals were enacted, chastity observed, and, crucially, the fitting feelings repeatedly performed, female religious could become literally, by which I mean legally, married to Christ—not only in this life but for all eternity."[1] Men, especially monks, were certainly not barred from marrying Jesus symbolically. But men did not have available to them the embodied social status of *sponsa Christi* (bride of Christ) that women's bridal status conferred with all its legal weight. Thus medieval women had two marital routes available to them, one leading to God, the other to a human male.

Yet these two marital tracks did not always stay neatly separated. Two twelfth-century cases illustrate that Christian women could find themselves in polygamous arrangements, being simultaneously married to a human male and to Christ. In other words, internal to Christianity's officially monogamous tradition were bigamous possibilities. These unions involve emotions and desires that complicate any easy divide between celibacy and marital sexuality. These mixed marriages reveal the limits of framing *sponsa Christi* and marriage more generally through legal recognition alone, since issues around consent and desire as well as claims to the sacramental nature of marriage can make it difficult to determine whether a marriage is over or not and if a person is in more than one marriage at the same time.

When Tertullian (c. 160–220) introduced *sponsa Christi* as a metaphor for consecrated virgins, he had no intention of it taking on flesh. In inaugurating this title for women, Tertullian shifted the rhetorical field that the apostle Paul had initiated earlier. In Ephesians 5, Paul (or, more likely, someone in his name) depicted the congregation as a collective bride of Christ. Elsewhere Paul spoke of the soul as the divine's spouse (2 Corinthians 11:2). Over the centuries this approach to *sponsa Christi* bore rich exegetical fruit that harbored an array of male gender play and queer erotics.[2] Tertullian, however, developed a possibility latent in the discussion of widowhood in 1 Timothy 5 that transformed this metaphor from a gendered code applicable to any Christian to one that applied in a particular way to females.

Tertullian was not exactly a champion of marriage's spiritual possibilities. He designated certain religious women *sponsa Christi* in order to gain a measure of control over them. Because virgins were at this time considered more angelic than ordinary Christians who married, describing them as spouses pulled these women a little farther from heaven even as it tied them more closely to the divine.[3] Other early church fathers, such as Cyprian (c. 200–258) and Athanasius (c. 296–373), worked to control and cultivate the spiritual life of religious women, subjecting them to the church's inchoate judicial system and marking their presence under the terms of marriage and adultery.[4] By the High Middle Ages the legal marital status of religious women became substantial enough to undo marriages to humans. Such developments were possible because theologians in the Latin West were increasingly literal about religious women being Christ's brides and transformed female consecration ceremonies into nuptial rituals.[5]

During this same period the church took a growing role in the betrothal aspect of marriage in order to sanctify it and to articulate what Christian marriage was.[6] The church further increased its jurisdiction over marriage by creating and performing a marital liturgy in the early Middle Ages, and marriages were increasingly performed in sacred spaces. However, it was not until the twelfth century that the leaders of Western Christendom brought marriage fully under ecclesial control. Twelfth-century reformers labored to regularize the confusing and contradictory canon law that they had inherited, which helped lead to marriage being included among the seven Catholic sacraments.[7]

A major dispute arose during this period concerning whether consent alone or coitus in addition to consent was necessary for a complete, sacramental marriage. Pope Alexander III (c. 1100–1181) sided with the consent-only faction.[8] But some medieval theologians, such as the influential Hugh of Saint Victor (c. 1096–1141), found the social fact that Christ's *sponsae* were actually his wives unsettling. This marital literalism created an enduring potential for category confusion, which Hugh marked with the language of adultery.[9] The cases of Christina of Markyate and Heloise and Abelard demonstrate that his concerns were not idle theological speculation.

Christina of Markyate

As a child, Christina of Markyate (c. 1096-8—c. 1155-66) dreamed only of marriage to Christ, and she united herself with him during her adolescence. For much of her life, however, she was also married to a man named Beorhtred, a young nobleman from a prominent local family. Thus, she lived in a form of polyandry that might be termed a double marriage. The two marriages posed emotional challenges for Christina, since she found her affections (and others' interests in her) frequently pulling her in directions she did not wish to follow.[10] *The Life of Christina of Markyate*, written to cast Christina as saintly, gains much of its narrative force from the conflict between advocates for the respective unions.[11] Everyone in *The Life* wanted Christina to be married to only one person; they just could not agree if it should be Jesus or Beorhtred. Beorhtred, with the encouragement of Christina's friends and family, even attempted to rape Christina in order to render their marriage complete per twelfth-century English marital customs.[12] Her polyandry was socially unbearable to all.

Christina pledged herself to Christ during Mass in a village church, prompted by a desire to be like the monks she had visited in her childhood.[13] Upon returning home, Christina informed Sueno, her first spiritual friend and adviser, of her vow.[14] Her marriage now had social stakes between humans as well as among the heavenly community. But the union, while valid and licit, remained incomplete. As with marriages between humans, a marriage to Christ required more than a betrothal. In order to secure full social legibility as a *sponsa Christi*, a woman needed to undergo a ceremonial consecration led by a bishop. Sexual status mattered as well. In general, permanent virginity held pride of place, with chaste widowhood being second best when it came to a divine marriage. Virginity stands as a proof of marital loyalty to Christ in *The Life*, and Christina's efforts to preserve her chastity consume much attention. But how virginal was Christina according to medieval conceptions of chastity?

The omniscient narrator of *The Life* informs us that before the consecration ceremony Christina was troubled by unwanted sexual desires and what they meant for the spiritual status of her flesh.[15] The most explicit case of Christina's sexual desire came while she was living in hiding with an unnamed cleric. Both Christina and this cleric began to desire the other. In an attempt to purge herself of her desires, Christina undertook a fierce ascetic program that included fasting, rationing food and drink, sleepless nights, and self-scourging.[16] Christina's refusal to consent to her desire shows her to be a virgin spiritually as well as physically.[17] If Christina did not willfully desire the cleric, her bridal status would not be in jeopardy.[18]

These efforts, though, proved insufficient. Her divine spouse had to provide her permanent relief. Christina encountered Christ as an apparition while awake:

> In the guise of a small child, [Christ] came to the arms of his sorely tested spouse and remained with her a whole day, not only being felt but also seen. The maiden took the child in her hands, gave thanks, and pressed him to her bosom. And with immeasurable delight she held him at one moment to her virginal breast, at another felt him in her innermost being. . . . From that moment, the fire of lust was so completely extinguished that never after could it be revived.[19]

How Christ provided his bride succor in this episode is worth pausing over, since it sheds light on another aspect of being *sponsa Christi*. This positively charged erotic scene is the only one in *The Life* in which Christina engages in mystical sex, which Constance Furey defines as "the intense pleasure and pain that bodies inflict and receive . . . the ecstasy, standing outside oneself, the rhythmic arousal and breathless pleasure that come from and in this experience."[20] Mystical sex in *The Life* differs, though, from the better-known violent sex several thirteenth-century female mystics experienced with a feminized Christ.[21] In Christina's case, the sexual encounter is one of skin against skin and nongenital penetration—a point reinforced by Christ's apparition as a young child—that yielded a sense of intersubjective bliss. This lust-sating sex prevents Christina from consenting to her desire for the cleric and thus preserves virginal chastity.

Mystical sex is not a legal requirement for a *sponsa Christi* to be a literal wife of Christ, but it does serve as a relational component that mirrors what is expected for human-human marriages. Christina's encounter with Christ does not simply prevent a lapse into extramarital sex but also stands in contrast to Beorhtred's sexual advances toward Christina in her other marriage. When her desire for the cleric arose, Christina had not long been released from her marriage to Beorhtred. Hence, Christ's and Christina's marital sex places Beorhtred and Christina's unconsummated marriage into relief. In the context of the narrative, Christina's experience with Christ helps consolidate their union as a marriage in which the two become one.

Yet if Beorhtred and his supporters had had their way, it would have been otherwise. Christina's family and friends sanctioned marital rape. Her parents actively schemed to get Christina to consummate her marriage with Beorhtred by intoxication, pressure from powerful clergy, and even magic.[22] Christina had her own host of allies who actively sought to ensure that the young woman ended up safely with Christ. Holy men and women were happy to do what they could to assist Christina's escape from Beorhtred and her family.[23] Other helpers were supernatural. Throughout *The Life*, saints appear in visions to encourage Christina and terrorize her foes. Divine forces are behind the fires and fevers that prevent Christina's and Beorhtred's wedding celebrations from taking place.[24] Beorhtred only consents to the dissolving of his marriage because the Virgin Mary "had appeared to him in a terrifying vision, harshly reproving him for his needless persecution of the sacred maiden."[25] In short, Christina's sex life was a thoroughly communal affair. In the end, Christina's allies carried the day. Beorhtred released Christina from the marriage, and Christina was consecrated as Christ's bride. But for many years she was a polygamist, albeit a discontented one.

Heloise

In contrast to Christina, Heloise, abbess of the Paraclete, was an unwilling bride of Christ, one who continued to have spiritual sex with her human spouse, even as he tried to fob her off on Jesus. The famous tale of Heloise and Abelard could easily be told in a linear fashion, a shift from illicit lovers, to married couple, and then finally to religious. Abelard uses this basic structure to narrate their interlocked biographies in his self-serving autobiography *The History of My Misfortunes*, but the series of letters exchanged between Heloise and Abelard in the wake of *The History* tells a different tale. Try as they might to figure out how Christ would fit into their lives, they are unable to put their past relational identities behind them. From this mix a potentially heaven-bound bridal "whore" emerges, though the final recipient of her passions remains contested.

Abelard (c. 1079–c. 1142) and Heloise (c. 1090–c. 1164) met in part because of Heloise's reputation for learning. Abelard, whose fame as a philosopher was growing, arranged with her uncle Fulbert, with whom Heloise lived, to serve as her tutor in order to seduce her. Heloise appears to have fallen as much for Abelard as he for her. Their love affair became known to Fulbert, and a secret wedding was held to maintain the peace while permitting Abelard to run his school, an occupation that required at least the appearance of a celibate life. The marriage became public, however, and Abelard hid Heloise in a convent. Fearing that this was a de facto divorce, Fulbert and his kin castrated Abelard.[26] In the aftermath, Abelard and Heloise both officially converted to religious lives and remained in sacred orders thereafter.

Legally their marriage ended when they became religious, and Abelard, in his letters, distinguishes between their past and present social selves with concomitant shifts in how they should relate to each other.[27] Abelard's insistence that they are changed beings is fully on display in how he addresses Heloise: "To the bride of Christ, from His servant."[28] In this invocation their relationship is hierarchically triangulated through Christ. Heloise, the spouse of his lord, is ranked higher than Abelard. She had married up, leaving Abelard both behind and below: "It was a fortunate trading of your married state: as you were previously the wife of a poor mortal and now you are raised to the bed of the high king."[29] Elsewhere Abelard asserts that, as religious, they were now spiritually brother and sister.[30] Both of these (non–mutually exclusive) relational frameworks stress that he is *not* her husband.

Abelard also desired Christ to be Heloise's "friend," the word Heloise uses primarily to refer to Abelard as her past lover. To justify the switch, he redeployed Heloise's language about why she accepted Abelard as her friend or, to use another term she used when emphasizing her inordinate desire, "whore."[31] "[Christ] is the true friend who desires yourself and nothing that is yours."[32] This friendship then is eroticized—even if lacking a genital component—just as was Abelard's with Heloise. Abelard renders this eroticization of the divine lover-spouse more explicit in another passage when he writes of Heloise's having intimately joined the heavenly king in the bridal chamber.[33] If these terms stood unquestioned, Heloise would be the chaste bridal whore of Christ, and Abelard would be her servant brother with one marriage neatly following the end of the other.

Yet throughout their writings, this neat substitution of social positions breaks down. Indeed, Abelard's emphatic insistence on Heloise's position as the lover-bride of Christ was partially a response to her own emphasis on her continued sex life, which remained firmly focused on Abelard. She confesses, "Men call me chaste; they do not know the hypocrite I am."[34] Of course she is chaste in the simplistic sense of not engaging in direct bodily, especially genital, contact with another human. But she is not truly chaste, since she actively, even if not always intentionally, engages in what can be called spiritual sex:

> In my case, the pleasures of lovers which we shared have been too sweet—they cannot displease me, and can scarcely shift from my memory. . . . Everything that we did and also the times and places where we did it are stamped on my heart along with your image, so that *I live through them all again with you.* . . . Sometimes my thoughts are betrayed in a movement on my *body*, or they break out in an unguarded *word*.[35]

Spiritual sex is bodily and verbal even if it is a form of solo sex that makes present prior sexual encounters. If people know how to read the corporeal clues and listen for the verbal betrayals, they might pick up on her continued sex life despite her efforts to keep it hidden. Heloise is deadly serious when she says she is an unchaste abbess.

This issue of "times and places" points in another direction besides the phenomenological characteristics of spiritual sex. Although Heloise framed her past sexual escapades with Abelard in terms of their relationship as lovers, the illicit, secretive element of their nonmarital sex bleeds into their licit marital encounters as well. While Heloise was hiding at Argenteuil, she and Abelard had sex in the refectory at least once during their few "furtive" meetings as a married couple.[36] With their sex as both "friends" and spouses marked by semisecrecy, stolen moments, and improper places, there is no clear break between their premarital and marital sex lives. Heloise's spiritual sex likely feeds off her entire sexual history.[37]

Elsewhere in the letters Heloise more directly insists on her marriage to Abelard as something still existing despite her status as *sponsa Christi*. Notice, for example, how she addresses Abelard in her first letter to him: "To her lord, or rather father; to her husband, or rather brother; from his handmaid, or rather daughter; from his wife, or rather sister; to Abelard, from Heloise."[38] This series of titular terms calls attention to her dual status as his wife and fellow religious. She does this, moreover, in spite of her no longer being Abelard's legal spouse. Instead, Heloise grounds the continued reality of their marriage in its sacramental form: "Yet you [Abelard] must know that you are bound to me by an obligation which is all the greater for the further close tie of the marriage sacrament uniting us, and are the deeper in my debt because of the love I have always borne for you, as everyone knows, a love which is beyond all bounds."[39] She insists upon her mixed position, with both sets of vows placing competing demands on her behaviorally as well as emotionally. This comingled state of affairs has led some scholars to view Heloise as "the shell of a bride of Christ."[40] She betrayed no passion for her divine husband even as she fulfilled her uxorial duties to him as abbess and nun.[41]

In spite of his efforts to establish a decisive succession of social identities, Abelard also blurs them. Indeed, he argues that Heloise's status as his wife is crucial to *his* salvation.[42] Noting the efficacious nature of wives' intercessory prayers for their husbands, he makes the links between Heloise's husbands explicit.[43] "For we are one in Christ, one flesh according to the law of matrimony," Abelard reminds Heloise near the end of his second letter. "Whatever is yours cannot, I think, fail to be mine, and Christ is yours because you have become his bride."[44] In other words, Abelard and Christ reciprocally gain each other through Heloise's polyandry. Indeed, it is his conjugal relationship to Heloise that prompts Abelard to react so harshly to her spiritual sex, which threatens her standing as Christ's wife. Such sex not only renders Heloise potentially hell-bound but also potentially cuts him off from the full fruits of *his* marital relationship to Christ.

Yet, Heloise continued to direct her intense affections toward one spouse rather than the other. While Abelard envisioned Heloise as Christ's bridal "whore," Heloise insisted on being Abelard's special friend simultaneously to her being both males' bride. She and Abelard reached an impasse about how to conceive of and live their polyandrous lives. Their dueling conceptions of the situation reveal a disordered marriage in which emotions and desire short-circuit the possibility of inhabiting discrete social, religious, and legal selves.

Conclusion

The cases of Christina and Heloise and Abelard make clear that the history of marriage, especially Christian marriage, cannot simply be identified with the history of heterosexuality. It was once intelligible and possible for women to marry the divine as well as men, and their respective marital sexualities should not be confused. Chastity, especially in the form of virginity, was part of the *sponsa Christi* marital deal. But genital chastity did not foreclose sex as an option, be it with a human or God (via spiritual sex and mystical sex, respectively). Some versions of medieval sexualities may disturb our sensibilities, such as Christina's pedophilic sex with Christ. Yet more important than discovering unnerving Christian sexualities are the implications of these tales for tracking relationships and how they relate to desire. Situated in a marriage, as we have seen, desire can pull in promiscuous ways precisely because what appear to be sexual situations between two persons often involve others *in absentia*.

These cases also teach us something important about marriage. Even in the pursuit of monogamy, forms of polygamy can emerge. This phenomenon is all the more telling because it occurred precisely when Christians should have been least likely to have multiple concurrent spouses. The twelfth century speaks back to us, since many of us labor under similar monogamous demands, reminding us that it is not enough to recognize that marriage can be queered (i.e., expanded to include GLBT persons) or that wedding ceremonies can generate queer desires around the putatively heterosexual couple being united.[45] These two cases of *sponsa Christi* demonstrate that marriage can also queer us.

NOTES

1. Sarah McNamer, *Affective Meditation and the Invention of Medieval Compassion* (Philadelphia: University of Pennsylvania Press, 2000), 28. Consult, too, Thomas Head's "The Marriages of Christina of Markyate," *Viator* 21 (1990): 75–102.

2. Stephen D. Moore, *God's Beauty Parlor: And Other Queer Spaces in and around the Bible* (Stanford, CA: Stanford University Press, 2001), 21–89.

3. Dyan Elliott, *The Bride of Christ Goes to Hell: Metaphor and Embodiment in the Lives of Pious Women, 200–1500* (Philadelphia: University of Pennsylvania Press, 2011), 13–29.

4. Ibid., 32–34, 38–43.

5. Ibid., 46–47; and John Bugge, *Virginitatis: An Essay in the History of a Medieval Ideal* (The Hague: Martinus Nijhoff, 1975), 66.

6. Elliott, *Bride of Christ Goes to Hell*, 46, 48.

7. Penny S. Gold, "The Marriage of Mary and Joseph," in *Sexual Practices and the Medieval Church*, ed. James Brundage and Vern Bullough (Buffalo, NY: Prometheus Books, 1982), 102–17.

8. James A. Brundage, *Law, Sex, and Christian Society in Medieval Europe* (Chicago: University of Chicago Press, 1987), 267–69, 331–39.

9. Hugh of Saint Victor, *Hugh of Saint Victor on the Sacraments*, trans. Roy J. Deferrari (Eugene, OR: Wipf and Stock, 2007), 345–51.

10. My reading is partially informed by C. Stephen Jaeger's essay "The Loves of Christina of Markyate," in *Christina of Markyate*, ed. Samuel Fanous and Henrietta Leyser (New York: Routledge, 2005), 99–115.

11. On how *The Life* fits into the hagiographic tradition, see Samuel Fanous, "Christina of Markyate and the Double Crown," in *Christina of Markyate*, ed. Samuel Fanous and Henrietta Leyser (New York: Routledge, 2005), 53–78.

12. Samuel Fanous, Henrietta Leyser, and C. H. Talbot, *The Life of Christina of Markyate* (New York: Oxford University Press, 2010), 13, 48; and Christopher Brooke, *The Medieval Idea of Marriage* (Oxford: Oxford University Press, 1989), 145–46.

13. Fanous, Leyser, and Talbot, *Life of Christina of Markyate*, 5–6.

14. Ibid. 6, 4–5.

15. Ibid. 53 (emphasis added).

16. Ibid. 46–47.

17. For more on the medieval distinction between spiritual and physical virginity, consult Sarah Salih, *Versions of Virginity* (Cambridge: D. S. Brewer, 2001).

18. Barbara Newman, *From Virile Woman to WomanChrist: Studies in Medieval Religion and Literature* (Philadelphia: University of Pennsylvania Press, 1995), 28–45.

19. Fanous, Leyser, and Talbot, *Life of Christina of Markyate*, 48.

20. Constance Furey, "Sexuality," in *The Cambridge Companion to Christian Mysticism*, ed. Amy Hollywood and Patricia Z. Beckman (Cambridge: Cambridge University Press, 2012), 340.

21. Karma Lochrie, "Mystical Acts, Queer Tendencies," in *Constructing Medieval Sexuality*, ed. Karma Lochrie, Peggy McCracken, and James A. Schultz (Minneapolis: University of Minnesota Press, 1997), 180–200.

22. Fanous, Leyser, and Talbot, *Life of Christina of Markyate*, 10–11, 16, 19–20, 23–24, 63.

23. Ibid., 35–36.

24. Ibid., 13–14.

25. Ibid., 43.

26. For the complexity of these matters, see M. T. Clanchy, *Abelard: A Medieval Life* (Oxford: Blackwell, 1999), 191–96.

27. Ibid., 163.

28. Betty Radice, trans., *The Letters of Abelard and Heloise*, rev. ed. (London: Penguin, 2003), 72.

29. Ibid., 73.

30. Ibid., 35, 56.

31. For more on the implications of Heloise's use of a Latin term for "whore," see Clanchy, *Abelard*, 164. Her use of the word "friend" also carried connotations of mistress, as Morgan Powell notes: "Listening to Heloise at the Paraclete: Of Scholarly Diversion and a Woman's 'Conversion,'" in *Listening to Heloise: The Voice of a Twelfth-Century Woman*, ed. Bonnie Wheeler (New York: St. Martin's Press, 2000), 261.

32. Radice, *Letters of Abelard and Heloise*, 86, 51.

33. Ibid., 77. Abelard eroticizes this relationship through an allegorical but functionally literal commentary on the figure of the "black" bride in the Song of Songs (73–77).

34. Ibid., 69.

35. Ibid., 68–69 (emphasis added).

36. Ibid. 16, 80.

37. The convent is a highly sexualized place according to Heloise. See Karma Lochrie, *Heterosyncrasies: Female Sexuality When Normal Wasn't* (Minneapolis: University of Minnesota Press, 2005), 42–46.

38. Radice, *Letters of Abelard and Heloise*, 47.

39. Ibid., 50.

40. C. Stephen Jaeger, *Ennobling Love: In Search of a Lost Sensibility* (Philadelphia: University of Pennsylvania Press, 1999), 170. I diverge from the common

argument that Heloise only recognized herself as Abelard's lover. Clanchy, *Abelard*, 149–50; Elliott, *Bride of Christ Goes to Hell*, 125–49; Jaeger, *Ennobling Love*, 160–69.

41. On Heloise as good abbess, see Donna Alfano Bussell, *Heloise Redressed: A Re-examination of Letter V* (San Francisco: San Francisco State University Press, 1996); Linda Georgianna, "Any Corner of Heaven," *Mediaeval Studies* 49 (1987): 221–53; and Mary Martin McLaughlin, "Heloise the Abbess," in *Listening to Heloise: The Voice of a Twelfth-Century Woman*, ed. Bonnie Wheeler (New York: St. Martin's Press, 2000), 1–17.

42. Radice, *Letters of Abelard and Heloise*, 56.

43. Ibid., 57.

44. Ibid., 87–88.

45. Elizabeth Freeman, *The Wedding Complex: Forms of Belonging in Modern American Culture* (Durham, NC: Duke University Press, 2002).

6

Gay Rites and Religious Rights

New York's First Same-Sex Marriage Controversy

HEATHER R. WHITE

In April 1971, a bride and groom, both African Americans, stood before the altar of a New York City Episcopal church to exchange vows that consecrated their relationship before God. Barbara Trecker, a journalist with the *New York Post*, was on hand to report this notable event, and her article began with the most important detail: the weather was perfect. The bride looked stunning in a floor-length yellow gown and handmade veil, as did the attending bridesmaid attired in green satin. The groom wore a classic black tuxedo with a carnation in the lapel, and the happy couple was surrounded by beaming family and friends and popping flashbulbs. The simple liturgy of the ceremony—described as a "holy union"—followed the conventional exchange of vows "to love and to cherish in the sight of God." The ceremony had "all the trimmings of a conventional wedding," the journalist noted. Except for one important detail—the groom in that tuxedo was a woman—the event appeared in every respect like the typical wedding.[1]

It was that detail, of course, that sparked the ensuing controversy. The "union ceremony," as it was termed, for Bobbi Jean Sanchez and Joan Kearse, the bride and groom presented in the article, sparked controversy and confusion in various quarters. The press coverage of the ceremony brought it to the attention of public officials and religious leaders alike, and it was these authorities who were called to weigh in on whether the ceremony was actually a wedding and whether it was legal and licit for two women to consecrate their relationship. This ceremony, taking place during the heyday of gay liberation in New York, might appear to be a side story or an exception to a movement better known for its "Stop the Church" protests and its critiques of "organized religion." Looking more closely at the wedding and the controversy surrounding it, however, reveals an important story about gay and lesbian wedding practices. It also highlights a broader history of Christian support for the gay liberation organizing of the 1970s.

A Wedding? How Radical!

Kearse and Sanchez celebrated their union ceremony a little less than two years after the event that popularly marks the rise of the gay rights movement. In the early morning hours of June 28, 1969, a police raid on a Greenwich Village gay bar named the Stonewall Inn had unexpectedly turned violent. Instead of submitting to the usual humiliating litany of harassment and arrest, the bar patrons fought back and commenced demonstrations in the streets around the bar that lasted all night and into the next day. The Gay Liberation Front, an organization of young leftists formed the month after the bar raid took place, spoke of the moment as a turning point—even a radical new birth—to a new kind of gay politics.

The heady rhetoric overstated the innovation represented by Stonewall and the organizations formed in its wake—Stonewall hardly represented the first moment of resistance against a police raid on a gay bar, and gay liberation certainly was not the first stirrings of queer politics in the United States. Both took place amid gay and lesbian activism that began formally organizing after World War II. However, the newly radicalized leftists and members of existing gay and lesbian associations alike saw the Stonewall Riots as a potent symbol of a movement that was finally achieving national visibility. In the early 1970s, newscasts, newspapers, and national magazines reported on the growing gay liberation movement and its radical challenge to prevailing laws, policies, and practices that targeted homosexuals. At the same moment, however, those media channels also called attention to a related development: alongside and overlapping with the gay liberation movement, gays and lesbians were also boldly claiming as their own the very religious traditions that many onlookers, gay and straight alike, perceived to be the taproot of the cultural prejudice against homosexuality.

Media sources reporting on gay liberation also delivered news about a perplexing trend (sometimes on the same page)—same sex couples in locations from Los Angeles to Minneapolis were laying claim to marriage, that most traditional of religious institutions. The *Post* story about the Sanchez-Kearse union was New York's answer to a broad trend. This development, as it appeared in the popular press, was led by Troy Perry, an ousted Pentecostal pastor and founder of the gay-welcoming Metropolitan Community Church (MCC) in Los Angeles. The MCC's first service took place in October 1968, and national newspapers began reporting on this novel "homosexual church" in late 1969. Those first articles reported that Perry performed marriage ceremonies for gay couples.[2] According to his own account, Perry conducted ceremonies that declared same-sex couples to be "married in the sight of God."[3]

In June 1970 he took these nuptial blessings into public politics when he officiated at the marriage of Neva Joy Heckman and Judith Ann Belew, a lesbian couple who sought to have their marriage recognized by the State of California. Nowhere did the law specify that a "husband" and "wife" must be of the opposite sex, and so Perry led the couple in vows in which the women promised to faithfully uphold the respective "office of husband" and "office of wife."[4] Only a few weeks earlier, a gay male couple, Michael McConnell and Jack Baker, had applied for a marriage license in Minneapolis. As in California, nothing in the law specified different sex as a requirement for a license, and they managed to obtain a valid marriage certificate in advance of their scheduled December wedding.[5] News about these first gay weddings appeared in the very month that papers also reported on the public demonstrations commemorating the first anniversary of the Stonewall Riots. Newspapers across the country noted with wonderment that the seeming revolt against sexual morals was also accompanied by a "gay marriage boom."[6]

The juxtaposition of gay radicalism and gay weddings was jarring for several reasons. Weddings themselves were on the wane in the early 1970s. Dress designers as well as pastors and other religious leaders worried about the trends toward increasing divorce, premarital sex, and unmarried cohabitation.[7] *Brides* magazine, engine of the wedding industry that boomed just after World War II, was struggling to stay ahead of bankruptcy as a countercultural generation opted for unconventional ceremonies or chose to forgo marriage entirely.[8]

Gays seemed like the least likely saviors of the declining industry.
Marriage, for many gay radicals and lesbian feminists, was an institution of patriarchal oppression. Liberationists castigated marriage and
"organized religion" alike as institutions of sexual and gender oppression, and they proclaimed homosexuality and free love as liberating
alternatives to those confining traditions. Mainstream reporters were
not alone in wondering about the gay marriage boom. Many gay and
lesbian liberationists also watched with perplexity as a segment of the
movement eschewed liberation for a blessing on their relationships.

A Union, a Friendship, or a Marriage?

The trend in same-sex ceremonies, however, also pointed to more
subtle developments. At the foreground of that trend was a quiet story
of established church support for gay liberation. The Kearse-Sanchez
union testified to this development. The ceremony took place in the
sanctuary of the Church of the Holy Apostles, an Episcopal congregation in the Chelsea neighborhood of New York. Just a few months after
the Stonewall Riots, the church opened the doors of its mission house
to the Gay Liberation Front (GLF), which had outgrown its loft space at
Alternative University. The group arranged, for a nominal fee, to lease
space from the church to hold dances and meetings. Robert Weeks, the
church's newly arrived rector, made the arrangements with the consent
of the church vestry and the knowledge of diocesan officials. During the
heady months immediately following the Stonewall Riots, the church
received a steady stream of such requests. In addition to the GLF, the
church provided space for discussion sessions and dances by the West
Side Discussion Group, a homophile organization founded in the 1950s.
The Gay Activist Alliance (GAA), a splinter group from the GLF, also
requested meeting space at the church. Over the course of the next few
years, nearly a dozen gay and lesbian groups cycled through the church.
Gay newspapers in the early 1970s simply designated events that took
place on the church premises with the acronym "CHA," for Church of
the Holy Apostles. The movement sparked by a bar raid found a temporary home in a church.

Holy Apostles was not exceptional. Progressive churches in other
cities also provided meeting space to gay and lesbian groups. These

arrangements often benefited all parties. Many of those urban congregations struggled to stretch donations from dwindling congregations to take care of aging buildings. But the relationship went well beyond material benefit. Urban ministers, working at the forefront of progressive movements in their denominations that emphasized social justice, understood their relationships with communities outside their churches in terms famously declared by liberal theologian Harvey Cox—churches needed to open their doors to the revolution taking place around them. This embrace of revolution certainly informed the activities of Holy Apostles' rector. Weeks attended meetings of the gay liberation groups and participated in political rallies. More than passively providing meeting space, the rector participated in the facilities arrangement as an outreach ministry.

In the spring of 1970, another kind of gay organization had sought facility use from Holy Apostles. Robert Clement, a gay man and a former priest in the Polish National Catholic Church, approached Weeks for permission to use the church's sanctuary for the services of a new congregation named the Church of the Beloved Disciple, which promoted itself as "a church for gay people." With some trepidation that the new gay congregation would siphon off some of Holy Apostles' own members, Weeks and his vestry agreed to host the services. Clement widely publicized the new gay church, and its first service, which took place on a Sunday afternoon two weeks after the first anniversary of Stonewall, drew hundreds. The congregation of the Beloved Disciple quickly outpaced its host, as queer New Yorkers flocked to see the elaborate liturgical services of a congregation that visibly proclaimed a welcome to gay people. The bulletins of service every Sunday repeated the proclamation, "Gay People This Is Your Church!" and the choir wore lavender robes. It soon became unclear, at least to outsiders, which congregation was the guest and which the host. The gay church outnumbered and outpublicized the host congregation, and in the common parlance of gay community members, the church was simply known as the Church of the Beloved Disciple.

Like Perry before him, Clement, in his role as priest, officiated over union ceremonies for same-sex couples. Unlike Perry and other ministers in the MCC, Clement opted to emphasize the distinction between the "holy unions" he officiated and the "marriage ceremonies" of heterosexual couples. Clement made this distinction clear in the service that was covered in the *New York Post*. The ceremony, Clement told the *Post*, was "not just a parallel of straight marriage. . . . Let us not bring into our beautiful gay parish all the faults and problems that sometimes beset marriages." Even as he distanced the ceremonies from hetero-sexual marriage, however, Clement took up the language of sacrament, a term that echoed the marriage theology of Orthodox and Roman Catholic Churches. The union ceremonies, Clement insisted, provided "a blessing of the love of two people sacramentally in the eyes of God and in the Church."[9] It was a paradoxical move—the MCC, following Protestant traditions, did not speak of marriage as a sacrament. How-ever, the "holy union" of the Beloved Disciple, while not a marriage, was indeed a sacrament, a means of divine grace for the couples that exchanged vows.

The *Post* article offered no quibble to this unorthodox marriage theology, but it did reveal another surprise—Weeks, the rector of Holy Apostles, also officiated in blessing rites for same-sex couples. Weeks admitted to the journalist that his numbers were much lower than his counterpart's. He also chose a different name, calling the rituals "ser-vices of friendship," reflecting a more modest relationship theology. However, the liturgy of the service differed very little from the service of holy matrimony provided for heterosexual couples. Weeks sent a copy of the service to New York's Episcopal bishop Paul Moore with an explanation of its meaning. "This blessing service cannot be considered either in the eyes of the Church or in the Law as being 'marriage,'" he indicated. The ceremony was simply "a public blessing of two persons who desire to love, uphold, forgive and help one another."

The language of Weeks's liturgy borrowed from the conventional marriage ceremony but with some important innovations. The gen-dered language of "husband" and "wife" and the designation of "spouse" or "partner" were avoided. The liturgy went instead with the more generic terminology of "friend." So, each participant vowed to "take this friend . . . to live together after God's holy ordinance and as the Church permits." Participants also promised, in conventional language, "to love, comfort, honour, and keep in sickness and in health; and, forsaking all others, keep only to this friend." The final clause of the vow—"as long as ye both shall live"—was put in brackets. As Weeks explained in the letter to Moore, most couples desired to make the vow to a lifelong fidelity. However, some did not, and so he offered it as an option. There were, however, some requirements: Weeks asked all couples to undergo several hours of counseling, and he only agreed to officiate at a service once he felt confident that the two people "really desire[d] a faithful relationship." He also would not permit either partner to cross-dress—something that, he explained to Moore, "I don't regard . . . as being in good taste for a public Church service." It was not only the pastors of new gay churches who were blessing same sex relationships; Weeks was one of a handful of mainstream clergy who understood his support for gays and lesbians to include consecrating their relationships.

Thus, both the new gay church and the established Episcopal congregation offered rites of blessing for same-sex couples. Both clergy distinguished these blessings from marriage, albeit for different reasons. Clement performed a sacramental rite that marked gay relationships as unique and distinct from the "faults and problems" of heterosexual marriages, while Weeks distinguished his "services of friendship" from the marriage ceremonies of heterosexual couples to sidestep those who would see the same-sex ceremonies as a violation of a hallowed tradition. Even as Weeks claimed a different meaning for the rite, however, the liturgy was little more than a gender-neutral version of the conventional marriage ceremony. Neither the "holy union" nor the "service of friendship" was a marriage, but the pains taken to mark the distinction also pointed directly to the possibility of confusion. Could a ceremony be a marriage in everything but name?

A Boundary between Religious Rites and Civil Rights?

The careful distinctions between "marriage ceremonies," "holy unions," and "services of friendship" were lost in the outraged responses to the ceremonies. The *Post* drew a denunciation from Herman Katz, the city clerk of New York, whose office was responsible for issuing civil marriage licenses. Katz, in a statement to the press, accused Clement and Weeks of performing illegal marriages and threatened arrests if the ceremonies continued. The practice of recognizing same-sex relationships—at a moment when New York laws still forbade practices of "sodomy"—expressed a potent political challenge to the legal status quo.

Alongside this legal challenge, the Episcopal bishop of New York also faced a barrage of angry letters. One irate inquirer demanded to know why the bishop would permit a gay group to "distort the sacraments of the church" in an Episcopal Church sanctuary.[10] Further inquiry pressed the bishop to attend to the rogue Episcopal priest who was also conducting union services for same-sex couples.

The most public response to the controversy came from the Gay Activist Alliance. Most gay liberationists had no interest in horning their way into an oppressive patriarchal institution. They didn't want to advocate gay marriage, but Katz's comments were discriminatory. The GAA responded by launching one of its most creative "zaps," gay liberationist parlance for creative protests. GAA members converged on Katz's office at the municipal court to celebrate an engagement party for two same-sex couples, a gala protest complete with wedding cake, music, dancing, and a mock invitation to the event from Katz himself.[11] This sort of queer activism is part of a familiar story, and it played well with the press.

Other responses shed more light on the significance of these early gay unions. Clement and Weeks's official response to Katz took a more sober-minded approach. They contacted a lawyer to defend themselves against the charge that they had violated the law by "unlawfully solemnizing a marriage." The lawyer's letter took a rather remarkable legal approach. The response ceded the question of civil recognition to focus, instead, on religious rights. Civil law, in using the terms "husband" and "wife" to designate a legal marriage, implied that a ceremony, in order to be a marriage, required participants "to take each other as husband and wife." Perry's marriage ceremony, which led participants to take the "office" of husband and wife, may have been the implied example here. The letter emphasized that the ceremonies conducted by Clement and Weeks were emphatically not civil marriages. Rather, "a fair characterization of the ceremony would be that it is an ecclesial recognition and blessing of the relationship between two homosexuals." Indeed, because the ceremonies were ecclesial and not civil, the clerk's office was overstepping its legal bounds. Katz's threat amounted to "an unjustified and dangerous attempt to interfere with the internal operations of a church."[12] Gays and lesbians' *religious* rights, that is, gave them authority to participate in ceremonies that consecrated their relationship.

The question of religious rights has different valence within religious communities themselves, where decisions are not bound by questions of equal legal recognition. Bishop Moore, however, carefully engaged the language of rights in his responses to discomfited conservative Episcopalians. The bishop's response to these offended church members carefully argued that both the Beloved Disciple and the Holy Apostles congregations ought to be granted the freedom to act upon their convictions. They should be free to make their own decisions, even if they were poor ones. The holy union service, he admitted, was "in bad taste." He wrote: "I believe that the homosexual community . . . [has] a right to express their religious beliefs in their own way. If a parish wishes to allow this ministry to occur within their building even though it may cause some embarrassment to others, we feel it is a plus, not a minus." As for Robert Weeks's participation, the bishop carefully stipulated that the services in question were not actually marriages but (merely) blessings for "the deep relationships which some of these people develop between each other."[13]

In both Weeks's and Clement's responses to Katz and Bishop Moore's response to conservative Episcopalians, it was "religious rights" that authorized both officiants and couples to take part in same-sex ceremonies. The ceremonies—precisely because they were religious—could not be prohibited. Because they were religious and circumscribed to the realm of conscience and private practice, they did not pose a threat to the meanings of marriage for the purposes of the law. That very recognition also circumscribed their public influence, however. To keep those religious ceremonies in their properly private place, Bishop Moore sent further admonishment to Weeks: whatever form of ceremony either church practiced, they should not, in the future, invite the press. The infraction was not the nature of the ceremonies but that the public knew about them.

The controversy and its resolution draw attention to a very different piece of legal terrain than that navigated by same-sex couples in their recent successful efforts to obtain legal recognition for their relationships in a number of states. This legal battle was not over the right for legal recognition for the ceremony, but the right to have it at all. And the religious recognition granted to the services marked yet another boundary around marriage that made it distinct from the ceremonies performed for same-sex couples. In the aftermath, Moore declined to censor Weeks's "services of friendship," and Katz refrained from pressing charges against Weeks's or Clement's "holy unions." Moore and Katz acknowledged that both were indeed religious ceremonies, and couples had a "right" to practice them. Both ministers were thus permitted to continue, but with a circumscribed legitimacy that restricted the meaning of these ceremonies to the realm of personal and thus private conviction. Marriage, in contrast, was public—a ceremony of legitimacy performed before the eyes of the state, the denomination, and the press.

Recovering the Religion of Gay Liberation

The controversy over the "holy union" service held on that bright April day highlights the contested place of religion in the gay liberation movement and illuminates the difficult terrain on which clergy and couples claimed divine recognition for same-sex relationships. Clergy and couples, in various ways, stood between contending discourses of the gay liberation movement, established religious institutions, and the state, each of which vested marriage with different meanings. Gay-welcoming clergy and congregations navigated those contending discourses in various ways, from the MCC's emphatic claim to marriage to the Beloved Disciples' unique sacrament of a "holy union" to the more modest "service of friendship" offered by Holy Apostles. All of these ceremonies rehearsed familiar liturgies and pronounced a divine blessing over a couple's union. However, each ceremony claimed subtly different religious meanings for the exchange of vows. The public controversy that responded to the "holy union" ceremony in New York ultimately assured it provisional private meaning. Same-sex couples, averred representative authorities of both church and state, had the right to hold religious ceremonies blessing their relationships. However, the meaning of those ceremonies should also remain personal and private.

The concerted push for legal recognition of same-sex marriage gained public momentum in the early 1990s, when the question of same-sex marriage began to draw attention as a matter of public policy. Historian George Chauncey points out that it was only in the aftermath of the HIV/AIDS epidemic and the lesbian baby boom of the 1980s and early 1990s—events that brought to the surface couples' material needs for relationship recognition—that a nationwide "marriage movement" began to take place. The investment in legal recognition, argues Chauncey, was a material one—same-sex couples were acutely aware of the ways that the lack of legal recognition made their relationships vulnerable.[14] Without sidelining these material investments, the account of earlier couples' earnestly sought ceremonies for religious recognition adds an important dimension to this history. As the marriage movement focused on the material benefits of civil recognition, the religious history of gay marriage has become paradoxically invisible. The dominant discourses of marriage equality advocates circumscribed religion to the private sphere and emphasized that civil marriage, as a status granted by the state, is not beholden to the religious teachings that had long undergirded heterosexual marriage. In making such arguments, however, marriage equality advocates obscured the witness of the movement's own religious traditions and again circumscribed the history of religious blessings for same-sex couples.

The history of those religious practices, however, suggests something else. The wedding practices of same-sex couples and supportive clergy have played a long and important role in battles for relationship recognition in both religious institutions and civil law. The exchanges of vows, along with the various "trimmings" of flowers, wedding gowns, and carefully pressed tuxes, tell another important story of marriage and its politics in the United States. These affective and quotidian practices have never been easily or neatly quarantined from the realm of public politics and civil law.

NOTES

1. Barbara Trecker, "Two Women Are Joined in 'Holy Union' at Church," *New York Post*, April 19, 1971, 3, 47.
2. John Dart, "A Church for Homosexuals," *Los Angeles Times*, December 8, 1969.
3. A. B. T., "Bold New Church Welcomes Gay," *Advocate*, February 1968, 2–3.
4. "Two L.A. Girls Attempt First Legal Gay Marriage," *Los Angeles Advocate*, July 8–21, 1970, 1.
5. Rob Cole, "Two Men Ask Minnesota License for First Legal U.S. Gay Marriage," *Advocate*, June 10–23, 1970, 1.
6. "An Advocate Interpretive: Gay Marriage 'Boom': Suddenly, It's News," *Advocate*, June 10–23, 1970, 6.
7. Rebecca Davis, *More Perfect Unions: The American Search for Marital Bliss* (Cambridge, MA: Harvard University Press, 2010), 174–75.

8. Cele Otnes and Elizabeth Hafkin Pleck, *Cinderella Dreams: The Allure of the Lavish Wedding* (Berkeley: University of California Press, 2003), 49.

9. Barbara Trecker, "Gay 'Marriages' Catching On," *New York Post*, April 14 1971, 3, 53; Trecker, "Two Women Are Joined in 'Holy Union' at Church," 47.

10. Antonio Ramirez to Right Reverend Horace W. B. Donegan (April 19, 1971), Bishop Donegan Papers, Archives of the Episcopal Diocese of New York, file: Holy Apostles.

11. Pete Fisher, "Gay Couples Celebrate Engagement at Marriage Licensing Bureau," *Gay* 2, no. 54 (July 5, 1971).

12. Frank Patton to Corporation Counsel, April 27, 1971, Paul Moore Papers, 75-11 Holy Apostles, New York.

13. Paul Moore to Mr. Marc Hass (April 22, 1971), Paul Moore Papers 75-11, 1–2.

14. George Chauncey, *Why Marriage? The History Shaping Today's Debate over Gay Equality* (New York: Basic Books, 2004).

7

Beyond Procreativity

Heterosexuals Queering Marriage

TERESA DELGADO

Do as I Say, Not as I Do . . .

On December 31, 2013, just hours before ushering in the new year at New York's Times Square, Justice Sonia Sotomayor of the U.S. Supreme Court issued a temporary injunction against the U.S. Department of Health and Human Services, blocking it from enforcing "the contraceptive coverage requirements imposed by the . . . Affordable Care Act."[1] This action was in response to a court action filed on behalf of the Denver chapter of the Little Sisters of the Poor, a Roman Catholic religious order, which was concerned about its perceived requirement to facilitate contraceptive coverage for its employees. It is anticipated that other religiously affiliated not-for-profit organizations will follow suit and challenge the mandate of the Affordable Care Act to provide coverage for artificial contraception.

The concern about artificial birth control among Roman Catholic organizations seems at odds with recent data, particularly a Guttmacher Institute study on the use of artificial birth control among women of childbearing age.[2] The report found that approximately 68 percent of self-identified Catholic women in the study (between fifteen and forty-four years of age) had used a form of artificial birth control to avoid pregnancy. Only 2 percent had utilized natural family planning (NFP), the only form of birth control that conforms with the official church teaching. An earlier Gallup poll (2007) also indicated that 54 percent of Catholics said a smaller family (between zero and two children) is ideal, while 34 percent said a larger family (three or more children) is ideal.[3]

The percentage of artificial birth control use among Roman Catholic women has changed little since the first National Center for Health Statistics (NCHS) study was administered in 1973 among married women,[4] just five years after Pope Paul VI's *Humanae Vitae* affirmed the church's official prohibition against artificial contraception.

An Issue of Rejection or Reception?

The statistics illustrate that a consistent majority of Roman Catholic women who can get pregnant are making distinct reproductive choices. Assuming that these women are heterosexually identified (at least we know that to be the case when the study was first administered in the 1970s), we are faced with a significant number of heterosexual Catholic women who are not following the teaching of the church regarding contraception. Their act of choosing artificial contraceptive methods makes a statement without saying outright, "I do not accept the official Catholic teaching on artificial contraception as good, and thus cannot confirm that teaching with my actions."

At its core, this statement is affirmed by the church's own canonical doctrine of reception, which, "broadly stated, asserts that for a law or rule to be an effective guide for the believing community, it must be accepted by that community."[5] This is no modernist idea. The origins of this doctrine date back to the writings of John Gratian in the twelfth century. Informed by the theological treatises of Saint Augustine (fifth century), it is based on the premise that the laws of the church are intrinsically different—in nature and purpose—from the laws of the state. Whereas the latter are imposed by a governing authority to ensure order and the rule of law, the former are decreed by authority with the added purpose of the spiritual fulfillment of its members. The members themselves, as part of the community of believers through whom the Holy Spirit is active, are empowered through their faith to confirm the validity of the law. The law "must be received to be effective."[6] Thomas Aquinas affirmed this principle through a definition of law which orders all things toward the common good and which is maintained by the community, which is responsible for the common good. A law is a law when it is instituted by a legitimate authority within the church. However, it is only legitimized or obligatory when it is received by those for whom the law is intended, and that full reception of the law is evidenced by action.

With Gratian's definition of reception as the basis upon which the fundamental intrinsic and extrinsic qualities of canon law are understood, the insistence of official Roman Catholic hierarchy that the law must be obeyed solely on the grounds that church authority has mandated it is baffling. The faith community has not simply rejected authority for the sake of rejection, or as an expression of rebellious disobedience and subversion of authority. Rather, the 68 percent of Catholic women using artificial birth control as a means of responsible parenting, in addition to the 54 percent of Catholics who believe two or fewer children represents the "ideal" family unit, are expressing a refusal to receive, and thus validate, a doctrine that disregards the lived, embodied experience of the community and thus undermines their mature, prudent, and reflective assessment of the most appropriate means to achieve what is best for that community.

Their refusal to validate this doctrine provides an opportunity to build bridges between heterosexual Catholics and LGBTIQ or "queer" Catholics. Through the act of being who they are and loving who they love, queer Catholics are similarly stating that they do not accept the official Catholic teaching on heterosexual normativity as good and thus cannot confirm that teaching with their actions. Nevertheless, given official teachings, heterosexual and queer Catholics hold distinct places of power and privilege in the church community. The heterosexually identified hold greater power and privilege. Thus they have an ethical responsibility to act on behalf of those who have been relegated to the margins of the church, namely, queer Catholics.

Heterosexual and Queer

In my own work and my life I claim that ethical responsibility as my own by furthering the dialogue around sexuality within the Roman Catholic Church. Although the church's present state does not seem to reflect such divergent opinions, the history of the church in the world has had a tremendous variety of perspectives on sexuality. In a way, the history of Christian traditions regarding sexuality has been a "queer" history. From its earliest formations, the Christian community has repeatedly found itself on the outskirts of the status quo, defying societal norms and exploring new ways of being in community.

Within theological circles, "queer" is an expansive term reflecting postcolonial critique of hegemonic norms and universalizing categories. It represents a rupture to these categories, a decentering, a liminal place of radical subjectivity. "Queer" is a term that accommodates the fluidity of sexuality and sexual identity even within one's lifetime. I am fully aware of the limitations of the term: its relative newness in academic discourse, its history as a pejorative term for so many, its potential to dilute the particularity of each individual mode of self-identification and experience, its disconnectedness from the experience of those persons whose self-identity is powerfully enmeshed with the clear naming and speaking out of a particular reality. Nevertheless, it has become a useful term in articulating resistance to anything and anyone that seeks the imposition of authoritative control over another.

Who I am and how I self-identify shape my theology and ethics. I am Latina of Puerto Rican ethnicity, born in New York City. My sexual orientation is heterosexual. I have been in a monogamous marriage with a Congolese man for the past twenty-five years, and we are blessed with four beautiful children. I stand in solidarity with my queer sisters and brothers toward full recognition and equality by the law of the land and by the church. I am Roman Catholic by upbringing and practice, raising my children in its traditions. I am grateful for its social justice legacy, while very saddened by its continued misogynistic, hierarchical, and abusive exclusivity. I stand at both margin and center, exercising a hermeneutic of suspicion from any vantage point, knowing that the ground is unsettled and moving when it comes to the church and questions of sexuality. I am "queer positive."[7]

To be queer positive is to be heterosexually identified while acknowledging that this identity holds a privileged place in the church as "normative." Queer positivity rejects the normative status of heterosexuality and uses one's access and privilege as heterosexual to undermine its normative place. My place of privilege is not an occasion for further exclusion but rather an opportunity to broaden the circle of those embraced by the Catholic community. Queer positivity is a powerful and conscious act of solidarity and subversion.

Queer Eye toward Church Doctrine

Let me return with a queer-positive eye to a catalytic moment in a debate that has been raging in and out of the Roman Catholic Church for nearly fifty years: Pope Paul VI's publication of *Humanae Vitae* (July 25, 1968). The tenets of the doctrine on marriage and sexuality affirmed in this papal encyclical bear upon the questions of what is considered good, natural, and moral within our sexuality and our sexual expression as Catholics, including the acceptance or rejection of Catholic doctrine. The encyclical also provides a crucial point of reference regarding the doctrine of reception, since it gave voice—with the expectation of full acceptance by the faith community—to the official teaching of the church on the purpose of sexual expression and the related prohibition against artificial contraception.

In 1963 Pope John XXIII created a special commission to assess the church's teaching on birth control. Including bishops, laypersons, and theologians, this commission recommended in overwhelming fashion that the teaching be changed.[8] Pope Paul VI ignored the recommendations of the commission. In *Humanae Vitae*, he speaks of marriage as a holy bond between a man and woman, reflective of a cosmological complementarity of male and female that reflects the divine plan of the natural order. Marriage is much more than just a social institution—it is sacramental, a visible sign of an inward grace, bestowed by God and God alone. If faith is open to the mystery of God's grace at work in the sacrament of marriage, married couples are like an open window that allows the refreshing breeze of God's grace to wash over them. Marriage is centered on love of God, love of self, and love of the other, in a simultaneous Trinitarian relationality. As each expression of love is enmeshed and enfleshed with the other, marriage necessitates an embodied, incarnate love.

This embodied love takes on its most immanent and transcendent expression of God's love through the powerful gift of sexual expression. *Humanae Vitae* asserts that the human person does not have unlimited dominion over his or her own body. Humanity's sexual faculties with the capacity to bring forth new life are even more intimately governed by God's natural law:

The Church, nevertheless, in urging men to the observance of the precepts of the natural law, which it interprets by its constant doctrine, teaches that each and every marital act must of necessity retain its intrinsic relationship to the procreation of human life. This particular doctrine, often expounded by the magisterium of the Church, is based on the inseparable connection, established by God, which man on his own initiative may not break, between the unitive significance and the procreative significance which are both inherent to the marriage act.[9]

The church affirms that sexual communion and the gift of giving physical pleasure to one's beloved are part of the natural ordering of God's creative energy in which couples fully participate, as made in God's image. In the marital act of physical communion, couples participate in the unity, or oneness, of God. However, this affirmation of pleasure is incomplete without its corollary, procreation:

The reason is that the fundamental nature of the marriage act, while uniting husband and wife in the closest intimacy, also renders them capable of generating new life—and this as a result of laws written into the actual nature of man and of woman. And if each of these essential qualities, the unitive and the procreative, is preserved, the use of marriage fully retains its sense of true mutual love and its ordination to the supreme responsibility of parenthood to which man is called.[10]

The type of sexual expression that is considered moral presupposes a male/female complementarity that, in the words of *Humanae Vitae*, reflects the oneness of God. Pope John Paul II reasserted this physical complementarity in glowing terms in his *Theology of the Body*.[11] Male and female together reflect the oneness of the Creator; married couples participate in that creative power through their procreative potential.

The hierarchy of the church continues to assert these teachings. In *Familiaris Consortio* (1981), Pope John Paul II repeated Pope Paul VI's condemnation of contraceptive interventions but in more personal terms. Sexual intercourse is a language that "expresses the total reciprocal self-giving of husband and wife," but in the use of contraceptive intervention this language is overlaid and contradicted by another language, "that of not giving oneself totally to the other." Thus, every sexual act must maintain the dual purposes of unity and procreation to be considered ethical within the context of marriage. As Tatha Wiley notes, the operative and only legitimate question open to the married couple within the Roman Catholic Church is "Should we have sex?"[12] In other words, are we open to both purposes of sexual expression at this moment?

Some theologians held out hope that *Humanae Vitae* would prove itself the deepest, more enduring truth. Richard P. McBrien expressed the hope in 1968 that it would generate a "consensus of approval throughout the whole church." Four decades later, he recognized "that the teaching has still not been widely received by those to whom it was originally directed, namely, Catholic married couples of child-bearing age."[13] Catholic married persons have not confirmed through their actions the doctrinal teachings on sexuality as articulated in *Humanae Vitae,* leading McBrien to lament that the needed, open discussion of the issue has not been permitted, and that the credibility of the magisterium has been weakened as a result.

Silent Dissent through Dissenting Action

The insistence of the magisterium of the church on the inseparability of unity and procreation exemplifies what Eleazar S. Fernandez has termed "disembodied knowing," a universalizing of principles and norms that does not take into account how the application of those principles and norms affects our very bodies. The lived experience of Catholic bodies in relation, married or not, cries out that our doctrines need to be critiqued through the lens of an embodied epistemology, a way of knowing that "sees reality through the configuration of our bodiliness and seriously considers the effects of ideas as they bear on bodies and vice versa, especially the disfigured bodies of the marginalized," one that "pays attention to radical plurality, particularity and the differences between human beings."[14]

The privilege of normativity requires a responsibility to pay attention to those who have been "disfigured" by their treatment in the church, both queer and heterosexual. If our theologizing is to begin with the lived experience of those on the margins, with radical plurality as Fernandez describes, with the subjectivity of those whose moral agency is questioned at best and suspect at worst, we can start by examining the

silent dissent among married heterosexual Catholics on the issue of contraception. Married heterosexual Catholics have been "closeted" in their
rejection of a teaching that prioritizes "means" over intention. If married
heterosexual couples not open to procreation at a given moment were to
ask the question posed earlier, "Should we have sex?" they would say
"no"—unless it was a time when conception would be less likely. But are
the means of contraception—of thwarting conception or, in the words
of the magisterium, frustrating the natural end of the act of sex itself—
any more ethical when they are natural rather than artificial? Perhaps
the intention to thwart conception is not the real issue. Given that the
majority of Catholics consider two children or fewer as the "ideal" family unit, it is clear that heterosexual married couples have weighed in on
which is the greater priority. Heterosexual Catholics have also dissented
from the church's teaching regarding what type of sex is licit, engaging
not only in penile/vaginal intercourse open to procreation at all times
but in other forms such as anal sex, oral sex, and masturbation—either
singularly or mutually. Thus the unitive function of sex is being priori-
tized independently of its openness to procreation.

Yet heterosexual Catholic couples do not talk about it. We are silent
in our refusal to accept these categories as relevant to our intimate
expression in relation to the partners we love. Why? Because we maintain the privilege of our heterosexual status by doing so. Our silence
suggests that we accept the normative framework of complementarity,
of procreation and unity, of natural contraception as ethical means for
parental planning, of penile/vaginal intercourse as the only licit form of
sex. However, our actions suggest nonacceptance of that same framework. In fact, since *Humanae Vitae*, our intentional actions have repeatedly refused to confirm official teaching while our voices have lagged
behind despite our own church's history—the doctrine of reception—as
weighty precedent. It is time to speak the truth that we cannot confirm
official teaching with our actions.

A Vocation and Occasion of Solidarity

If heterosexual Catholics were willing to "come out" from behind the
guise of pretending to affirm the teaching of the church on matters of
sexuality—particularly regarding birth control and modes of sexual

expression—we would acknowledge the deep value of our experiential understanding of the good of sex. Embodied epistemology tells us that the intention behind married heterosexual Catholics' use of birth control, engagement in oral sex, and so forth is good, natural, and moral.

Suppose we imagined the marriage question in terms of vocation rather than complementarity of male and female, or procreative and unitive. Queer and heterosexual Catholics would then have a unique opportunity to consider places of strategic convergence and occasions for solidarity. In order to "queer" our current understanding of the purpose of marriage, I would begin by elevating its meaning as a *vocation*: as *vocare* (to call, or to give voice to) *and* as *vocare* (to call out to the world, to shout from the mountaintop the joy of loving another and wanting that love to sustain for a lifetime). By giving voice and calling out this shared, mutual, and reciprocal love and commitment, we come out of the closet to challenge the silence that has enveloped both the heterosexual Catholic community and so many in the queer community. We offer a corrective to the sexual ethics of the Catholic Church.

What if married heterosexual persons were courageous enough to acknowledge their silent dissent and affirm that the sexual expression of two people who love each other into their own being, who wish to give and receive physically intimate joy and pleasure from their beloved, is an expression of sacramental communion, of unitive oneness, "and the two shall become as one," and that this oneness is good in and of itself? What seems like living a lie because of past silence is revealed as something neither selfish, dishonest, nor unfaithful.[15]

What if the good of procreativity is truly, at its core, an overturning of a self-centered, narcissistic understanding of sexuality that is focused exclusively on the "what's in it for me" question? This is the meaning of procreation conveyed so beautifully by Margaret A. Farley when she speaks of "fruitfulness" as an appropriate corrective to the traditional and more limited view often associated with the term "procreation." Farley poses the following questions to challenge our understanding of procreation while signaling to the potential solidarity between heterosexual and queer Catholics:

> How, then, can [procreation] constitute a norm for sexual activity and relations? Even if it were recognized as a norm for fertile heterosexual

couples, what would this mean for infertile heterosexual couples or for heterosexual couples who choose not to have children, for gays and lesbians, for single persons, for ambiguously gendered persons? For these other individuals and partners, would it signal, as it has in the past, a lesser form of sex, and lesser forms of sexual relationships? Or is it possible that a norm of *fruitfulness* can and ought to characterize all sexual relationships?[16]

Farley continues with an explanation of this corrective norm of fruitfulness as a measure of all interpersonal love that moves beyond the egotistic "as long as I get mine" attitude, toward a generative understanding of love, including sexual love, that brings "new life to those who love."[17] It can include the bringing forth of children biologically but is not limited to that alone. It can even include the raising of children within queer families, a broader and more inclusive understanding of family planning than articulated by official church doctrine. This fruitfulness of love is the potential of all lovers—queer and heterosexual alike—who are willing to take responsibility for and affirm the other in their relational, and sexual, expression of love.

Such a "queering" of procreation into a broader, more fluid, expansive, generous, and fruitful understanding leads us to see within it a reflection and image of a loving, generous, and generative God. It discloses places of solidarity that already exist between heterosexual married Catholics and queer Catholics. In our actions—our refusal to accept the authority of *Humanae Vitae* by embodying the reception of a more authentic understanding of the good of sex—we come together through an understanding of loving sex that is mutual, generative, and good, whether or not it is open to the physical begetting of offspring.

Tatha Wiley has suggested a starting point for such a disclosure—a reexamination of the resources of Aquinas's moral teleology. In Aquinas's understanding of the purpose and end of human existence in the journey to God we find an understanding of happiness as nothing less than subjective authenticity, of being true to one's truest self. Applying this norm to a Catholic sexual ethic, we could turn our attention away from the physicalism of most natural law understandings of moral/ immoral sex acts and toward the potential of those acts to either fulfill or limit our authenticity. "Authenticity is realized when judgments of value are the product of responsible choices and actions, locating that responsibility in the couples' own complex discernment of authentic value."[18]

An alliance of queer and heterosexual Catholics around our lived norms of ethical sex, norms that extend beyond procreativity/unity, can present a credible and powerful challenge to the doctrine of *Humanae Vitae*. Our alliance gives voice to a common dissent, one based in our lived experience, against the limiting norms of sexual morality present within the doctrine for both heterosexual and queer alike. It also challenges the church hierarchy's norms of authentic selfhood in relation to embodied experiences that we have found truly fulfill our selves and the common good. Both challenges reflect the ancient yet often overlooked Catholic doctrine of reception by allowing our embodied epistemology to test the norms of sexuality theologized by the teaching authority of the church, allowing the actions our bodies to either confirm or reject those norms. In our faithful lives as sexual Christians, whether heterosexual or queer, we are not ignoring or evading Catholic theology of sex but discerning a deeper, truer theology, one the magisterium has yet to hear. And our alliance shares a common goal: recognizing the generative, creative, and unitive power of sex that is good in its mutuality, natural in its embodied fulfillment, and moral in its reflection of the creative image of a just and loving God. We have a responsibility to insist that our words—our voice, our advocacy, our theology—finally catch up with our actions.

NOTES

1. Tom Howell Jr., "White House Urges Supreme Court to Reject Nuns' Appeal for Birth Control Exemption," *Washington Times*, January 3, 2014.
2. Guttmacher Institute, "Supplemental Tables on Religion and Contraceptive Use," www.guttmacher.org/media/resources/Religion-FP-tables.html.
3. Joseph Carroll, "Americans: 2.5 Children Is 'Ideal' Family Size," Gallup News Service, June 26, 2007.
4. National Center for Health Statistics, "Contraceptive Utilization, United States (Data from the National Survey of Family Growth)," Vital and Health Statistics, Series 23, No. 2 (1979), www.cdc.gov/nchs/data/series/sr_23/sr23_002.pdf.
5. James A. Coriden, "The Canonical Doctrine of Reception," www.arcc-catholic-rights.net/doctrinc_of_rcccption.htm; see also James A. Coriden, "The Canonical Doctrine of Reception," *Jurist* 50 (1990): 58–82.
6. Coriden, "The Canonical Doctrine of Reception."

7. This term was first introduced to me by Robyn Henderson-Espinosa as a way to describe those who are allies with/for the queer community.

8. See Robert McClory, *Turning Point: The Inside Story of the Papal Birth Control Commission* (New York: Crossroad, 1995).

9. Pope Paul VI, *Humanae Vitae* (July 25, 1968), www.vatican.va/holy_father/paul_vi/encyclicals/documents/hf_p-vi_enc_25071968_humanae-vitae_en.html.

10. Ibid.

11. Pope John Paul II, *Man and Woman He Created Them: A Theology of the Body,* trans. and intro. Michael Waldstein (Boston: Pauline Books and Media, 2006), 257.

12. Tatha Wiley, "Humanae Vitae, Sexual Ethics and the Roman Catholic Church," in *The Embrace of Eros: Bodies, Desire and Sexuality in Christianity*, ed. Margaret D. Kamitsuka (Minneapolis, MN: Fortress Press, 2010), 112.

13. Richard P. McBrien, "*Humanae Vitae* after 40 Years," *Tidings*, July 25, 2008, https://www3.nd.edu/~newsinfo/pdf/2008_07_25_pdf/Humanae%20Vitae%20After%2040%20years.pdf.

14. Eleazar S. Fernandez, *Reimagining the Human: Theological Anthropology in Response to Systemic Evil* (St. Louis, MO: Chalice Press, 2004), 13.

15. Lisa Sowle Cahill, quoted in Richard A. McCormick, "'Humanae Vitae' 25 Years Later," *America*, July 17, 1993.

16. Margaret A. Farley, *Just Love: A Framework for Christian Sexual Ethics* (New York: Continuum, 2006), 227 (emphasis added).

17. Ibid., 227–28.

18. Wiley, "Humanae Vitae, Sexual Ethics and the Roman Catholic Church," 113.

8

Disrupting the Normal

Queer Family Life as Sacred Work

JENNIFER HARVEY

"Family" is one of the most powerful cultural sites at which heteronormativity and normative gender expression are reproduced and enforced. The power of the discourse surrounding it is one reason tension exists within queer communities over the issue of marriage equality and the visibility of queer families with children that has attended that equality struggle. Long and legitimate debates have raged within LGBT communities as to whether political battles to broaden the legally recognized definition of family are a compelling issue of rights or an assimilationist lure.

It is within this larger context that this chapter reflects on one family's experience—that of my own queer family. I begin with three glimpses into the day-to-day encounters of one two-person set of white, middle-class lesbians, one Christian, one not, married and raising two young children in the heart of the Midwest. A poststructuralist understanding of sin provides the framework through which I engage these experiences to reflect on the normalizing gendered, raced, classed, and heterosexual contexts within which queer family life unfolds. The project of queer family can be understood as sacred work, work that should pursue being recognized as "legitimate" while eschewing the desire to be "normal."

A Glimpse: On Relationship

A few weeks after marriage equality was legalized in Iowa, I was standing outside the home my partner and I were trying to sell. It was spring

2009. We had a new baby. My neighbor pulled up in his pickup truck. I did not know this neighbor beyond the "hello" we always said when we encountered each other on the block. He was friendly enough, though I assumed our worlds were rather different. Our racial identity was the same, but visible markers signified that our class experiences diverged— his daily garb suggested he worked in construction, while I donned that more typical of a college professor. I therefore assumed (without realizing I had assumed it) that our politics similarly diverged. Thus my surprise when he leaned out of his truck and said to me: "So, you are moving? You and . . . well, is she your wife now?" He smiled at me.

Though my partner and I had had a nonlegal wedding two years prior to publicly ritualize our commitment, we were not legally married at the time of this encounter. Neither of us refers to the other as wife. But I was stunned by this neighbor's vulnerability, his willingness to risk such language in my presence. I interpreted his act as a nod to his recognition that the changes consuming the state impacted me, and to his desire to positively acknowledge this. I felt seen by him in a way I had not expected.

"Yes," I said. "My wife."

A Glimpse: On Gender

We have two young children: girls being raised by two moms, each of whom has an outward appearance that does not conform to standard notions of gender. My partner is sometimes mistakenly called "sir." I have very short hair and tend to wear clothing considered boyish. We both have face piercings. We have both been followed into bathrooms by helpful restaurant staff who, in trying to stop us from embarrassing ourselves, end up themselves embarrassed when they realized their error.

When our first baby was born, I realized how endless the issues and questions about gender were going to be. To give just one example, the most mundane question of how to dress our baby girl seemed large to me. What does it mean to put a dress on a child who cannot make a choice about her clothing and when dresses are not something either parent associates with her sex/gender expression? But what does it mean to refuse to put her in a dress either?

It is in this context that the following conversation with my then three-year-old took place while driving one day. We pulled up behind a truck, and my daughter asked me something about the driver. I couldn't see the driver well and so was curious when she referenced him as male.

ME: "How do you know that driver is a man?"
SHE: "He has short hair. Boys all have short hair."
ME: "They do? What about girls?"
SHE: "Girls have long hair."
ME: "Really? So, how would you describe my hair?"
SHE: "Well . . . you have short hair."
ME: "So what does this tell you about me?"
SHE (SOUNDING LIKE SHE WAS THINKING THIS THROUGH FOR THE FIRST
    TIME): "Well . . . you're kind of a boy-girl, Mama."
ME: "Oh! I see. What about Mommy?"
SHE (sounding more confident): "Oh, she's definitely a boy-girl."

A Glimpse: On Race and Class

For race and class I can provide no specific glimpse, a fact that is itself significant. We have had few overly negative experiences with homophobia. And yet were my partner or I, or either of our children, persons of color or not so clearly identifiable as middle-class, this glimpse would undoubtedly include a story. I hold the space for it here to mark the presence of whiteness and class privilege. Although white class-privileged queers tend to forget this, the normalizing discourses with which queer families dance are always as much about race and class as they are about gender and sexuality.

The Sacred Work of Disruption

It may be surprising that I propose engaging these family experiences through a framework of sin, but in some ways sin is a "natural" starting point. Queer family almost immediately invokes discussion of the sea change taking place in the United States in regard to legally recognized same-sex marriage. Meanwhile, given Christianity's obsession with sex and the teaching that the only "good" sex is that which takes place within a committed, potentially procreative, heterosexual marriage, changing notions of marriage might mean changing notions of sin. At the same time, sin as a starting point here is utterly "unnatural." Christianity's long history of denigrating the lives of those who are lesbian, gay, bisexual, or transgendered, or who otherwise experience nonheterosexually focused attraction or live differently gendered lives, gives good reason for those of us who live such complex identities to run fast away from it. "Sin" has bludgeoned many lives.

Natural or not, sin enables me to explore what it means to live out resistant, insurrectional responses to systems that relentlessly produce the "normal" while marginalizing that produced as "deviant." My use of sin does not signify traditional Christian notions. Instead, I am compelled by theologian Margaret D. Kamitsuka's poststructuralist understanding of sin. Kamitsuka rejects the idea that a pregiven human subject exists prior to or outside of the power and knowledge discourses through which human subjectivity is produced and performed. But she is determined to hold strongly to human agency as well as to the *imago dei*. Thus, she writes, "To say that our humanity is created in God's image means that our performativity has the possibility of being 'an icon of who God is.' . . . we have a lifelong project of performing the image of God."[1] The feminist liberationist tradition teaches us how the "normal" enacts and ratifies injustice. The thoughtlessness of the normal adds to its sinfulness. Divine performativity has the potential to disrupt it.

In poststructuralist understanding, power is neither good nor bad. It circulates and disciplines. While power constitutes regimes characterized by oppressive social structures and formations, these regimes are also the terrain in, on, and through which insurrection can and must take place. And this is where sin enters. If godly performativity is the form of agency to which Christians are called, to sin is to choose inappropriate postures relative to the disciplinary regimes of power through which human subjectivity is formed. These would be postures that impede justice or the flourishing of all, postures that distort human relations.[2]

Sin can be a manifestation of *either* "undue" or "underdeveloped cooperation" with disciplinary power. The former of these might be more obvious. Undue cooperation suggests being overly compliant with oppressive power formations, in the process harming others.[3] But underdeveloped cooperation is equally sinful. If resistance can only arise in and through the discursive processes that produce the "normal" human subject, underdeveloped cooperation is agency that evades the realities of power or knowledge production. Such agency also evades the "conditions necessary for resistance"[4] and thus fails to engage in godly performativity.

To illustrate underdeveloped cooperation, consider the example of race. Someone racialized as "white" might want to disavow the disciplinary regimes of white supremacy. To respond to such a desire, however, by refusing to take white racialization seriously—for example, to say "I am color-blind" or "I don't think of myself as white"—would be to underdevelop one's cooperation. Such a response relies directly on the privilege that makes it possible for whites to disregard their whiteness. By failing to engage racial discourse on its own terms, such a response cannot disrupt it and thus contributes to the entrenchment of white supremacy.

In theological terms, disrupting the normal might be conceptualized as sacred work. Any agency lived in a manner that sustains normative whiteness, normative gender constructions (and the sexism intrinsic to such), normative heterosexuality, and normative notions of the family unit (however the unit is constituted) distorts human relations and narrows the possibilities for all of life to flourish. Given the constitution of normalcy in U.S. public life, to perform the "normal" is to sin. In contrast, ways of being, living, and performing that disrupt the production of the normal, whether in the most subtle or magnificent manner, might be described as godly performativity.

Locating such performance in the context of notions of the sacred is consistent with my own relationship to Christianity. However diverse this tradition, and however contended the *meaning* of the claim might be, Christianity makes some sort of claim about right relationships to neighbor and the significance of humans bearing the image of God. This claim invites me to understand disrupting normalcy as sacred work.

Queer family is a uniquely interesting project though which to consider such work. Family is a site at which a diverse array of powerful and normalizing discourses come together. Queer theorists describe this phenomenon as the pervasive existence of "familialist ideology."[5] It takes few examples to expose American familialist ideology. What does a good mother look like? Is she middle-class or on food stamps? Single or partnered? What does it mean to be a real man, and how does the presence or absence of such a man impact boy children? Which of these is a "real" family: a nuclear family or a household constituted through extended kinship relations? What color is that family? Familialist ideology produces the normal in regard to everything from appropriate adult gender roles to gender in children, from obsessions about the morality of certain kinds of sexual activity to the morality of families living in diverse economic conditions or household arrangements.

Queer families—my focus is on those that involve daily living with and caring for children—are immersed with particular intensity in the disciplinary streams in which such familialist ideology swims. Sex, gender, children, race, class: they are all in there, accompanied by powerful public assertions about what and who is "good" and "bad." In turn, these assertions have real material implications as legal policies confer different kinds of political access and rewards on different families.

It is no surprise, then, that scrutiny of queer families does not come only from heterosexist society but also from other queers. The stakes are high when it comes to public recognition of family forms. In some readings, two women taking civically approved nuptials supports heterosexist and racialized familialist ideology by endorsing the idea that long-term, monogamous sexual relations are the only "good" relations and nuclear family the only form that deserves legal support.[6] In race and class terms, at least, the couple seems "normal" enough. In other readings these same two women epitomize subversion as they undermine sexist notions of gender complementarity on which heterosexist familialism depends and has nothing implicitly to do with race at all (i.e., the assumption here would be that women of any race getting married subverts the sexist paradigm).[7]

Reading these debates as a parent can lead to a kind of "deconstruction fatigue." It is so easy for abstract theory to trap queer families in an assimilation/subversion binary. Valerie Lehr's *Queer Family Values: Rethinking the Myth of the Nuclear Family* is a perfect example. Although Lehr begins with a powerful critique of the belief that marriage rights

can address the myriad social injustices queers face, by the time she fin-
ishes, she manages to imply that lesbians who give birth are buying into
a discourse of natural gender and warns that those who see their interests as mothers as superseding their interests as lesbians are "politically
devastating."[8] (I have yet to meet such a lesbian, since encountering the
world as a lesbian mother makes it impossible to separate these.) Lehr's
work was early, but similar issues and lack of nuance raged in the recent
Proposition 8 debates in California.

My fatigue in the face of these battles comes in part from my immediate experience of life as a day-to-day parent. I think: "Okay, call me
conservative, call me radical. Either way I have to go home, make the
macaroni and cheese, and get the kids to bed." A real debate continues
in regard to whether or not "same-sex marriage" or "marriage equality"
can ever actually disrupt "normalcy" given the powerful history of marriage as a heterosexual, patriarchal institution. While specific dimensions of that debate (as well as its quality) are outside the specific foci
of this chapter, I reject any position that attempts to cast the marriage
debate through an either-or (assimilationist/subversion) lens.[9] More
to the point, my fatigue signals how dangerous it is to theorize about
queer families without rooting theory in the real material experiences
of actual and diverse families. For many queer parents, having children
in one's life means less choice about living in greater contact with institutions particularly invested in producing the "normal" (schools, medical establishments, play groups, adoption agencies, kids sports teams)
than one might otherwise have. Queer theory unconstrained by these
concrete realities oversimplifies complex ethical dilemmas queer families face and rhetorically disfigures us.

Stephen Hicks warns against the exclusionary tendency to represent queer parents' lives as "essentially conservative, essentially radical, essentially egalitarian, essentially challenging of gender norms,
essentially . . . anything."[10] To make any such arguments is to "thingify"
such families.[11] His interviewees are all deeply aware that homophobia
is something every member of a queer household has to negotiate and
in regard to which each takes up different postures in diverse contexts.
Hicks's warning serves as a Kamitsukian reminder.[12] All of us—the
single, the partnered, the multiply partnered, even the heterosexually
constituted parental unit—swim in disciplinary streams of familialist

ideology that we have no choice but to engage to make sense of our lives. The question is not whether queer families are assimilationist or subversive. The question is one of undue or underdeveloped cooperation with sinful normalcy. To what extent can and do we enact agency that disrupts the disciplinary powers that produce race, class, gender, and sexual orientation constantly even while being honest about the constraints imposed by the discursive terrain in which our lives unfold?

Thinking Sin, Thinking Sacred

The glimpses with which I began this chapter reveal the presence of disciplinary power in queer family life and, more important, moments in which disruptive agency becomes available. For example, there are good reasons my partner and I do not use the language of "wife." "Wife" as a concept, its history, the images it conjures—the weight of such a term discursively signifies submissive woman in the context of heterosexual marriage. Regardless of the behavior of *actual* married women, "wife" is complicit in distorting human relations. It is only recently that a vow to "obey" ceased to be standard in Christian marriage ceremonies. Study after study shows that even when both parents work outside the home, women continue to do the lion's share of in-home unpaid labor.[13]

But particularities of race and class reveal that "wife" can have other implications. Women of color and working-class women have always worked outside the home and been, therefore, relegated outside the circle of who is meant by "good wife." In addition, according to Mignon R. Moore, equitable division of work inside the home has rarely been the primary concern of African American women because other areas of inequity have been more salient. For black lesbians, "economic independence, rather than the egalitarian distribution of household chores, is the primary feminist organizing mechanism in these families."[14] The whole debate is thus vexed by intersecting disciplinary streams relative to normative race and class as much as gender. These need to be acknowledged to avoid prioritizing a set of racially and economically privileged concerns about the question of whether or not queers should aspire to the status of "wife."

What, then, are the implications of my "yes" to my neighbor? All kinds of risks were present in regard to compliance with disciplinary power, including the possibility that my "yes" normalized one family form in a manner that relegated those without a "wife" as deviant. And yet "no" would have created different problems. It would have failed to engage my neighbor's risk-taking public indication of his support, or to affirm the real disruption that was taking place in Iowa at that moment. The disorientation of city hall clerks scrambling to cross out "wife" and "husband" on marriage applications the day the Iowa Supreme Court declared marriage open to all revealed this moment as anything but one of assimilation. Saying so does not mean claiming marriage equality as a radical political accomplishment, but it highlights the reality that even a concept as laden as "wife" can be used to send familialist ideology into chaos. My "yes" endorsed such chaos. While it rested on preexisting discursive terrain that makes it less than ethically clear from a liberationist perspective, in that moment it was sacred work—liberative work performed in a thoroughly sin-laden context.

Similar dynamics can be seen in the conversation with my three-year-old. The possibilities created by a young child discerning that a "boy-girl" exists, and declaring as much without any concern about experiencing chastisement or correction, represents a truly liminal and sacred moment. I claim it as a godly performance. My partner and I are not *essentially* subversive. But our daily living does disrupt normative gender constructs in a manner that has made a different world available to our daughter. Meanwhile, this world is not stable, permanent, or comprehensive. The enduring power of gender discipline could not be clearer than the recitation of the mantra that boys have short hair and girls have long by a young child who lives in day-to-day intimacy with mothers such as us. Gender discipline has already exerted its intent to secure her cooperation.

Endless questions emerge in this moment in which normative gender production becomes visible. These include questions pertaining to what the most liberating ways of articulating the meanings of sex/gender are and how to articulate these in developmentally meaningful ways with young children. What does it mean to parent such that the visibility of the "boy-girl" for a three-year-old is supported and sustained even while the equally real experience that the boy-girl does *not* exist, something she undoubtedly experiences at school, is also acknowledged? Honoring her experience is central in our vision of parenting.

At what point does insurrection become either undue or underdeveloped cooperation?

Moore's analysis of the effect of the constantly intersecting streams that produce subjectivity as "integrative marginalization" bears upon the extent to which dimensions of queer family life may or may not be sacred performance and addresses the empty space of my third "glimpse." In describing diverse manifestations of gender and sexual orientation among variously classed African American lesbian mothers, Moore emphasizes that marginalization has very different implications when one embodies statuses that can "compensate" for disparaged aspects of identity.[15] For example, a certain level of education and/or class status can compensate for lesbian identity, thus making it more tempting for some black lesbians to comply with certain class performances in order to maximize their being perceived as acceptable. Sullivan identifies a similar phenomenon among white lesbian mothers who distance themselves from working-class lesbians in order to secure their status as "normal" mothers.[16]

The complexities of integrative marginalization mean constantly assessing what and how ideological streams discipline if we are committed to sacred disruption. Such work might even reconfigure what queer family means. For example, to the extent that whiteness, class, and occupational status allow my family "integrative marginalization," the sacred work of *queer* means that I need to disrupt well beyond issues that pertain "only" to my sexuality and gender. What happens in my daughter's classroom around gender and family forms is of a complex piece with what she encounters in teachings about Thanksgiving and Native peoples, nationalist recitations of the Pledge of Allegiance, or relations with a child of color who also comes from a lesbian home. While the "nature" of queer family may make encounters with disciplinary power more obvious and stark than do other family formations, the sacred work of disrupting the normal ultimately opens into an endless array of sacred performances seeking to create solidarity and just relations.

At the end of the day, the framework constructed here generates more questions and possibilities than answers. I have not offered solutions to the political debate about public policy options that attend the move toward public recognition of same-sex marriages and family formations. Whatever its policy implications, however, disruption of the normal as sacred work pushes against queer families presenting ourselves as "normal."[17]

The work is better understood as asserting our *legitimacy*. More forms of family than we can imagine are legitimate and legitimately demand recognition, respect, protection, and visibility. This can and should be done even while no final claims are made (and, indeed, final claims are actively resisted) about just what "good family" looks like. Rather than demanding recognition as normal and admission to normative race, class, or gender, the sacred work of disrupting the normal can assert, instead, legitimacy in a manner that subverts the equation. Insisting on legitimacy can be used to scramble and send into chaos the function of the discursive power that produces normalcy. The "boy-girl" is *not* normal. Asserting its legitimacy challenges normative gender (even while the presence and power of normative gender is acknowledged). Marriage equality veers dangerously close to pursuing normalcy and, with it, achieving allocation of public rights and resources to only certain kinds of families. True sin. Yet, in insisting that marriage—its meaning, function, familialism—change because of queer legitimacy, rather than that queers change in order to access it, we create the possibility that something more sacred might come to be even in this imperfect, incomplete, fractured political terrain. Taking up the challenge to make visible and protect the legitimacy of diverse queer families in this moment is godly performativity.

The issues raised in this chapter go well beyond the most immediate controversy around marriage rights. In the case of my queer family, "family" looks like an endless dance between sinfulness and divine performativity that is simultaneously boundless and limited, creative and constrained, angry and joyful. I am hard-pressed to imagine asking more of queer family than that it engage in such a dance with honesty about all of the complexities that emerge from the paradoxical terrain in which all of our sacred performances unfold.

NOTES

1. Margaret D. Kamitsuka, *Feminist Theology and the Challenge of Difference* (Oxford: Oxford University Press, 2007), 79.

2. Ibid., 72, 73.

3. Ibid., 74.
4. Ibid., 75.
5. See Stephen Hicks, *Lesbian, Gay and Queer Parenting: Families, Intimacies, Genealogies* (Houndsmills, Basingstoke: Palgrave Macmillan, 2011).
6. With some nuance, this is the overarching claim of Valerie Lehr's *Queer Family Values: Rethinking the Myth of the Nuclear Family* (Philadelphia: Temple University Press, 1999).
7. Maureen Sullivan, *The Family of Woman: Lesbian Mothers, Their Children, and the Undoing of Gender* (Berkeley: University of California Press, 2004).
8. Lehr, *Queer Family Values*, 12, 131, 67.
9. I have written on this elsewhere. See Jennifer Harvey, "Both/And Thinking on Same-Sex Marriage" (March 28, 2013) and "Waiting One More Day (on DOMA)" (June 25, 2013), both at huffingtonpost.com. For readers interested in understanding the debate more deeply, Huffington Post offers an excellent window into the many passionate and competing analyses and perspectives LGBT communities have on the marriage issue. See especially the section "Gay Voices."
10. Hicks, *Lesbian, Gay and Queer Parenting*, 217.
11. Ibid., 3.
12. Ibid., 22.
13. Sullivan, *The Family of Woman*, 98. See Lehr, *Queer Family Values*, 23, 27.
14. Mignon R. Moore, *Invisible Families: Gay Identities, Relationships, and Motherhood among Black Women* (Berkeley: University of California Press, 2011), 160.
15. Ibid., 222.
16. Sullivan, *The Family of Woman*, 123.
17. Here I agree with Hicks. Hicks, *Lesbian, Gay and Queer Parenting*, 81.

Healing Oppression Sickness

YVETTE FLUNDER

A few years ago my spouse was diagnosed with stage 4 breast cancer. Her mother and sister had died from breast cancer, and it seemed that the strain of cancer that plagued her family was particularly virulent. While she was undergoing chemotherapy and radiation treatment, my own mother was diagnosed with noncurative lung cancer and given a grim prognosis. My dog became ill during this same time period, and we discovered that she had a cancerous tumor in her leg that would require an immediate amputation, and it was very doubtful that the removal of her leg would eradicate the fast-moving cancer.

I was driving across the Golden Gate Bridge between hospitals in Marin County and San Francisco when I had what would best be described as an emotional breakdown. I wept bitterly, cried out to God, and asked, "What have I done to you to deserve this kind of compounded pain and loss?"

While my family circumstances justified an emotional response, what surprised me was an accompanying wave of self-condemnation that suggested I was enveloped in this cloud of suffering because I am a lesbian. After being in a loving relationship with my spouse for twenty-five years, raising two beautiful daughters, being on the front line in the fight for LGBT moral and political equality, and planting affirming churches in the United States and beyond, I could not believe I could be revisiting this kind of God-based self-loathing. I was shocked and amazed at how deep the tentacles of this kind of self-defeating thinking can go. Although it took an extreme set of circumstances to bring them to the surface, the "stinking thinking" was still there.

This experience allowed me to reflect deeply on the origins and power of being colonized and deeply scarred by the self-hatred and self-loathing associated with learning about God in the context of what might be called conditional acceptance. Trying to establish a relationship with a God who tolerates you but cannot truly accept and certainly will never celebrate you can do incredible damage to your self-esteem. The tortured historical and theological view that suggests that some people are just flawed or born to be the underclass and should never expect to be on God's A-list has been the convenient method used to hold women, immigrants, the poor, and LGBT people in chains of self-depreciation.

When this kind of thinking takes root, it encourages a life narrative that says that certain people should not expect to excel and that the desire for acceptance and equality is a waste of time. My maternal grandfather loved me and demonstrated his love in many ways, yet when I talked to my grandpa about my desire to go to college, he told me I would do better to pursue vocational school because "white folks don't like smart Negros and men don't want a wife with too much education." He said he wanted me to have a good life. I was encouraged to "go along" with my God-ordained diminished state so I could "get along" in the world. LGBT or Same Gender Loving (SGL) people in many faith communities struggle constantly against a similar internalized oppression and colonization exacerbated by an environment that will use their skills but won't celebrate their personhood. There is a constant requirement to "go along" in order to "get along."

When existing communities are not even conditionally accepting, marginalized people must seek to develop community for and among themselves. Where people are giving birth to a fresh, emerging Christian community, old barriers must be overcome with extravagant welcome and radical inclusivity. At the risky experiment called City of Refuge UCC Church, founded in San Francisco in 1991 and now in a beautiful new home in Oakland, we have a saying that we welcome you and all your baggage for we are here too with all our baggage—working toward a personal and intimate relationship with God.

City of Refuge was and is a response to several fundamental questions: How do we create a spiritual community that will embrace our collective cultures, faith paths, gender expressions, and sexual/affectional orientations while simultaneously freeing us from oppressive theologies that subjugate women, denigrate the LGBT community, and disconnect us from justice issues locally and globally? How do we embrace liberation and liberating theologies and celebrate indigenizing our faith? People sometimes wonder how and why we, in what I call the African American Metho-Bapti-Costal (Methodist Baptist Pentecostal) church, cherish embodied worship. Others wonder why we stress indigenizing our faith. Sometimes nothing less is required to take down that "stinking thinking" for a community where the edge gathers.

Oppression Sickness

The theology of those at the center of society often characterizes people on the edge as enemies of God. This is especially true when individuals or groups unrepentantly refuse to conform to the dominant definition of normativity. Overcoming internal and external oppressive theology, a theology that excludes certain people, is primary in creating a Christian community for people visibly on the periphery. Those who promote theologies that exclude certain races, cultures, sexual and gender orientations, and classes in the name of Jesus would do well to remember that Jesus himself was from the edge of society, with a ministry to those who were considered least.

Oppression sickness is internalized oppression that causes the oppressed to be infected by the sickness of the oppressor. The effort to mimic the dominant Christian culture or those 'truly favored' by God has infected the African American church tradition with classism, sexism, hetero-privilege, patriarchy, and closed doors. How does an inferior-feeling group of people feel superior? By finding someone else to make inferior to *them*. Accordingly, light-colored people feel superior to dark people. Educated people feel superior to undereducated people. Men lord over women. Straight people bash SGL people. Whoever is considered the "gentile" in our midst is oppressed.

Contempt for the church and all things religious often stems from exposure to oppressive theology, biblical literalism, and unyielding tradition. A person, church, or society can do extreme harm when that harm is done in the name of God and virtue and with the "support" of scripture.

In *The Good Book*, Peter J. Gomes reflects on an old aphorism he heard from a friend: "A surplus of virtue is more dangerous than a surplus of vice, because a surplus of virtue is not subject to the constraints of conscience."[1] Many people rejected by the church got their burns from Bible-believing Christian flamethrowers. Marginalized people, now as in the time of Jesus's earthly ministry, respond to a community of openness and inclusivity, where other people from the edge gather. In such an atmosphere people feel it is safer to be who they are. A liberating theology of acceptance must be embodied in the atmosphere of a liberating Christian community.

In the Metho-Bapti-Costal tradition there is a form of oppression sickness that masquerades as virtue. The ancestors of present-day African Americans were taught to cover up in the daylight and were often sexually and physically abused behind closed doors at night. This brought about shame and guilt regarding the body, but what was worse was what went on behind those doors late at night. Africans came to feel that virtue was a white thing for white people and did not extend to the slave; the rules came in different colors. Sin and evil were black; goodness and virtue were white.

Slaveholders were the people who taught Africans brought to the Americas about Jesus, a Jesus who loved Africans as long as they were content to be slaves, a Jesus who supported the snatching of babies from their mothers' breasts and selling them downriver. Folks who could sing "Amazing Grace" on the deck of a slave ship or at a burning, beating, or lynching were the examples of good moral Christians. John L. Kater rightly asserts that all theology serves someone. The question is, Whom does it serve? Who benefits, and at whose expense? When we are finished cooking up and serving our theologies, who reigns and who suffers? According to Kater, "Both Jesus and the prophets before him knew well that it is possible to practice religion without seeking Justice."[2]

The slave's understanding of a God who could allow such atrocities would have to be joined with internalized inferiority. In 1706, six colonial legislatures passed acts denying that Christian baptism made slaves equal to whites. Baptism began for many with the following proclamation:

> You declare in the presence of God and before the congregation that you do not ask for the holy baptism out of any design to free yourself from

the Duty and Obedience that you owe your master while you live, but merely for the good of Your Soul and to partake of the Graces and Blessings promised to the members of the Church of Jesus Christ.[3]

Preachers allowed to preach to slaves had to constantly remind them that they were never going to be equal to their masters—neither now nor in the hereafter. A slave named Frank Roberson paraphrased the kind of preaching slaves were subjected to:

> You will go to heaven if you are good, but don't ever think that you will be close to your mistress and master. No! No! There will be a wall between you; but there will be holes in it that will permit you to look out and see your mistress when she passes by. If you want to sit behind this wall, you must do the language of the text "Obey your masters."[4]

In order even to preach to the slaves the preacher had to convince the slaveholder that Christianity would produce a more docile, obedient slave.

It is impossible to come into the Christian faith through the slave door and not have a skewed view of the relationship with the Creator and a sideways interpretation of virtue. Women's experience led to a particularly tortured relationship with white "virtue." According to M. Shawn Copeland:

> Black women's suffering redefined caricatured Christian virtues. Because of the lives and suffering of Black women held in chattel slavery—the meanings of forbearance, long-suffering, patience, love, hope, and faith can never again be ideologized. Because of the rape, seduction, and concubinage of Black women under chattel slavery, chastity or virginity begs new meaning.[5]

Just as child abuse passes from one generation to the next, so does spiritual/theological abuse and the resulting oppression sickness that can make the oppressed a "virtuous" oppressor.

The pulpit often becomes a place of monarchy, not ministry—particularly when the pulpit is the only place where the minister has value. When a low sense of self-worth is present, it often seems necessary to stand tall on someone else's back. In the world of church, regardless of the ethnicity or culture, those backs often belong to the people who do not fit—the ones who are obviously, visibly "other." Lording it over the "have-nots" makes people feel like "haves." As Elias Farajaje-Jones has said, "Expressing homophobia/biphobia to reaffirm their heterosexual privilege is often the only situation in which many Black Christians feel that they have any form of privilege at all."[6]

This is a peculiar paradox as the African American church has a long history of fighting for the rights of those in its pews and community. For more than 400 years the African American church has been the principle source of sanctuary, education, socialization, information, and community for people of African descent in this country. Most of the great African American civil rights leaders, such as Martin Luther King, Barbara Jordan, Rosa Parks, and Jesse Jackson, are products of the black church. Yet this black church community that endured so much oppression during its development on the margin has become an oppressor for many. In *Unrepentant, Self-Affirming, Practicing*, Gary Comstock revealed the findings of Michael Dickens's survey of SGL men of African descent in Connecticut. Especially because of the leading role of the black church in "all progressive changes in civil rights since the days of slavery," Dickens reflected, "we begin to understand how truly devastating it is for someone to be condemned for their homosexuality by an institution that has long been in the vanguard of the cause of justice."[7]

This oppression is rooted deeply in the African American community's spirit. African Americans demonstrate certain characteristics of African Spiritualism such as ecstatic, cathartic behavior in worship, with dancing and "shouting" behavior very similar to and central to the liturgy of West African peoples. Yet we are told what Africans do is demonic while what African Americans do is the Holy Spirit. We have systematically been taught that all indigenous African expressions of faith are heathen, demonic, or ignorant. Some African American churches refuse to sing songs with call-and-response or long repeating choruses because it has been suggested that only ignorant people sing the same thing over and over. Yet the repeating chant is much more than just a significant part of our musical history. The African village concept of community was demonized along with African religion. So much was lost in the crossing of the Atlantic.

Cathartic Vulnerability

In order to create community among people on the margin, it is essential to adopt a theology that seeks to identify and eradicate oppression sickness no matter what the root cause may be. Oppressive theology, or a theology that welcomes those who fit a normative definition of the dominant culture while excluding those who do not, is a ball and chain on the heart of the body of Christ, and with it we keep each other in bondage. The Church of Jesus Christ is in the midst of change, not all of it for the better. Any theology that suggests that God receives some and rejects others is not reflective of the ministry of Jesus Christ. Comstock insists "that the church has simply gone astray from a basis, center, origin in a common carpenter who welcomed, included, and healed the broken, outcast and needy."[8]

Jesus established the role of ministry that was being ushered in by the phenomenon of God being made flesh when he read from the scroll of Isaiah one Sabbath morning. Jesus said the Spirit of the sovereign God was upon him to

> Preach good tidings to the meek
> Bind up the broken hearted
> Proclaim liberty to the captives
> Open the prison to them that are bound
> Proclaim the acceptable year . . . the year of jubilee
> Comfort all that mourn
> Give beauty for ashes and the oil of joy for mourning
> Give a garment of praise for the spirit of heaviness
> Make us trees of righteousness, plantings of the Lord. (Luke 4:18, 19;
>   Isaiah 61:1–3)

These priorities must also be the priorities of an oppression-free Christian community. How can we be the Church of Jesus unless we reflect the ministry of Jesus? Is the church a radical incarnation of the ministry of Jesus or a private social club?

It is crucial in the formation of community that those who were and are oppressed seek to overcome the theological millstones tied around their necks. It is equally important not to adopt pejorative assumptions toward others in community who are different; this passes on the sickness of oppressive theology. Donald N. Chinula asserts that oppression manifested as an unjust use of authority or advantage "seeks its own advantage at the expense of the oppressed and strives to perpetuate itself."⁹ Stereotyping allows the oppressor to stand apart from the oppressed and to categorize and pigeonhole a group of people. This oppression is particularly insidious when the Bible is used to defend it. This cycle of naming and blaming marginalized people has historically been the biblically based justification of the violence perpetrated against individuals, races, and nations.

The principal message that goes out from the Church of Jesus Christ should declare: freedom in Christ is freedom in life. All are welcome at the table.

I am often asked, "If we resist the oppression sickness that was handed down to us and made us feel rejected by the church and just barely received by God . . . if we dispel that defeatist thinking, will we retain the atmosphere, style, sound, and feel of the church as we know it?" I have found that it is quite possible to have the style, sound, and feel of the Metho-Bapti-Costal Church without the oppression perpetuated by some in these traditions. The preaching, the song, and the dance are media through which the Spirit moves. *They are ours*, and they should remain. God can move through any culture. When Ghanaian womanist theologian Mercy Amba Oduyoye was challenged about the church in Africa demonstrating too much traditional African spirituality, she replied: "The Owner of the Church will purify and use it as He sees fit." It is not necessary to choose between a Spirit-filled oppressive church and a cold, dead, liberated church. Church can be effervescent and joyful while simultaneously being theologically liberating, justice oriented, culturally appropriate, and inclusive.

Often when someone is introduced to the possibility of being accepted in a Christian community, after being rejected for so long, there is a period of what I call "cathartic vulnerability." During this time, people take every opportunity to tell their story, one that has possibly been bottled up for years. Stories of oppression, fear, guilt, self-hatred, survival, and hope surface. People compare scars. When the stories begin to flow out of one experience to another, and from one person to another, similarities emerge around which people can identify and community can form. Community, then, is a circle of open huts around a central welcoming table where everyone has a place to come to be healed. There is no more need to put forth a pathetic, halfhearted effort to be accepted; individuals' seats at the table are not given *in spite of* who they are but *because of* who they are.

Part of the thorough colonization of African Americans in the United States included making the slaves feel that their indigenous faith was ignorant, substandard, and demonic. Many African American and other colonized people learned Christianity in the context of this oppression and sought to abandon the ways of their ancestors. Yet our style of worship is heavily influence by our historic cultures. We mimic our predecessors while being discouraged from celebrating them. The intent of City of Refuge Church is to celebrate our pre-Christian-influenced cultures *and* our deep roots in the churches of our youth. We celebrate all of our gender expressions and all of our sexualities. We have carved out a theology of radical inclusivity, extravagant grace, and relentless hospitality while actively working for justice and peace for all.

We have deep roots in the Pentecostal, Baptist, Methodist, Adventist, and Spiritualist movements. Our histories and our current worship are filled with choir and usher processionals, Mother's Boards, self-proclaimed prophets, clapping on the second and fourth beats, chants, moans, songs with few verses and long repeating choruses, wood floors so we can hear our feet, drums, jazz organs, and dancing. Our cultures include sermons with call-and-response in which people talk back to the preacher and the sermons end in a celebration catharsis for the week to come. We touch and care for our dead. We lovingly regard, respect, and welcome the presence of our ancestors. We have prayer vigils called "shut-ins." We have visions, we lay our hands on each other when we pray, and we baptize by immersion.

We are black, white, Asian, brown, Christian, Cherokee, Muslim, Jewish, Yoruba, Candomblé, Kemetic, Wiccan, Catholic, Universalist. While we were in exile from our faith communities, we saw the value and importance of synergy and syncretism (the bringing together of disparate religious traditions). Our strong desire is to find and embrace the spiritual threads that have historically held communities on the margins together—what we call the common Christ. There is no map for where we are going, but we are not lost, for we are here—holding on to some things that were almost snatched from us and simultaneously letting go of those things that stand between us and our loving God.

*   *   *

With joy I can say that God did not leave me comfortless on the Golden
Gate Bridge, in my moment of despair. I received two revelations before
I came to the end of the bridge. One said that God does not punish other
people on my account; I now call this displaced religion-based ego. Second, I was experiencing life, and I was assured that blessing would come
from this, no matter how horrible things appeared. My spouse of thirty
years is cancer-free and still with me, Mama transitioned beautifully and
pain free the morning of her wedding anniversary, and we determined,
while our dog was in surgery, that the cancer was too far gone. We were
allowed to come into the surgery room and kiss her as the doctor administered the medication to end her life. Thanks be to God!

> For I am convinced that neither death nor life, neither angels nor demons,
> neither the present nor the future, nor any powers, neither height nor
> depth, nor anything else in all creation, will be able to separate us from the
> love of God that is in Christ Jesus our Lord. (Romans 8:38–39)

NOTES

1. Peter J. Gomes, *The Good Book: Reading the Bible with Mind and Heart* (New York: William Morrow, 1996), 51.
2. John L. Kater, *Christians on the Right: The Moral Majority in Perspective* (New York: Seabury, 1982), 116–17.
3. Edgard Legare Pennington, *Thomas Bray's Associates and Their Work among the Negros* (Worcester, MA: American Antiquarian Society, 1939), 25.
4. John B. Cade, "Out of the Mouths of Ex-Slaves," *Journal of Negro History* 20 (1935): 329.
5. M. Shawn Copeland, "Wading through Many Sorrows," in *A Troubling in My Soul: Womanist Perspectives on Evil and Suffering*, ed. Emilie Townes (Maryknoll, NY: Orbis, 1993), 124.
6. Elias Farajaje-Jones, "Breaking Silence: Toward an In-the-Life Theology," in *Black Theology: A Documentary History*, vol. 2, *1980–1992*, ed. James H. Cone and Gayraud S. Wilmore (Maryknoll, NY: Orbis, 1993), 141.
7. Gary David Comstock, *Unrepentant, Self-Affirming, Practicing: Lesbian/Bisexual/Gay People within Organized Religion* (New York: Continuum, 1992), 190.
8. Gary David Comstock, *Gay Theology without Apology* (Cleveland, OH: Pilgrim Press, 1993), 92.
9. Donald M. Chinula, *Building King's Beloved Community: Foundations for Pastoral Care and Counseling with the Oppressed* (Cleveland, OH: United Church Press, 1997), 2.

PART III

Promiscuities

Traditional Christian morality has relegated all sexual expression out-side celibacies and matrimonies to the residual category of sexual sin. Thought to be at once insatiable, formless, and sterile, it has seemed an existential threat not only to the states of life of celibacies and matrimo-nies but to the very *idea* of states of life. The chapters in this part push back at these judgments.

This was the hardest part to name, perhaps because it recognizes loves that historically could not speak their names. "Promiscuities" won the day, but only after having been dismissed and retrieved and dismissed again. This very contention struck us as important. Queer people have claimed pejorative terms before, but few queer Christians we knew of would choose this word. Yet a number of theologians have insisted that the Christian message is nothing if not promiscuous—extravagant, undiscriminating, even excessive—in its welcome, affirma-tion, and self-giving. The plural "promiscui*ties*" here makes us aware of the forms queer Christians have found to test, share, and learn from the transgressive potential of all desire.

The chapters in this part shed light on the Christian potential of promiscuities from a number of unexpected vantage points. Michael F. Pettinger casts an unflinching eye on the vagaries of sexual desire in all its forms and finds an unlikely resource for understanding and cel-ebrating it in the idea of sin and grace in the work of a theologian often thought to be the greatest enemy of queerness, Augustine of Hippo.

Mary E. Hunt celebrates the expansive category of friendship, arguing that understanding "sex" and "friendship" independently of each other has proved disastrous for both. Nicholas Laccetti argues that a critical appreciation of the engagement of BDSM (a culture embracing bondage, discipline, dominance, and submission, sadism, and masochism) with the power dynamics inherent in all relationships can shed unexpected light on the redemptive potential of the cross and Eucharist. Finally, Elijah C. Nealy reclaims the category of "promiscuity" itself as a description of the way Christians are called to live as they negotiate the challenges of identity and relation in an unjust world.

More open, differently structured, and generously lived forms of sex and friendship have much to teach about both queerness and Christianity.

9

Double Love

Rediscovering the Queerness of Sin and Grace

MICHAEL F. PETTINGER

Queerness teaches us that norms exist to be broken, boundaries are fields of play, lives are performances, and identities are fluid. This is metaphoric language, of course, meant to describe a queerness that will not be pinned down by words. Metaphors serve to help you recognize queerness when you experience it, but without experience, talk of boundaries, performances, and fluidity turns as hard and inert as the norms queerness is supposed to resist. At least this was the case with me. But in the middle of a queer life that had grown hard and inert, I found love. And love made me into someone I could scarcely imagine in my younger days—a gay Augustinian.

For a long time I resisted that love. In college and graduate school I had plenty to say about Augustine, some of which can still be found in notes I furiously scribbled in the margins of my brother's copy of *The City of God* before I finally threw the book against a wall. I didn't get past the first hundred pages. I didn't even reach the place where Augustine observed that "when Lot had escaped from Sodom, there came down from heaven a torrent of fire, and the whole region of that ungodly city was turned to ashes. For it was a place where sexual intercourse between males had become so commonplace that it received the license usually extended by the law to other practices."[1]

A hundred pages of *The City of God* is nothing in the vast corpus of Augustine's work. Augustine was prolific, and his writing grew organically from the concerns and controversies in which he engaged. It resists easy systematization, and as a student looking for systems, I had little patience for him. What I read of him was filtered through the work of other scholars who told me what to expect—authority and authoritarianism, penal notions of sin and redemption, and, most grievous of all, sex negativity. My understanding of Augustine followed and reproduced theirs because their experiences seemed more substantial and real than my own.

But after I finished my doctorate, I met Augustine again. I decided to put his work *On Christian Teaching* on the syllabus for an undergraduate seminar in medieval vernacular literature. My motivations, as far as I understood them, were strictly academic. Written in the 390s, the first three books of *On Christian Teaching* constitute a manual for the interpretation of scripture. The fourth book, written almost thirty years later, is a guide to preaching. It seemed a perfect introduction to the aspects of medieval literature that would be least familiar to undergraduates—allegory, oral performance, and the rejection of the refined pleasures of literary Latin in favor of the vernacular language. I didn't expect my students to take Augustine's theology seriously, and I had no interest in pressing the matter. In those days, after all, I considered myself an agnostic.

Yet my students found the literary issues less compelling than the theological ethics that underlie Augustine's work. In the first book of *On Christian Teaching*, Augustine divides all things into two classes—those that are to be enjoyed and those that are to be used. "Enjoyment" is the great motivating force of all human activity. "To enjoy something is to hold fast to it in love for its own sake."[2] Enjoyment should result in "bliss." Other things are available for use in our efforts to attain this bliss, but only one thing is worthy of enjoyment, or rather, three in one: the Holy Trinity. "If indeed it is a thing, and not the cause of all things, and if indeed it is a cause. It is not easy to find a name for such excellence."[3] The love that clings to God inspires love for anyone else capable of sharing that love, so that the love of God gives rise to the love of others. This double love not only is the key to Augustine's ethics but becomes his hermeneutic principle for reading the Bible as well. "Anyone who thinks that he has understood the divine scriptures or any part of them, but cannot by his understanding build up this double love of God and neighbor, has not yet succeeded in understanding them."[4]

The questions that troubled my students had also troubled me. If God alone is to be enjoyed, were all other kinds of enjoyment sinful? Can we love others without enjoying them? Where does that leave sex? Sex became the practical test by which my students—and I—determined whether Augustine's ethics were plausible. My students seemed to think that they failed that test. One asked if we could not be good enough to reach heaven without forsaking other pleasures. Another put the matter more graphically: "Isn't it enough that I'm thanking God for this beautiful man on top of me?"

Like any professor who wants the reading taken seriously, I defended Augustine. But there was a passion in my performance, detectable to my students and baffling to me, that suggested that my defense was not strictly academic. My students seemed to enjoy the exchange. For my part, I felt like a middle-aged man who had defended his faith. That seemed to be my colleagues' impression as well. "You're such a devout Catholic!" one of them exclaimed in the middle of a conversation, seemingly apropos of nothing. This was news to me. At the time I refused to set foot in a church. I would hurl the epithet "you Catholics" at family members when they pissed me off. I told my brother on Christmas Eve that the Virgin Birth was a "fraud." But apparently my performance as an agnostic was not entirely convincing.

My attachment to Augustine seemed at odds with my positions as a gay man and an agnostic. I felt as if it undermined my authority as an "objective" performer in the classroom. It even dulled my instincts as a pedagogue. When my student asked if we couldn't be good enough for heaven without forsaking other pleasures, I should have asked, "Exactly how good would you have to be? What could you possibly do to guarantee yourself the endless bliss of 'heaven'? Why believe that such bliss was even possible?" Her statement assumed that if such bliss existed, it was something she might be entitled to enjoy—at the right price. That annoyed me. But why?

The only way to answer that question was to read more Augustine. I added the *Confessions* to my syllabi and quickly realized how incomplete my understanding of Augustine had been. On that sweaty night, writing in my brother's copy of *The City of God*, I had not encountered the protagonist of the *Confessions*—grace. Grace is the subject of the opening rhapsody of the *Confessions*, which concludes with a prayer to God who is most high, utterly good, utterly powerful, most omnipotent, most merciful, most just, deeply hidden yet most intimately present, perfection of both beauty and strength, stable and incomprehensible, immutable yet changing all things, never new, never old, making everything new and "leading" the proud "to be old" without their knowledge; always active, always in repose, gathering to yourself but not in need, supporting and filling and protecting and creating and nurturing and bringing to maturity, searching even though to you nothing is lacking; you love without burning, you are jealous in a way that is free of anxiety, you "repent" without pain of regret, you are wrathful yet remain tranquil.[5]

A God, in short, who pours forth a stream of favors, some harsh, some sweet, and whose grace completely queers the ethics of use and enjoyment. A soul cannot simply choose to fix lovingly on the invisible God who baffles all categories of thought. It needs that God to fix it on unchanging divinity. The only worthy "object" of human enjoyment is not the passive destination of the soul but the one who truly acts.

Grace not only destabilizes the "self" as an autonomous subject but destabilizes the self's relationship with others as well. Neither self nor other can be objects of enjoyment without drawing attention away from the unchangeable and fixing it on what changes.[6] This need not translate into a lack of love either for oneself or for others. Whether it is the self or others, "any other object of love that enters the mind should be swept towards the same destination as that to which the whole flood of love is directed."[7] This sweeping love extends to the flesh, which no one truly hates. "Some say that they would prefer not to have a body, but they are mistaken. For what they hate is not their body, but its imperfections and its dead weight. What they want is not to have no body at all, but to have one free from corruption and totally responsive; they think that if the body were such a thing it would not be a body, because they consider such a thing to be a soul."[8] For Augustine, the body that perfectly responds to the promptings of the soul is no mere philosophical speculation. It is the body of the resurrected Jesus. Belief in him might be a reason for my student to believe that endless bliss is possible. It might even convince me.

Against the sweep of grace stands sin. Sin is not the choosing of evil, since evil has no existence in itself, but rather the choice to cling to lesser goods over and against the call to something greater. To cling to lesser goods, even the best of them—oneself, one's body, or the souls and bodies of others—does more than set up rivals to God. Such enjoyment becomes a form of "use," even "abuse." It assigns to these things a fixed identity, one that serves the selfish needs of the person who claims to love them while depriving them of the fluidity they need to respond to God's transformative activity. It stands in the way of their bliss and gives rise to a desire to control them. The self usurps the place of God, and "concupiscence of the flesh" kindles "concupiscence of domination." But even if this unjust domination harms the soul, it can be useful to others, since resistance to injustice clarifies commitment to the divine. "The martyrs," for example, "certainly, did not love the wickedness of those who persecuted them, but used it to win their way to God."[9]

The question, then, is whether sexual desire is selfish abuse or the prompting of grace to a greater good. A number of Augustine's contemporaries argued the latter position, especially Julian of Eclanum, a younger bishop from southern Italy who engaged in a heated debate with Augustine in the last years of the older man's life.[10] Julian was a defender of Pelagius, the British monk who had objected to Augustine's teaching that the sin of Adam and Eve left an inborn flaw in the will of their descendants. According to Augustine, this flaw, manifest in every aspect of human life, is particularly evident in sexual desire. While Augustine believed that sexual desire before the Fall would only arise at the goodwill of the innocent soul, Julian believed that humans experienced sexual desire exactly as the first couple did, as a good created by God.

For Julian, what mattered was the use we made of sexual desire. "For, as we receive the image of God by the reason of the mind, so we experience our unity with the animals by the affinity of the flesh. Though its form is different, it is, nonetheless, the same substance with regard to the material of the elements, destined of course, in accord with the rational mind to see eternity, either wretched with pains or glorious with rewards."[11] A just God would not condemn the rational soul for spontaneous sexual impulses over which it has no control but would reward the merits of the soul that puts those impulses to the good use of reproduction in marriage.

For Augustine, the desire described by Julian only demonstrates the soul's impotence. Humans who are healthy and free can use eyes, lips, hands, and feet in seamless accord with the will. Why is it, then, that, "when it comes to begetting children, the organs created for this purpose do not serve the nodding of the will, but must be waited upon, so that pleasure, as if by right, should make them move? And sometimes it will not do so when the spirit wills, and other times it does so when the spirit wills not?"[12] Julian thought that Augustine's teaching on the original sin undermines notions of free will, merit, and what Peter Brown calls "the equity of God." Augustine objected that Julian ignored the ways in which the comings and goings of desire limited the freedom of the rational soul.

The hardened differences between the theologies of Julian and Augustine have often been explained in terms of their supposedly different experiences of sex. Julian, a bishop's son, had been married to Titia, apparently the daughter of another bishop. Paulinus of Nola praised the way their wedding avoided the bawdiness and luxury supposedly typical of non-Christian weddings.[13] But he exaggerates the differences. Whatever dirty songs were customary at weddings, traditional Roman notions of matrimony subordinated the desires of the couple to the demands of procreation and family continuity. Even shorn of gross celebrations, the marriage portrayed by Paulinus was still the same sort of parentally arranged union idealized by well-to-do "pagan" Romans.

In the *Confessions*, Augustine provides what might be a more honest portrait of late-Roman marriage. He complains that his parents neglected to arrange a proper marriage for him, fearing that it would stand in the way of his career.[14] They left him free to be an enthusiastic and shameless pursuer of love.[15] Eventually he established a monogamous relationship that might have been considered a marriage, were it not for his own refusal to commit.[16] More than a decade later, after his unnamed partner had borne him a son, Monica, Augustine's surviving parent, finally negotiated a respectable marriage for Augustine in much the same way that Julian's father would. Forced to renounce his earlier relationship, Augustine claims that he was left with a heart dripping blood and a sexual dependency exposed and vulnerable.[17] How much of Augustine's subsequent shame at his sexual past, and his skepticism of sexual desire, was rooted in despair at the ways traditional, respectable Roman marriage made cruel use of human beings, subordinating ties of love and affection to the demands of status and progeny?

Perhaps, as some scholars argue, we should not take Augustine's story at face value, but he is certainly more forthcoming than Julian. To claim alongside Elaine Pagels that "Julian was evidently restrained in sexual matters" confuses his marital ideology with his actual experience of marriage.[18] Based on his own experience of sexual impulses, Augustine is more critical. When Julian claims that celibates restrain desire by virtue, while those who are married use it with honor, Augustine snaps: "Is that your experience? Is then this evil, or this good of yours, not reined in by married couples? I suppose that married couples lie down together, whenever they like, and enter each other whenever the desire moves them. This desire for intercourse is not postponed even for an hour; rather the union of their bodies is seen as permissible at the very moment when this natural good of yours is spontaneously aroused."[19] Augustine had asked in the *Confessions*, "Can it be wrong at any time or place to love God with all your heart and all your soul and with all your mind and to love your neighbor as yourself?"[20] For Julian to admit that he had to restrain desire even in marriage would imply that sexual impulses are not simply the promptings of double love, which are just at all times and in all places.

Even Julian's claim that procreation in marriage is the right use of sexual desire falls short in Augustine's eyes. Despite a common notion that Augustine saw procreation as the true end of marital intercourse, he is quick to argue that a Christian couple that produces a child but does not see to its baptism fails to share their love of God with their off-spring.[21] Yet baptism and the final bliss of their child are likely the furthest things from the minds of most Christians in the throes of passion. In the less heated context of his work *On the Good of Marriage*, Augustine calls the gap between the couple's intentions in the midst of sex and the final good of their child a "venial" sin, pardoned by the grace of God without the rites of sacramental penance for the sake of the sacramental fidelity of marriage.[22] But it is hard to conceive of a couple sexually aroused at the hope of their child's final bliss, a bliss that depends, after all, not on them but on the ceaseless working of grace.

Augustine's critical doubt in the face of Julian's claims reminds me of that second student, who asked if it was not enough that she thanked God for the beautiful man on top of her. With Augustine I want to ask—is that really your experience? I do not expect the two of them to produce a child for which they are probably unprepared. But I do wonder if, in the heat of passion, she is really thanking God. And if she is, is the beautiful man joining in her prayer? Is either of them prepared to bear the weight of what it means to be a gift of God's grace to another person? And what will happen to that grace if their desire fades? The questions sound harsh, but they arise, as I believe they arose for Augustine, from a certain kind of experience. So rather than lend them a false and disembodied authority, let me ground them in a confession.

For years I believed, much like Julian, that my sexual desires were simply "natural," a fairly typical position for a gay man coming out of the closet in Nebraska in the 1980s. I believed that I could trust and use them in ways that were loving and liberating. Thirty years later, my right to be sexual with other men guaranteed by the Supreme Court, my right to marry assured by the State of New York, and my sexuality virtually normalized in the minds of a younger generation, I have to say that I don't feel liberated, and I am not loving. I did love, and was loved by, a man who walked away from me. I was told that this was normal, and I tried to love again—and again—and again—and again. My desires drove me to return to sex over and over with someone who made me ashamed of everything I loved. Desire would not move in me for someone I loved, even though he did love and desire me. I turned to anonymous sex and found moments of ecstasy that left me feeling liberated. But I felt compelled to see if I could repeat those experiences, and when they failed, I felt compelled to see if they would fail me again. I can name men that I have abused. And if anyone who shared those moments with me thanks God for the beautiful man who was lying on top of him—how would I know? Neither my attempts at matrimony nor my promiscuities have brought me lasting bliss, and the times I have sworn celibacy have left me restless. No matter the form my life has tried to take, the problem of sin has remained. Augustine's model of a desire that is skewed from true enjoyment has proved truer to my experience than Julian's confidence.

This has nothing to do with being gay. I know that when Augustine looked for an example of something that could never be an act of double love, he found it in the same-sex acts of the men of Sodom.[23] But Augustine has taught me that heterosexual desire is no less skewed from double love than same-sex love, a truth confirmed in films, pop songs, books, and an entire culture hell-bent on making the heartbreak and violence of concupiscence look like nature. Perhaps it was the brokenness of Augustine's own desire that led him to cast out queerness so that heterosexuality might seem "normal," even "holy," in comparison. But while resistance to this perverse domination can be useful in the pursuit of true enjoyment, simply denouncing the domination of a heterosexist society—even one grounded in an understanding of Augustine—leaves the root of the problem untouched. It also leaves me doing exactly what has been done to me, a point deeply impressed upon me by James Alison's reading of the dynamics of exclusion in the story of the Man Born Blind.[24]

Augustine, my companion in returning to faith, has taught me that a reading of my experience that is queer because it is Christian must go further. It cannot rest until it finds a lesson on double love, even in the places it was told not to look—whether those places are sex clubs or the writings of Augustine himself. He traces a line from the dangerous stirrings of desire, through the commingling of persons and the communions of sacrament, to the eschatological fulfillment of offspring in the kingdom of God. It's a thread so tenuous that it seems a miracle. It fills me with longing. Compared with Augustine, the work of too many LGBT theologians reads like Julian—a little too confident in their use of sexual desire, a little too good to be true just yet. I don't deny the possibility that others have found lasting joy in their relationships, or promiscuity, or celibacy. I have seen joy after all. But I wonder about the broken hearts left behind them and the unearned gifts of God that they enjoy. Even more, I look for a queer theology that can stand up to my own experience and show me how the ceaseless activity of God might be transforming the impulses of my own desire into the stuff of the kingdom of heaven.

NOTES

1. Augustine, *The City of God against the Pagans*, ed. and trans. R. W. Dyson (Cambridge: Cambridge University Press, 1998), 743.

2. Augustine, *On Christian Teaching*, trans. R. P. H. Green (Oxford: Oxford University Press, 1997), 9.

3. Ibid., 10.

4. Ibid., 27.

5. Augustine, *Confessions*, trans. Henry Chadwick (Oxford: Oxford University Press, 1992), 5.

6. *On Christian Teaching*, Green, 17.

7. Ibid.

8. Ibid., 18–19.

9. Ibid., 18.

10. Useful discussions of the argument between Julian and Augustine can be found in Peter Brown, *The Body and Society: Men, Women, and Sexual Renunciation in Early Christianity* (New York: Columbia University Press, 1988), 408–27; and Elaine Pagels, *Adam, Eve, and the Serpent: Sex and Politics in Early Christianity* (New York: Vintage, 1989), 127–50.

11. Augustine, *Unfinished Work in Answer to Julian*, trans. Roland J. Teske, in *Answer to the Pelagians, III: Unfinished Work in Answer to Julian* (*The Works of Saint Augustine: A Translation for the 21st Century*, ed. John E. Rotelle, pt. 1, vol. 25) (Brooklyn, NY: New City Press, 1998), 419.

12. Augustine, *Marriage and Desire*, trans. Roland J. Teske, in *Answer to the Pelagians, II: Marriage and Desire, Answer to the Two Letters of the Pelagians, Answer to Julian* (*The Works of Saint Augustine: A Translation for the 21st Century*, ed. John E. Rotelle, pt. 1, vol. 24) (Brooklyn, NY: New City Press, 1998), 33.

13. Paulinus of Nola, *Carmen* 25, trans. P. G. Walsh in *Poems of St. Paulinus of Nola* (New York: Paulist Press, 1975), 245–53.

14. *Confessions*, Chadwick, 28.

15. Ibid., 35.

16. It is often claimed that Augustine's partner was of the wrong social class for the relationship to be recognized as a legitimate "marriage," but he seems to argue otherwise, at least for sacramental purposes. See Augustine, *On the Good of Marriage*, trans. P. G. Walsh in *De Bono Coniugali: De Sancta Virginitate* (Oxford: Clarendon Press, 2001), 11.

17. *Confessions*, Chadwick, 109.

18. Pagels, *Adam, Eve, and the Serpent*, 141.

19. Augustine, *Answer to Julian*, trans. Roland Teske, in *Answer to the Pelagians, II: Marriage and Desire, Answer to the Two Letters of the Pelagians, Answer to Julian* (*The Works of Saint Augustine: A Translation for the 21st Century*, ed. John E. Rotelle, pt. 1, vol. 24) (Brooklyn, NY: New City Press, 1999), 355.

20. *Confessions*, Chadwick, 45.

21. See, e.g., *Answer to Julian*, Teske, 353.

22. *On the Good of Marriage*, Walsh, 13–15.

23. *Confessions*, Chadwick, 46. Mark D. Jordan correctly notes that the reference to same-sex acts is not explicit (*The Invention of Sodomy in Christian Theology* [Chicago: University of Chicago Press, 1998], 34). But see the commentary on the passage in James O'Donnell's "The *Confessions* of Saint Augustine: An Electronic Edition" (www.stoa.org/hippo/comm3.html#CB3C8S15).

24. James Alison, "The Man Blind from Birth and the Creator's Subversion of Sin," in *Faith beyond Resentment: Fragments Catholic and Gay* (New York: Crossroad, 2001), 3–26. See John 9.

10

Love Your Friends

Learning from the Ethics of Relationships

MARY E. HUNT

My lawyer reports that people under age thirty-five plan to get married regardless of the gender constellation of their mates. Her older clients, like me, are ambivalent at best about marriage to anyone. We prefer to live out our affective relationships without benefit of clergy and outside the law, at least until it becomes too costly to do so. The Internal Revenue Service's decision to open joint tax filings to all married people, the potential to receive a partner's Social Security benefits if she or he predeceases one, and the ease of transferring major assets without tax consequences make it hard, finally imprudent if one has children, to resist marriage's charms. How romantic!

Opening marriage to more people, while a social justice victory on its face, on more careful examination is a chance to think about what kind of society we really want. I want one with lots of friends, some of whom might choose to marry, many of whom will not. Marriage does not make people friends. It creates legal ties that govern shared property, inheritance, and the like. The rest one has to do for oneself and/or with the support of a community.

Friendship, not coupled love, is the normative adult human relationship in my view.[1] I have lived in a committed relationship with the same person for more than thirty years. Given how strongly we feel about the centrality of friendship, we were faced with whether to marry or not. Many of our friends are in the same boat. When we talk about our partners, our friends, our significant others, whether one or more, we mean the terms in robust, multidimensional ways, terms of endearment that are at least as significant as "spouse," "wife," or "husband" but not nearly so laden with baggage. Most of us are deciding to marry for economic reasons, which we in no way confuse with love and care. Friendship, not marriage, undergirds our commitments.

Friendship remains largely unexplored from a postmodern ethical perspective. A feminist exploration of the phenomenon from a lesbian Catholic perspective is an invitation to broaden what friendship means in common experience and parlance, indeed, to increase its normativity both in and outside of marriage. Same-sex marriage raises questions for everyone, about just what our most intimate and committed bonds mean. Yet, as same-sex marriages increase, I fear the loss of any such discussion. It's a conversation worth having especially with younger friends/colleagues who have grown up expecting that same-sex couples can marry. Why would they necessarily think beyond the box? But what might they miss? Let me begin such a conversation now.

My starting point is as a theologically trained person who works at the intersection of scholarship and activism. As the longtime codirector of the Women's Alliance for Theology, Ethics and Ritual (WATER), I am privileged to lecture and write without the usual constraints of academia or a religious tradition, in my case Catholicism.[2] I can extend and expand the contours of my tradition without worrying that authorities will revoke my tenure or pull my license to teach. This allows me to listen to the *sensus fidelium*, the real-life experiences of people, and craft theological possibilities accordingly. WATER's goal is to promote the use of feminist religious values in the work of social change. We do so through both scholarship and activism, both pastoral ministry and collaboration with other justice seekers of many and no religious commitments. Perhaps our most important effort is to live the future we envision, especially in a small office where we have welcomed people of many relational commitments. The operative word is "welcomed," as the commitments can and do change.

In this chapter I look carefully at things Catholic with regard to friendship. My reason is twofold. First, the misuse of the term "friendship" by some Catholic hierarchs muddies the waters, distracting from the real issue, which is that institutional Catholic teaching has been antiqueer, anti-body, and antifemale for generations. Second, recent off-the-cuff comments by Pope Francis on sexuality have astonished many people around the world.[3] He seems to walk away from his recent predecessors' notion that same-sex love is "objectively disordered." When such a simple, obvious statement as "Who am I to judge?" makes front-page news, I must conclude that the institutional Catholic Church, especially the pope, still exercises more clout than I wish it did. If this is to persist, then it is important to clarify what is useful and what is not, and to emphasize that just because something comes from the hierarchy of the Roman Catholic Church does not mean it is accepted Catholic teaching.

Friendship in Context

The history of Christian considerations of friendship is not terribly robust.[4] Most scholars trace the roots to Aristotle. His *Nicomachean Ethics* contains a rigorous discussion of various kinds of friendships, culminating in "virtuous" ones that unite good people.[5] Aristotle and early Christian writers who based their thinking on his work did not have women at the forefront of their imaginations. Women were not envisioned as friends with one another, and the social superiority of men was thought to preclude their friendship with women. Hence the history of Christian thinking on friendship was predicated on male-male relationships in a heteronormative world that did not include a sexual dimension.

Of course some male owners had sex with their male slaves, male teachers with their male students, and the like, but those were quite different from the friendships of virtuous men. Friendship was seen as a category distinct from romantic love and was not envisioned as a hallmark of same-sex love. Marriages were not usually contracts between friends but between those whom families deemed convenient for business and/or social purposes. What were often called "loveless marriages" are better described as unions lacking in friendship. Thus, a theology of marriage arose completely divorced, as it were, from friendship.

Contemporary feminist theological studies of friendship have challenged this one-sided approach to the topic. In her book *Just Good Friends: Towards a Lesbian and Gay Theology of Relationships*, British theologian Elizabeth Stuart looked at the complexity of weaving sex into friendships.[6] She writes: "We are called to be passionate friends to each other and to God who is Passionate Friend."[7] Stewart bases her theology on the experience of lesbian, gay, and bisexual people at a time of homohatred. But there is every reason to think that the insights that accrue from such friendships are broadly applicable. Margins are often zones of creativity, as the LGBTIQ community has proved over and over. While same-sex marriage will function to dull the edges of such difference, I am hopeful that even this gentle reminder of a proud history of same-sex loving friends will catalyze imitation.

My own early work on friendship, *Fierce Tenderness: A Feminist Theology of Friendship*, is based on the claim that friendships include love and power, embodiment and spirituality.[8] I see generativity as a hallmark of friendship.[9] Sex is an integral component of friendship, since erotic attraction is an embodied expression of how love, power, and spirituality configure. Women experience these dynamics to various degrees in every friendship. This is not to say that every friendship involves genital sexual expression, but rather, that sexuality, as most women see it, is an integrated part of everyday human interaction— whether touch, embrace, caress, or more intimacy. This prioritizing of friendship based on women's experiences offers a different starting point for sexual choices. Friendship becomes the bedrock of all love relationships. It is a good foundation. It is articulated in a range of ways, including a range of erotic expressions. There is no reason to single out a sexual partnership as somehow qualitatively different from other friendships. Rather than separating sex as something one engages in with a lover, it is far healthier and safer to see friendship as the basis on which one engages in sex.

Many progressive theo-ethical scholars have raised serious questions about same-sex marriage. We are in agreement with the equality dimension,[10] but we are concerned that the focus on couples takes away from the common good. We worry that replicating the privileges of heterosexual marriage for same-sex couples is simply adding to those who are advantaged (in inheritance, some tax situations, etc.) rather than reconfiguring society to level the playing field for all. Pressure to marry for economic reasons increases with equal marriage. One couple I know has been together for more than thirty years. If they marry, they will lose access to the Social Security benefits of one person's former spouse. If they don't marry, they can no longer share the insurance coverage that was permitted them as domestic partners. Because "all" can marry in their state, the insurance company now requires that people be married in order to take advantage of the benefit. Rethinking the whole matter of social connections as if friendship, not marriage, were foundational would result in justice for many more people.

Marriage is still generally perceived to be the default adult human relationship. But census data for 2010 show that only 48 percent of U.S. households are made up of people who are married.[11] As same-sex marriage becomes increasingly available in the states, this percentage may go above half again, but the trajectory seems clear. Other ways of organizing daily life are increasingly chosen by (or imposed on) more people. Some of these ways fail as friendships, as, for example, women with dependent children whose partners (usually male) shirk their responsibilities. But in the main, relational variety, from single to polyamorous, from hetero-coupled to same-sex coupled, from community to cosmos, is increasingly normative, if not economically feasible.

Friendship is a broad rubric that encompasses all of these options and need not be confined to any of them. More variety can be expected as gender and sexuality are increasingly understood as fluid, changing, dynamic. Previously fixed categories fly out the window, and new, brilliant expressions of friendship flourish for which most people do not have names. People who change genders reconfigure their friendship constellations accordingly. For example, in a M-F (male-to-female) trans case, the husband becomes a wife. The original or initial wife goes from being heterosexually identified to being lesbian identified because her spouse is now a woman. Is that how she sees herself? This is not a trivial matter, but rather a lesson to all who bond, including heterosexually married people. As stories begin to emerge, it is clear that many couples who stay together through one person's transition (perhaps both people in some cases) emerge as friends even though public categories that formerly defined them have changed. We learn that friendships can endure and be constitutive of many good long-term relationships without reliance on gender categories.

The trans example shows how feeble are our efforts to name and categorize people, how precarious our insights into human relationships, how shaky the scaffolding of our society if we put too much credence in defining others rather than letting them define themselves. The wife of the trans-woman did not magically decide she was a lesbian. She could be a heterosexual woman who simply loves her friend who was her husband. Formerly useful explanatory constructs like heterosexual and homosexual are rapidly coming to the end of their usefulness. How a friendship is sexual is the concern of those who are involved, not those who would seek to label.

Playing the Friendship Card

Conservative culture shapers, especially some religious leaders, are visibly nervous because so little of what they have to offer is useful in a society far more complex than their narrow categories can stretch. Rather than keep a respectful silence in the face of what they do not understand, many have taken the role of opposing same-sex marriage. Ironically, they are vocal against what is arguably the most conservative aspect of this changing friendship picture, namely, the various gender combinations of those who marry. For example, the logic of the Roman Catholic hierarchy's pro-marriage position would seem to encourage, not discourage, same-sex marriage. What better way than marriage to maintain a two-by-two social structure and social constraints on sexual expression outside of marriage? I understand the hierarchs' arguments about the need for a man and a woman, but contemporary studies, queer theory, and other sources have rendered their anthropology outdated. It's enough to make me wonder if, once they figure out just how conservative same-sex marriage really is, they will not become its biggest proponents in the world.

Catholic hierarchs know that same-sex marriage is virtually a done deal in the United States. Seeing this handwriting on the wall, there is a new "charm offensive" by the bishops that offers friendship, not marriage, to same-sex loving people. On the ABC News program *This Week* on Easter Sunday 2013, Cardinal Timothy Dolan was asked, "What do you say to a gay couple who says, we love God, we love the church, but we also love each other and we want to raise a family in faith?" He replied:

> The first thing I say is, I love you, too. You were made in God's image and likeness. We want your happiness. And you're entitled in friendship.

> But we also know that God has told us the way to happiness, in terms of
> sexual love, that is intended only for a man and a woman in marriage
> where children can come about naturally.[12]

I am not quite sure what the odd phrase "entitled in friendship" means,
but I get Cardinal Dolan's drift: heterosexual people can have sex without necessarily being friends, while same-sex loving people can have
friendship without sex. Marriage is the prize; friendship is the "also ran"
that benevolent people permit those who are less fortunate, that is, not
heterosexual.

The archbishop of Westminster, the leading spokesperson for Catholics in England, has expressed a similar view.[13] The language is so similar
to Cardinal Dolan's that it is as if it comes from a postmodern Christian
playbook in which sexless friendship is fine for same-sex loving people
but sexed marriage is only for the heterosexually inclined. But their formulations are mistaken in a number of key ways.

First, no one is "entitled" to friendship as if some people are not
so entitled. Friendship is a human experience available potentially to
everyone without needing the permission of anyone. To suggest that
friendship is for one group and marriage, with its many civil perks, is
for another group is either bigoted, absurd, or both. Second, religions
have no direct line to the divine. While a cardinal may affirm a certain
religious tradition that teaches that marriage should be between people
of different sex/gender, at issue today is a legal matter in democratic
countries. No religious group is free to dictate its views to the larger
public, a lesson the Catholic hierarchs in the United States are learning
state by state. Third, it is disingenuous at best, pernicious at worst, to
claim to love people and want their happiness and then urge rank discrimination against them. One simply cannot have it both ways. To use
the guiding metaphor of this discussion, it is not something that friends
do. Sociology, psychology, and anthropology have produced data and
theories that prove same-sex love to be healthy and natural to the satisfaction of most people. Lived well, all love can be conducive of the
common good.[14]

But the greatest gap in their logic is the reality of sex in friendship, not to mention the lack of it in some marriages. The distinctions that the bishops rely on simply do not exist anywhere but in their

imaginations. It is a category error to separate friendship from marriage. "Profound friendship" is not antithetical to marriage but integral to it, or so I would recommend from a Christian perspective. Whether or not friendships include genital expression is the business of those who are in them. But there is no basis for thinking that some people are eligible for friendships and others are eligible for marriage. When everyone can be a friend, and equal legal marriage is increasingly available, the distinction does not hold up.

Catholic hierarchs can hold their views, but they must not labor publicly under the delusion that their actions are experienced as loving by those whose rights they seek to limit. Nor should they be permitted to turn the tables by complaining that that they do not like to be called bigots when they offer no plausible explanation for why they seek to discriminate.[15] Hiding behind theological assumptions long since jettisoned by most adherents of their own faith will not suffice. Such tactics are transparent and have no place in Christian relational ethics. To call them unfriendly is to understate the case.

If I were advising conservative culture critics, I would tell them to embrace same-sex marriage with both arms, as it will keep society virtually the way it has been in the past several hundred years. After all, marriage focuses on couples, not single people or groups. Marriage is presumed to be monogamous, while friends who are sexual might not be. If they really want to create change, the hierarchs ought to look more closely at friendship.

Let Friendships Flourish

Difficult as the struggle for relational integrity is in Catholic circles, I am delighted to see that several decades since I first attended to friendship as a key theo-ethical matter, it is becoming a central concept. Work remains to be done in rethinking sexual ethics as if friendship and not marriage were normative. Some contours are helpful to start the process. Biblical texts are one starting point. "Love your enemy" is a widely used Christian biblical quote (Matthew 5:44; Luke 6:27). However, it is striking that there is no concomitant biblical invitation to "love your friends." Like so many dimensions of Christianity, the injunction to love those who act against us leads to widespread confusion. Loving enemies is not appropriate in every instance. In cases of sexual abuse, especially incest, loving the enemy can put one in danger. On the other hand, biblical texts that focus on laying down one's life for one's friends, not being servants but friends, invite critical analysis as resources for relational ethics. "Love your friends" would be a very useful thing to teach, possibly redundant, but a good reminder of the obvious.

The witness of so many good people's lives serves as data for relational ethics. Those are the "texts" that persuade me. I marvel at the blessing of more than three decades of committed friendship with my partner. But I also rejoice in forty-plus years of friendship with two high school classmates, more than fifty years of friendship with a grade school friend, lifelong strong bonds with several family members. Longevity is not the measure of friendship, but when coupled with faithful companionship through thick and thin, it is important. The stories of how friendships play out over time are many and varied. I know friends who lived on different continents and made technology work for them, phoning, e-mailing, even Skyping when it became possible, though they were of an age when it was almost unheard of. I know a friend who continues to visit regularly and maintain ties with a friend who developed dementia, sure that if the shoe were on the other foot, the other friend would do the same. I know friends who retired together, pursuing different interests but relishing a drink and dinner together at day's end. I know friends who shared many great years, a robust family, and plenty of international travel. When one died, the other went literally to the end of the earth to scatter the friend's ashes. These are fierce and tender loves. Try to figure out which of these people were married or not, which were couples of women, of men, or mixed couples. Marriage is immaterial or, better, only material. Friendship is the crucial tie in each case.

Young people are forming all manner of friendships with sexual and gender permutations the likes of which most people over forty can scarcely imagine. For example, I worked with a young lesbian woman who wanted to be a man so she could marry her girlfriend and share the benefits that were prohibited to her in a state without same-sex marriage. They remain happily married friends regardless of their genders. There are people who find that they want to be in more than one sexually intimate friendship at a time. I have rarely seen polyamory sustained over a long period, but there is no point in denying the cases where it does work. For one set of friends I know, having more than one partner for one of them helps offset the negative aspects of putting too much expectation on one person for sexual and emotional intimacy. Another set of friends found that with children involved it was difficult to explain, hard to orchestrate. They found other ways to be friends. There is newfound interest in those who declare themselves asexual.[16] They, too, form friendships but apparently do not consider sex an important component. Variety is the name of the game. The task of postmodern Christian relational ethics seems to be to figure out how to create and sustain a just and welcoming society based on more, not fewer, options. These are real human situations that deserve respect, support, and an open mind toward what is possible even if one does not embrace it for oneself.

Many religious and even secular conservatives reject such relational variation as a sign of moral decay. I propose that we celebrate the flourishing of friendship against great odds—the marriage-industrial complex, the economic pressures to prioritize career over family, and the rape culture that commodifies women's bodies for men's pleasure. Friends are an antidote to all of those things. Reshaping our economy to accommodate everyone instead of privileging a few more people via marriage equality is a dream worth having. As a step in this direction I encourage using the term "friend" as often as possible. I want to get people accustomed to it as one default norm, to value friends as much as partners, to see spouses as first and foremost friends, and to reflect on the various dimensions of their own friendships. Seeing friends in a new light, including the erotic, that is, in a bodily expressed way, points toward the love and care present among friends rather than pining for marriage that is not all there is.

I trust that these insights will go a long way toward replacing outmoded ethics with useful models of human relating. At least there will be conversations in which loving friends will be engaged about loving friends! My friends and I will be grateful.

NOTES

1. See Mary E. Hunt, *Fierce Tenderness: A Feminist Theology of Friendship* (New York: Crossroad, 1991).

2. The Women's Alliance for Theology, Ethics and Ritual (WATER) is a nonprofit educational organization in Silver Spring, Maryland. www.waterwomensalliance.org.

3. See Mary E. Hunt, "Will Francis' Statements on Women and Gays 'Make a Mess' inside the Church?," July 29, 2013, www.religiondispatches.org.

4. For some of the background, see Paul J. Wadell, *Becoming Friends: Worship, Justice, and the Practice of Christian Friendship* (Grand Rapids, MI: Brazos Press, 2002).

5. Aristotle, *Nicomachean Ethics,* especially book 8, chaps. 2 and 6.

6. Elizabeth Stuart, *Just Good Friends: Towards a Lesbian and Gay Theology of Relationships* (London: Mowbray, 1995).

7. Ibid., 246.

8. Hunt, *Fierce Tenderness*, chap. 4.

9. Ibid., 99.

10. Mary E. Hunt, "Same-Sex Marriage and Relational Justice," part of "Roundtable Discussion: Same-Sex Marriage," *Journal of Feminist Studies in Religion* 20 (2004): 83–117.

11. www.nytimes.com/2011/05/26/us/26marry.html?_r=0.

12. http://abcnews.go.com/ThisWeek/video/cardinal-timothy-dolan-week-interview-easter-sunday-18849751.

13. www.telegraph.co.uk/news/religion/9147559/Gay-couples-are-just-lifelong-friends-says-Catholic-leader.html.

14. Mary E. Hunt, "Just Good Sex," in *Good Sex*, ed. Patricia Beattie Jung, Mary E. Hunt, and Radhika Balakrishnan (New Brunswick, NJ: Rutgers University Press, 2001), 158–73.

15. This was attempted successfully by Cardinal Donald Wuerl, Easter Sunday 2013, on Fox News Sunday, www.foxnews.com/on-air/fox-news-sunday-chris-wallace/2013/03/31/mark-kelly-whether-call-action-gun-control-fading-cardinal-donald-wuerl-new-pope#p//v/2268240676001.

16. See the website for the Asexual Visibility and Education Network, www.asexuality.org/home/.

11

Calvary and the Dungeon

Theologizing BDSM

NICHOLAS LACCETTI

At any one of the many BDSM[1] conventions or dungeons that one might find in any major American city, the paraphernalia of bondage, domination, submission, and sadomasochism intermingles with the paraphernalia of lived Christianity, past and present. A naked, blinded, long-haired man with his arms bound to two columns, tormented by the memory of a stereotypical Delilah, might be a biblical scene; it might also be a BDSM scene in a local hotel convention center. A priest in the confessional might be practicing certain unsavory methods of reconciliation with his penitent, but the setting of the confessional might be more nightclub than cathedral. A bloody crucifixion scene might take place, but do the blood and sweat that land on those who lay prostrate at the foot of that cross wash their sins away and free them from the powers of death and hell? What does it mean to reproduce these things in the dungeon, and what happens to the meaning of the original scenes that they are copying, the antitypes of these tableaux of torture and violation? And how does any of this relate to that *other* cross, on the hill of Calvary outside the city, to which—some of us have been told—we must send up our sufferings, with much rejoicing?

It is perhaps too much of a cliché at this point to connect the dots between the pious Christian and the sadomasochist; the cultural links between the two are by now well established in pop culture and fetishism. That theologians, even academic theologians, should become enamored of the discourse of BDSM is not surprising; their interest in a practice that intimately involves the exploration of bodily and psychological suffering, power dynamics, hierarchy, gender roles, and sexuality should be obvious. Yet theological reflections on BDSM are mainly moral judgments or justifications, or the use of BDSM trappings to illustrate theological points that have little to do with BDSM as done by real-life practitioners. Following an overview of the primary theories of BDSM in feminism and cultural studies and their use in queer theology, this chapter will provide an analysis of BDSM that reads the practice through the lens of the cross and the traditional doctrine of God's impassibility—producing a Christological reading of BDSM that respects it as a lived practice embedded in material social realities while drawing on the theoretical insights raised by it into the theological meaning and role of suffering.

Theories of BDSM

Past theological writings on BDSM have usually accepted one of two theorizations of the practice. One, often the position of radical feminists, states that BDSM is a mere repetition, and reproduction, of the social inequalities and oppressions with which it plays.[2] The other, often the position of queer theorists and liberal feminists, states that, due to its emphasis on consent, the BDSM scene[3] is a bracketed space, at a clear remove from the structural oppressions that it draws on for its material.[4] For those who take the latter position, BDSM is either neutral—a "private" activity with no connection to the world outside of the bedroom or the dungeon—or a subversive activity that undermines the status quo through its transgression of societal boundaries and norms. Karmen MacKendrick, for example, has theorized BDSM as a "counterpleasure"— a destabilizing, counterintuitive pleasure not normally seen as pleasurable, thus transgressively working against the grain of the totalizing discourses of pleasure and power that regulate our societies.[5]

As Margot Weiss explains, such theorists see the BDSM scene as "a 'break' with both subjectivity and capitalist productivity . . . a break from social relations," and in fact a way to undermine such normative social relations.[6] Practitioners like Lea D. Brown (a Metropolitan Community Church pastor from San Francisco) suggest that BDSM uniquely recognizes the "dangerous dimensions of both human sexual need and desire," providing "a safe and creative container in which to experience and explore all of who we are"—a bracketed space of play and exploration.[7]

When theologians have positively engaged with BDSM, they have frequently taken the view of BDSM as transgressive as their theoretical starting point. Queer theologians often emphasize the way in which Christian doctrines can be subversive and boundary-breaking. As Patrick Cheng explains:

> Queer theology, like queer studies and queer theory, erases boundaries by challenging and deconstructing the "natural" binary categories of sexual and gender identity. Indeed . . . Christian theology itself is a fundamentally queer enterprise because it also challenges and deconstructs—through radical love—all kinds of binary categories that on the surface seem fixed and unchangeable (such as life vs. death, or divine vs. human), but that ultimately are fluid and malleable.[8]

Queer theology emphasizes transgression as a theological method and category: Christian doctrines queer normative boundaries and thus undermine the structures of power that work to oppress sexual minorities and other marginalized peoples. Some queer theologians have found in BDSM a language with which to express the supposed subversiveness of Christian doctrine. For instance, Theodore Jennings and Roland Boer queer traditional Christian doctrines about the omnipotence of God by conceptualizing God as a "top" and humans as God's "bottoms."[9] Cheng situates this kind of theological use of BDSM in his discussion of "parody," what Elizabeth Stuart calls "extended repetition with critical difference."[10] Couched in BDSM language, traditional doctrines are restated by queer theologians "with a critical difference," and these queer parodies "dissolve categories because they attempt to replicate the thing to be parodied, but the copy is ultimately transformed into a new creation."[11]

Beyond Oppression and Transgression

Ultimately, both the radical feminist anti-BDSM position and the queer or liberal feminist pro-BDSM positions are reductive. Margot Weiss's ethnography of San Francisco's pansexual BDSM scene shows that "BDSM scenes 'play with' real power to produce legible scenes."[12] Weiss retains the radical feminist insight that "SM is produced through social power, that sexuality (scenes, erotics, desire, and fantasy) is always social, and that "none of us is exempt" from this condition. In this, SM sexuality is like all sexuality: it is not possible to sever sexuality from power; sexuality is a social relation within an already existing social world."[13] The BDSM scene is not a bracketed space somehow disconnected from the social inequalities and power relations from which it draws its material. BDSM is not *inherently* transgressive—every BDSM scene really reproduces the social relations it is meant to parody.

Weiss parts ways with radical feminists, however. BDSM "is not a repetition of social power" in the radical feminist sense, for "it carries and produces the complexities of social relationships, relationships shot through with contradictions unresolved—indeed, erotically and politically powerful precisely because they remain in tension."[14] All sexuality—BDSM included—is constituted by the material social relations of our society; all sexual acts repeat these social relations with a difference. There is no originary power structure behind the repetition, and thus neither the BDSM scene nor the radical feminist utopia could be bracketed off or disengaged from the "already existing social world."

This argument seems to repeat the claims of queer theologians who argue that all parodies are transgressive because they "dissolve categories." Yet sometimes the critical difference produced by the parody not only reinforces social inequalities but establishes further "forms of disavowal and unknowing that enable social privilege and help to justify it." This is precisely the danger that arises when a practitioner or theorist reflexively suggests that the BDSM scene is bracketed off from the social real. Sometimes, however, the opposite happens, and the BDSM scene subversively disrupts the status quo of the social relations that are being parodied. In the end, "there is no single reading of the SM scene, because scenes depend on the active production of the materiality of social differentiation by players, audiences, and readers."[15] What happens during the BDSM scene depends too much on the material relations and consciousness of its participants to be generalized about.

For queer theology, Weiss's insights suggest that it is dangerous to utilize BDSM discourse with the expectation that it will be inherently transgressive, that the critical difference produced through the use of such a discourse to recapitulate Christian doctrines will always dissolve the oppressive categories that such doctrines have previously upheld. Perhaps the omnipotent God as an S/M top is still just the omnipotent God, with an added layer of "disavowal and unknowing." Or perhaps the added difference that is produced by conceptualizing the omnipotent God as an S/M top *does* queer the traditional doctrine in a way that is liberatory, not oppressive. As Weiss concludes, *it depends*. Each case of such theologizing is unique, for each theologian inhabits a social location and an experiential standpoint that is particular to that theologian and her community.

Crucifixion Play: The Cross as the Ultimate S/M Scene

Once one has moved beyond the reductive notion that BDSM can provide us with a sure space from which to reconceive oppressive social norms, whether these norms are social relations or traditional Christian doctrines, where should one take up the task of theologizing BDSM? I suggest that we examine the site that ultimately provides, for Christians, the clearest source of the longtime relationship between BDSM and Christianity in the first place—Jesus Christ's cross on Calvary.

As has been observed by many people, critical of Christianity or not, Jesus's consensual sacrifice on the cross can be seen as a deeply masochistic activity. Womanist theologian Delores S. Williams's classic critique of the cross retains its power and challenge today: Jesus is "the ultimate surrogate figure," who "stands in the place of someone else: sinful humankind."[16] Because oppressed people—especially black women, who have a history of being coerced or forced into surrogacy—are constantly being asked to passively accept their suffering, is it fitting for them to recognize Jesus as bringing redemption through *his* passive acceptance of suffering, through his role as the ultimate surrogate? For Williams, the answer is a resounding no. "There is nothing divine in the blood of the cross." To glorify the cross is "to glorify suffering," to render black women's exploitation sacred.[17] Williams's position on the cross is analogous to the radical feminist position on BDSM. According to the radical feminists, the BDSM scene is nothing more than a glorification and reproduction of suffering, specifically women's suffering.

This position is starkly different from MacKendrick's queer theoretical interpretation of the masochistic abandonment of the cross as the ultimate example of "the resistant, subject-shattering power of pain and restraint." For MacKendrick, the cross is the "perfect abandonment" that transgresses the boundary between human and divine. As a counterpleasure it "returns us to ourselves"; it is death without dying, "the ultimate stage of life."[18] Though she does not explicitly use the term, "resurrection" seems constantly to be on the tip of MacKendrick's tongue during the last few pages of *Counterpleasures*.

These views of the cross thus parallel views of BDSM. What might a theology of the cross that takes into account Weiss's insights on BDSM have to say? As we have seen, all BDSM scenes draw their erotic power from social norms and inequalities; there is no clear disconnect between the BDSM scene and the structures of power that surround it. Weiss's argument that all sexuality is social and that "none of us is exempt" reminds one of the Augustinian doctrine of original sin: each repetition propagates the (fallen) social relations of the thing being copied. None of us is exempt from sin. The fallenness of our world is thus the raw material of the BDSM scene, and it constitutes the scene as an event with vast productive power. BDSM sexuality is like all sexuality, but "the spectacularity of SM's play with social power" renders its use of such social relations uniquely visible; the BDSM scene is "a crowded social field."[19] The cross of Calvary is the BDSM scene par excellence— on the cross, all of the world's brokenness, its sin, its fallen social relations, are taken up in a single event, Christ's consensual torture and sacrifice. It is no wonder that such a scene produces vastly different, and equally passionate, responses.

The Cross and God's Impassibility

The cross may be the ultimate BDSM scene, but we have seen that this does not alone tell us whether the event is oppressive or transgressive. In putting the traditional doctrine of the cross in dialogue with BDSM, I intend each discourse to interrogate the other, raising its own unique insights on both, and on suffering itself. Such a dialogue clarifies certain choices in soteriology, Christology, and sacramental theology. For one thing, affirming the traditional doctrine of the cross in dialogue with

BDSM will of necessity mean affirming a doctrine that relates to the cross but is often discarded in contemporary discussions of God and Christ—the impassibility of God, "the teaching that God is, in [God's] nature, impervious to any external force of change—any pathos or affect—and is free of all reactive or changing emotions."[20] By affirming God's impassibility, one affirms that God in God's self does not suffer; Christ suffers fully on the cross in his human nature but not in his divine nature, which suffers no change.

Contemporary theologians often reject impassibility for describing what they see as a cold and unfeeling God, a God who only pretends to share in humanity's suffering. As Thomas G. Weinandy explains, "The catalyst for affirming the passibility of God, one that is still intensely operative, is human suffering. God must be passible for [God] must not only be in the midst of human suffering, but [God Godself] must also share in and partake of human suffering."[21]

This demand that God suffer in God's very being along with humanity—for Christ to suffer in his divine nature as well as in his human nature on the cross—has well-meaning advocates, theologians who want to ensure that human suffering is not forgotten, who find human suffering monstrous and do not want a God who cannot absolutely identify with such suffering. Advocates of the passible God want a God fully implicated in the human social relations and social inequalities that constitute the event of the cross.

For the most radical of these theologians, the Incarnation and the Crucifixion mean that God is fully immanent in the material world. For example, queer theologian Marcella Althaus-Reid—one of the most prominent of the "transgressive" theologians who utilize BDSM discourse to reconceptualize theology—locates God in the messy, immanent sexual relations of human beings: "God is desire in history and in the events of everyday life in society." For Althaus-Reid, "revelation reveals (unveils, undresses) God in our historical circumstances, and assumes a materialist twist in our understanding. That is the point of doing theology from people's experiences and from their sexual stories."[22]

Yet such a passible, immanent God falls right into Delores Williams's critique of the oppressive masochism of the cross. If God is absolutely identified with human suffering in the cross, the cross serves to reconcile God and humanity to suffering; the cross legitimates suffering and death as holding ultimate meaning. Suffering and death are raised into the Godhead, or the Godhead, in stooping down to earth in Christ, is ultimately lost among the crowd in our fallen cosmos. This passible God is, like human beings, not exempt from material social relations and inequalities. And because these social relations are always imbricated with structural oppressions and toxic power dynamics, a passible God has nothing much to say about our suffering, because that God, like the cross and like the BDSM scene, is constituted in its very being by that suffering. As Stuart explains, Althaus-Reid's vision of human social relations "holds the divine without remainder" and thus "offers no horizon to redeem that which causes pain or exploitation" in such relations.[23]

The passible God does not ultimately dissolve the rigid boundaries between life and death, divine and human—does not really queer them—because, like BDSM, the passible God is not inherently transgressive. Being susceptible to human emotions and to change, a passible God the Father is implicated in the material social relations that led Jesus of Nazareth up to Calvary. Paradoxically, it is only in a passible conception of God that God the Father is *actually* a sadist—the favorite critique of new atheist Internet commentators everywhere—a divine dominant desirous of the blood of his messianic submissive. In the impassible conception of God, the apathetic Father's "sadistic" role in the Crucifixion has more in common with the (humanly) impossible, platonic ideal of the S/M literary dominant—Sir Stephen of the *Story of O*, for example—who inflicts his punishments on his submissive with a seemingly clinical, detached air, void of explicitly erotic intent.[24] The apathetic dominant—itself a rather queer role, a sexual agent with a rather indifferent sexuality—is the BDSM type of the heavenly Father. Fallen human dominants, whose erotic desires are messy, complicatedly involved in real social baggage and oppressions, and whose arms get tired and brows get sweaty, simply do not compare.

Jesus Christ as fully impassible God and fully passible human being, meanwhile, is also a truly queer being—a true masochist who can fully absorb all the sin of our human social reality on the cross without being ultimately consumed by it, because he is fully the God who cannot change. As Weiss shows us, no human dominant or submissive could hope to participate in such an S/M scene as the Crucifixion without being altered by the social power that constitutes that scene. Only the impassible God can do this. As David Bentley Hart proclaims, God in the cross

> subverts death and makes a way through it to a new life. The cross is thus a triumph of divine *apatheia*, limitless and immutable love sweeping us up into itself, taking all suffering and death upon itself without being changed, modified, or defined by it, and so destroying its power and making us, by participation in Christ, "more than conquerors" (Rom. 8:37).[25]

The way out of the imbricated material social relations that constitute the suffering of BDSM and the cross is participation in Christ's particular, unique suffering on that cross, the BDSM scene unlike any others.

The Eucharist as Eschatological Repetition

Theologically, the Eucharist is the avenue of our participation in the cross. If understood as transubstantiation, the sacrament is a truly transgressive BDSM scene. It is the only scene that parodies oppressive social relations—the social relations of the cross—without really parodying them, as it allows us to really enter the reality of Calvary rather than merely act as a repetition-with-a-difference of that event. As the Catholic Catechism explains, the Eucharist "*re-presents* (makes present) the sacrifice of the cross"; "the sacrifice of Christ and the sacrifice of the Eucharist are *one single sacrifice*."[26] Every Eucharistic celebration *is* the reality of the cross because the cross is the eschatological reality—the originary event of the new cosmos, as Stuart explains, "stretching vertically to the spiritual and horizontally to the physical, and meeting at the absurdity point, the point of the Christ who fully exists on both planes. There is no space that it does not touch."[27] The Eucharist is thus unambiguously transgressive in its eschatological nature, unlike the BDSM scene, and it, rather than any human sexual relation, is what dissolves the "dualism between material and spiritual, divine and earthly." Through the Eucharist "all and everything are caught up in this great drama of salvation"—the drama, the S/M scene, of the cross of the impassible God.[28]

If we follow our dialogue between BDSM and Christianity to its end point, the theological choice for the Real Presence and the sacrificial nature of the Eucharist over against memorialization is necessary. Without these doctrines, our participation in the one truly transgressive scene of Calvary falls back into the fallenness of human parodies and repetitions of oppression. It would not be participation in the eschatological cross of Christ but in a human representation of a historical event, even if that representation, like the secular BDSM scene, carries with it some energy of the originary event. Consuming an icon of Christ would not have the same effect as consuming the consecrated Host, even if the icon of Christ—in Orthodox theology, for example— does provide a real link with its prototype. To break out of the cycle of fallen repetition and reproduction, which Augustine understood so well in terms of physical sex and procreation, we require true contact with the impassible God's sacrifice on the cross. The Real Presence of the Eucharist repeats the sacrifice of Christ without really repeating it; it is a re-presentation rather than a representation.

Conclusion

As we have seen, BDSM scenes have real social effects, both on the communities that practice and witness them and on the dominants and submissives who take part in them. To play with the raw stuff of a deeply embedded social oppression in a scene is not something that participants can leave behind in a bracketed safe space—it will remain with those participants far beyond the scene, for better or worse. This chapter would simply be another case of a theologian overlaying a point about Christian doctrine with the trappings of BDSM if I were to suggest that a BDSM practitioner—dominant or submissive—could somehow take on God's impassibility during a BDSM scene. Instead, I offer the potentially queerer suggestion that one particular event, one particular experience of suffering—one particular S/M scene—*does* break out of the circuits of sin and fallenness: the cross of Calvary. This scene is truly transgressive in a liberating way, but only because this particular suffering is suffered by a particular person, Jesus of Nazareth, fully impassible God and passible human. This is masochism without masochism. By participating in *this* suffering—through the eschatological repetition that is the Eucharist—one may truly transgress the boundaries of life and death, divine and human, the brokenness of pain and the pleasure of new creation. The cross of Calvary is a repetition of the sin of the world with a critical difference. God suffers fully, but does not suffer at all, and thus breaks the bonds of suffering once and for all.

Does my dialogue between BDSM and Christian theology offer any viaticum for the fallen denizens of the dungeon at the BDSM convention and the human players in consensual scenes of human suffering and exploitation? I have not offered a new moral take on BDSM. If BDSM does not break out of the circuits of material social relations, if the S/M scene is not a safe container, neither is traditional marriage or church-approved sexuality. As other chapters in this volume make clear, the cosmic disease of original sin passes through church-sanctioned heteronormative intercourse just as well as sin passes between queer, unmarried lovers or between a dom and a sub in a dungeon. The peculiar—a synonym is queer—gate of heaven is found elsewhere, on the hill of Calvary, in that "pallid wafer that at times, one would fain think, is indeed the 'panis caelestis,' the bread of angels."[29]

NOTES

1. An acronym embracing bondage and discipline, dominance and submission, sadism and masochism.
2. Robin Ruth Linden, Darlene R. Pagano, Diana E. H. Russell, and Susan Leigh Star, eds., *Against Sadomasochism: A Radical Feminist Analysis* (East Palo Alto, CA: Frog in the Well, 1982).
3. A "scene" is a BDSM term for a specific time period of BDSM activity. For a useful discussion of BDSM terminology, see Margot Weiss, *Techniques of Pleasure: BDSM and the Circuits of Sexuality* (Durham, NC: Duke University Press, 2011), vii–xii.
4. See, e.g., the classic anthology by the lesbian-feminist S/M Samois organization, *Coming to Power: Writings and Graphics on Lesbian S/M* (Boston: Alyson Publications, 1981). For more recent takes, see Jaclyn Friedman, ed., *Yes Means Yes: Visions of Female Sexual Power and a World without Rape* (Seattle, WA: Seal Press, 2008).
5. Karmen MacKendrick, *Counterpleasures* (Albany: State University of New York Press, 1999).
6. Weiss, *Techniques of Pleasure*, 6.
7. Lea D. Brown, "Dancing in the *Eros* of Domination and Submission within SM," in *Dancing Theology in Fetish Boots: Essays in Honor of Marcella Althaus-Reid*, ed. Lisa Isherwood and Mark D. Jordan (London: SCM Press, 2010), 150.

8. Patrick S. Cheng, *Radical Love: An Introduction to Queer Theology* (New York: Seabury, 2011), 10.

9. Ibid., 51–52.

10. Elizabeth Stuart, *Gay and Lesbian Theologies: Repetitions with Critical Difference* (Farnham, UK: Ashgate, 2003), 108.

11. Cheng, *Radical Love*, 51–52.

12. Weiss, *Techniques of Pleasure*, 145.

13. Ibid., 154.

14. Ibid., 230.

15. Ibid.

16. Delores S. Williams, *Sisters in the Wilderness: The Challenge of Womanist God-Talk* (Maryknoll, NY: Orbis, 1993), 162.

17. Ibid., 168.

18. MacKendrick, *Counterpleasures*, 160.

19. Weiss, *Techniques of Pleasure*, 154.

20. David Bentley Hart, *The Doors of the Sea: Where Was God in the Tsunami?* (Grand Rapids, MI: Eerdmans, 2005), 75.

21. Thomas G. Weinandy, *Does God Suffer?* (South Bend, IN: University of Notre Dame Press, 2000), 2.

22. Marcella Althaus-Reid, *Indecent Theology: Theological Perversions in Sex, Gender and Politics* (London: Routledge, 2000), 148.

23. Elizabeth Stuart, "Making No Sense: Liturgy as Queer Space," in *Dancing Theology in Fetish Boots: Essays in Honor of Marcella Althaus-Reid*, ed. Lisa Isherwood and Mark D. Jordan (London: SCM Press, 2010), 115.

24. Pauline Réage, *Story of O*, trans. Sabine d'Estrée (New York: Ballantine, 1965).

25. Hart, *Doors of the Sea*, 81.

26. *Catechism of the Catholic Church*, 1366–67.

27. Stuart, "Making No Sense," 117.

28. Ibid., 121.

29. Oscar Wilde, *The Picture of Dorian Gray*, in *The Picture of Dorian Gray and Other Writings*, ed. Richard Ellmann (New York: Bantam Classics, 2005), 126.

12

Who Do You Say That I Am?

Transforming Promiscuity and Privilege

ELIJAH C. NEALY

About six months after beginning my gender transition, I went for routine blood work at a lab in Greenwich Village, New York City. By this time, I was consistently being read as male. The facility was in a cramped basement room with low ceilings. It was late morning on a hot summer day. I signed in and took a seat in the small, crowded reception area.

A short while later, I heard my name, "Elijah," called.

As I went to the front, the receptionist began to review my computer file. A puzzled look came over her face.

"You're Elijah?" she asked.

I nodded yes.

"But it says 'female' here," she said.

I took a deep breath and began, "I'm a transgender man, and my identity documents say male . . ."

Her immediate frown almost stopped me.

"My health insurance card stills has an 'F' on it, so I can be sure to have coverage if I need any gynecological care."

Tapping her pencil repeatedly on the desk, she stared at me and asked loud enough for everyone in the waiting room to hear, "Well, what are you then?"

*   *   *

160 <<

Fast-forward six years. I am living in Yonkers with my family. I've been involved in the alcohol recovery community for many years. When we moved, I found a great Saturday morning men's meeting nearby that's become the touchstone of my recovery. Every week the room is filled with men ranging in age from seventeen up to their seventies and eighties. The sharing is incredibly down-to-earth and brutally honest. No topic is off limits. I mean, when's the last time you sat in a room and listened to forty men talk about sex, drugs, and prayer in graphic detail all in one hour?

On the one hand, from the moment I walked through that door, I felt incredibly comfortable in this meeting. It seemed like home. I loved the combination of the laughter and the honesty, and I felt like I belonged there. On the other hand, I often thought about what these men would think if they knew my history as a transgender man. Would they still see me the same way? Would they still accept me? Would they still even want me in that room with them? I wasn't sure I wanted to find out.

I found a new sponsor there who's been an amazing gift in my life. You wouldn't think at first glance that we would hit it off. He's a sixty-eight-year-old straight white guy who grew up in the South in a conservative religious world. I wasn't sure we would have enough in common to work together, but when he talked about his life and his recovery, I felt like he was telling my story. I began to share much of my life story with him, but I didn't disclose my transgender history. Sometimes it didn't seem relevant, but mostly I was afraid this one fact would change everything between us.

Late one Sunday morning, we met for breakfast. It was a crowded suburban diner, packed with folks all dressed up coming in to eat after church. I had done some inventory recently, writing about some resentment I had with my partner and my youngest daughter. We had met today to discuss this and look at my part in these dynamics. In the middle of describing a conversation with my partner, it seemed clear my sponsor needed to know my history as a transgender man for him to really understand what I was feeling.

What followed was a conversation that was all too familiar to me. First off, he didn't understand what I was saying. He thought I was a man who wanted to be a woman. I kept trying to explain what "transgender man" meant, that I had been born in a girl's body but had always felt like a guy and some years ago transitioned to live as a man. But he just couldn't wrap his brain around it.

At one point, he questioned me at least three times, "But do you have a vagina? You know, Eli, a vagina? Do you have a vagina?"

Before I came out as trans, I had never been asked what my genitals looked like, but trans people are asked that incredibly invasive question all the time. That question, or the question of whether or not you've had "the surgery," carries the implication that the questioner wants to know whether you are "real" yet—as if the shape of our bodies is the sole determinant of what it means to be a man or a woman. It cuts to the heart of what transgender people face throughout their lifetimes, namely, "If I come out to you as a person of trans experience, will you still see me as a real man or woman?"

* * *

As I reflect on these experiences and the emotions they evoke, I am reminded of the story in which Jesus asks his disciples, "Who do the crowds say that I am?" The disciples respond, "Some say John the Baptist, some Elijah, and some say another one of the prophets." Then Jesus pointedly asks them, "But you, who do you say that I am?" (Matthew 16; Mark 8; Luke 9).

Jesus's life and ministry challenged those who encountered him. His teachings and actions didn't easily fit their definitions of good Jewish men or messiahs. Even those closest to him had difficulty understanding his true identity. I think of this interaction as the queer Christ's transgender moment: Jesus being called to give an account of himself. Jesus and trans people everywhere are being called not only to give an account of ourselves but literally to justify and defend our humanity and our divinity. "Who do you say that I am?" "Well, what are you, then?" "But Eli, do you have a vagina?"

Judith Butler writes:

> To counter oppression requires that one understand that lives are supported and maintained differentially, that there are radically different ways in which human physical vulnerability is distributed across the

globe. Certain lives will be highly protected, and the abrogation of their claims to sanctity will be sufficient to mobilize the forces of war. And other lives will not find such fast and furious support and will not even qualify as "grievable."[1]

Some lives count as more human than do others. Individuals of transgender experience challenge such simplistic and dualistic notions of humanity and the world. People who are gender different are stigmatized by the dominant culture. This marginalization silences the voices of transgender persons and renders their stories and lives invisible. The binary gender assumption marks trans persons as "other" and "queer." It classifies them as gender transgressors and subjects them to shame, ostracism, hatred, verbal, physical, and sexual assaults, and even murder.

Jesus, too, challenged the boundaries and binary constructs of his time. Patrick S. Cheng argues that the essence of both queer theology and Christianity is the reality of a God of "radical love" who dissolves all boundaries—between men and women, Jew and Gentile, rich and poor, heaven and earth, body and spirit, even life and death.[2] What does it mean to worship a God who dissolves the boundaries of our lives? What does it mean to follow a Christ who eradicates the binary constructs of our time and place? Does this notion of God's radical love dissolving boundaries have relevance for our nitty-gritty, day-to-day lives?

*   *   *

The word "promiscuous" has often been used to defame and debase the queer community. We have been denied the right to marry our partners and accused of being unfit parents because of the notion that we are inherently indiscriminate in our sexual relations. We have been caught in the crossfire of a binary construct that posits monogamy as the moral opposite of the immorality called promiscuity. Dictionary.com defines the word "promiscuous" as follows:

1. characterized by or involving indiscriminate mingling or association, especially having sexual relations with a number of partners on a casual basis;

2. consisting of parts, elements, or individuals of different kinds brought together without order;

3. indiscriminate; without discrimination. It is from the Latin root, "to mix."[3]

I wonder what might it mean to embrace ourselves as a "promiscuous" people, much as we have embraced the previously negative epithet "queer." Could we reclaim the notion of promiscuity? In her book *Our Tribe*, the Reverend Nancy Wilson writes about queer people's penchant for "promiscuous hospitality."[4] Vincent Cervantes writes about queer people "loving promiscuously."[5] Laurel C. Schneider posits a "promiscuous incarnation," suggesting the indiscriminate excess of divine love.[6] Anchoring my reflections in my own experience, I want to explore what it would mean to embrace promiscuity in our work for justice and hope. Queer folk know that greater justice can be done with category-confounding promiscuity than with marriage's exclusionary myth of equality. The queer Christ did, too.

*   *   *

A while back my twenty-five-year-old son, Alex, and I went to see Tyler Perry's movie *Good Deeds*. It is a challenging story layered with the complexities of race and class. It revolves around Wesley Deeds, a wealthy businessman who encounters (and falls in love with) a single mom who works as a janitor in his office building. The woman, Lindsey, is on the edge economically, often living in poverty despite the hours she puts in cleaning offices every night. At one point, she and her six-year-old daughter are evicted from their home. Homeless and living out of her car, Lindsey tries desperately to maintain a semblance of normalcy for her daughter, driving her to school each day, stopping at gas station restrooms so her daughter can wash up and brush her teeth each morning, tucking her in for the night in a utility closet in Wesley Deeds's office complex while she cleans. Upon discovering the family is homeless, a school official reports Lindsey to the child welfare department, and her daughter is taken away from her and placed in a foster home.

This is not just a scene in a movie but one that is repeated every day in real life. In the fall of 2011 my son's partner, their year-old daughter, and his partner's mother and younger sister were evicted. They spent several weeks in the shelter system simply because they were poor. The only reason my partner, a single mom for five years often stretched financially beyond her means, did not become homeless with her daughter was the middle-class privilege she inherited. What does it mean for our family to grapple with these realities? What does it mean to have a place called home, no matter how tight money feels sometimes? How do we as queer Christians reconcile our privilege alongside the poverty among us?

Alex came into my life through a New York City agency called You Gotta Believe! Its mission is to find a permanent family for every young person in foster care, even the eighteen- to twenty-one-year-olds whom other people have long ago given up on. Forty percent of the 25,000 kids in the New York state foster care system are fourteen years and older and unlikely to be returned to their birth families. When kids age out at twenty-one, they get a check for $750 and a studio apartment, and they're expected to be ready to live on their own, but few of them have the stable family connections that can support their independence. Most of the twenty-one-year-olds growing up today in stable middle- and upper-class families are not financially or emotionally independent, yet we expect youth with a long history of trauma and loss to be able to make it on their own. It is estimated that 50 percent of NYC's homeless population grew up in foster care.

I met Alex at a panel where young people talked about their experiences in foster care. He had a great smile and a sense of openness in his eyes. Alex was taken from his mother when he was five years old mostly because she was poor, Latina, HIV-positive, and drug addicted. Raised by an abusive foster mother until she "gave him back" at age thirteen, my son spent his teenage years in a residential treatment center parented by no one. The agency had been searching for more than four years to help Alex, about to turn twenty-one, find a permanent family to call his own.

A few weeks after that panel, the agency brought Alex and me together over a meal. The following weekend, Alex and a friend of his came to my place in Brooklyn. The next week I had a birthday barbeque. He stayed for the weekend and never left. Throughout those few short weeks, several friends advised me not to take a total stranger into my home and heart, but something was calling me to be promiscuous. In the years since Alex and I have been in each other's lives, I have struggled regularly with how to reconcile my class and race privilege alongside all the ways my son has been marginalized by the world I inhabit. How do I grapple with the oppressive aspects of my marginalized identity as a transgender man alongside my privilege as a white middle-class man?

Being a promiscuous queer Christian cannot simply be about sexual orientation and gender identity and expression. Promiscuity is about indiscriminately mixing and mingling and making the connections between all kinds of people and things. The God we worship is a God who promiscuously and indiscriminately brings us together, proclaiming, "My house shall be called a house of prayer for all peoples" (Isaiah 56:7). The Gospels are full of injunctions to be promiscuous with our privilege. Jesus asks the rich young ruler, "Will you give all that you have and come follow me?" (Matthew 19:21). "Will you be promiscuous with your privilege for the sake of the Gospel?" Over and over Jesus proclaims, "Those who would save their lives must lose them" because he knows that when we hang on to our privilege, we lose both our humanity and our divinity (Matthew 16:25; Mark 8:35; Luke 9:24).

The writer to the Philippians calls us to have the same mind among ourselves that was evident in Christ Jesus. The word choice is plural; the emphasis is on our communal lives. Elizabeth Shively notes, "Paul aims to form a collective mind that informs collective actions."[7] The writer goes on to uphold Jesus, "who being in the form of God, did not count equality with God a thing to be grasped, but emptied himself, taking the form of a servant, being born in the likeness of humanity" (Philippians 2:6–7). This passage, often called the Kenotic ethic, describes the way the Christ story "moves from separation to solidarity, and from difference to likeness."[8] A more accurate translation reads "because he was in the form of God." Because it is in God's very nature to love lavishly and promiscuously, Jesus did not consider his divine privilege something to be hoarded or protected, instead spending it promiscuously in the work of love, liberation, and justice. The story is one of God/Jesus in solidarity with humanity, calling each of us collectively to be in solidarity with one another.

I spent my formative years growing up as a girl-child in a fundamentalist Baptist home where we were taught that "JOY" was best achieved by placing *Jesus* first, *others* second, and *yourself* last. This passage from Philippians has long been used to perpetuate the self-sacrifice and obedience of women and other marginalized persons by urging them to follow Christ's example of obedience, even unto death. But Paul defines "he emptied himself" not by what Jesus gave up but by what he "took on"—the form of a servant/humanity.[9] Solidarity is about standing with each other. It's not about suffering, and it's not about sacrifice. It is a conscious choice made from a place of privilege.

I see the immense power of this in action all the time in my recovery. There's a slogan in twelve-step programs that says, "You can only keep what you give away." When one alcoholic helps another alcoholic, we don't do this from a place of privilege but because we literally need each other to stay sober (and alive—and human). Yet when I share my experience, strength, and hope with you, there's a sense in which I am sharing the privilege of the gifts I have been given in sobriety. I receive as much as I give away. This section of the Philippians passage moves toward a conclusion with the admonition to "work out your own salvation with fear and trembling" (Philippians 2:13). Salvation is not about a private, individual destiny; it is about the quality of our corporate life as it is lived within the present realm of God.[10] It is about the ways we give freely of ourselves to stand in solidarity with others.

In his book *The Cross and the Lynching Tree*, James Cone notes that white Christians of that era, as well as contemporary theologians, have been silent about the common historical practice of lynching black men, women, and children.[11] Cone's commentary made me think about my horror and revulsion as a teenager learning about the Holocaust. I couldn't imagine how any nation could exterminate 6 million people just for being who they are. Later I often wondered why I felt so gripped by what had happened in Nazi Germany. I realize now that it was easier, then and now, for me to focus on what happened somewhere beyond our borders than to face the violence my own race inflicted and continues to inflict on African American people at home.

Those of us who are queer theologians cannot afford to erase or distance ourselves from this history any more than we can afford to ignore the ways contemporary mob violence manifested itself in a brutal attack on a transgender woman at a fast-food restaurant while others watched and cheered. Or the ways homophobic and transphobic mob violence allows queer youth to be bullied in their schools and communities to the point of finding no way out but to take their own lives. We must name and call out the connections between all our stories. Those of us who are white can no longer do queer theology as if white queer voices represented all queer voices. Our oppression, and the violence directed at us, are inextricably linked.

I began this chapter looking through the lens of my marginalization as a transgender man struggling to be read as real in a world that often invalidates me. James Baldwin wrote:

> That man who is forced each day to snatch his manhood, his identity, out of the fire of human cruelty that rages to destroy it knows, if he survives his effort, and even if he does not survive it, something about himself and human life that no school on earth—and indeed, no church—can teach. He achieves his own authority, and that is unshakable. This is because, in order to save his life, he is forced to look beneath appearances, to take nothing for granted, to hear the meaning behind words.[12]

Black men, Latino men, queer men, trans men, indeed all those on the margins, female and gender queer too, all of us are forced to snatch our identities out of the fire of injustice and oppression. All of us are compelled to take nothing for granted. The struggle of trans people to be counted as "real" is the struggle of people of color and poor people and people with disabilities everywhere.

But clearly, this is not the only lens I possess. Luke 12:48 says, "To whom much is given, much will be required." I hated that verse growing up. It was used as a club against me to always demand more. But I also chafed against it because in many ways, it speaks the truth: I have been given much. I'm white. And despite our working-class and even poor roots, mine was and is a middle-class family. While I spent years visibly queer and living on the butch dyke margins, I live my life today with easy access to straight white male privilege—unless I make a point to come out as transgender. I have my health, despite an episode of Bell's palsy. I have two master's degrees and am finishing a PhD.

In an article on teaching white students about racism, Norma Akamatsu discusses the ways each of us has places of privilege in our lives and places of marginalization or subjugation.[13] It is hard to examine these places of privilege. We are much more comfortable focusing on the ways we have been marginalized. Have you ever been in a group in which white queer people derail the conversation about race by shifting the focus to how we are just as oppressed because of our sexual orientation? What if, instead of comparing and contrasting our oppressions, we became committed to following love's long arc toward justice for all humanity?

What if, like the queer Christ, we did not view our places of privilege as something to be hoarded and protected but instead promiscuously spent this privilege in the work toward dignity and liberation for all people? What would it mean if white queer people promiscuously used our racial privilege in the work for racial justice? What would it mean if queer people of means promiscuously and lavishly expended our privilege in making our world economically just? What would it mean if queer men—gay, bi, and trans—took seriously the pervasive and demeaning impact of sexism in our culture and promiscuously spent our privilege undoing the misogynist structures of our time? This kind of promiscuity is about a way of being in the world that can hold the complexities of both our privilege and our marginalization. It is a way of being in the world that calls us to love one another and fight for dignity and justice with the very queerest sense of passion.

*   *   *

Fast-forward to today. My son's mother-in-law and youngest daughter are back in their apartment, no longer homeless. Caroline, Alex, and now their two babies live with my partner, our nine-year-old daughter, and me. It's a full house, and we struggle monthly to make ends meet. Alex has been in drug rehab for six months now; he's finally getting sober after years of self-medicating the pain and loss of growing up in foster care. Caroline is in college pursuing her associate's degree in criminal justice. We all juggle the babies (three years and six months), shouldering the challenges of child care, diapers, and groceries. I think back on my friends' caution. It has been a lot to take a twenty-one-year-old stranger into my life, but I knew I had love to spend, and along the way my life has become immeasurably richer for loving Alex.

Butler writes that the critical ethical question facing each of us is, "What makes for a livable world?" She adds that it is not only about what makes my life bearable or human, "but from the position of power and point of view of distributive justice, what makes, or ought to make, the lives of others bearable?"[14] Have this mind among yourselves that was also in Christ Jesus who because he was in the form of God did not see this place of privilege as something to be grasped onto, but instead spent it promiscuously in the work of liberation and justice for all people. James Baldwin is right: in order to save our lives and the lives of those around us, we need to look beneath appearances and find the meaning behind the words. We need to embrace the very essence of our lavishly queer promiscuous selves. Then, and only then, will we achieve our own authority, and we will be an unshakable force for justice.

NOTES

1. Judith Butler, *Undoing Gender* (New York: Routledge, 2004), 24.
2. Patrick S. Cheng, *Radical Love: An Introduction to Queer Theology* (New York: Seabury, 2011).
3. http://dictionary.reference.com/browse/promiscuous?s=t, accessed February 10, 2012.
4. Nancy Wilson, *Our Tribe: Queer Folks, God, Jesus, and the Bible* (New York: HarperCollins, 1995).
5. Vincent Cervantes, "Loving Promiscuously: A Queer Theology of Doing It," http://blog.vincentcervantes.com/2011/08/loving-promiscuously-queer-theology-of.html#more, accessed February 10, 2012.
6. Laurel C. Schneider, "Promiscuous Incarnation," in *The Embrace of Eros: Bodies, Desires, and Sexuality in Christianity*, ed. Margaret D. Kamitsuka (Minneapolis, MN: Fortress Press, 2010), 231–46.
7. Elizabeth Shively, "Commentary on Philippians 2:5–11," Working Preacher, www.workingpreacher.org/preaching.aspx?lect_date=3/24/2013&tab=3, accessed March 24, 2013.
8. Susan Eastman, "Commentary on Philippians 2:1–13," Working Preacher, www.workingpreacher.org/preaching.aspx?lect_date=9/25/2011&tab=3, accessed September 25, 2011.
9. Shively, "Commentary on Philippians 2:5–11."
10. Eastman, "Commentary on Philippians 2:1–13."
11. James Cone, *The Cross and the Lynching Tree* (Maryknoll, NY: Orbis, 2011).
12. James Baldwin, *The Fire Next Time* (New York: Vintage, 1962), 98–99.
13. Norma Akamatsu, "Teaching White Students about Racism and Its Implications in Practice," in *Re-visioning Family Therapy: Race, Culture, and Gender in Clinical Practice*, 2nd ed., ed. Monica McGoldrick and Kenneth V. Hardy (New York: Guilford Press, 2008), 413–24.
14. Butler, *Undoing Gender*, 17.

PART IV

Forward!

The discussions of celibacies, matrimonies, and promiscuities in the preceding parts should have been stimulating and unsettling. If nothing disturbed you, or if one approach seemed cleanly to prevail, we have failed. We hope to have captured the ferment of queer Christian— indeed, of any embodied Christian—experience as it strives to articulate itself faithfully in new contexts. What are the next steps for scholars and theologians?

In this final part, ethicist Victor Anderson articulates an approach to Christian sexual ethics that is generous enough to embrace this ferment without losing sight of the realities natural law and subjectivist traditions seek to name. Contextual theologian Kathleen T. Talvacchia shows how queer Christian experience takes us beyond the theory-practice distinction through a careful analysis of how participation in a seemingly conservative practice led her to transgressive action. Finally, historian Kathryn Lofton places the project of this book in the longer history of academic efforts to understand queer religion and suggests new theoretical questions it makes possible.

13

Three Versions of Human Sexuality

VICTOR ANDERSON

Sex is a fact of our organic biological being. It is not a human imperative but a human condition; it is something like a profile of being human. It is in this sense, then, that sex might be said to be a human good that is premoral. However, when the good of human sex is theorized within a philosophy of the natural law, sex ceases to be simply a matter of biology and bodily sensations and becomes the subject of laws of nature. Thus, it was an easy step to move from regulating sex and sexuality by natural law, to regulation by something called sexual morality, which is the subject of Christian sexual ethics.

This chapter discusses three ideas of Christian sexual ethics: the physicalist, the ethical personalist, and the pragmatic naturalist versions of human sex and sexuality. For the physicalist, I reflect on sex and the natural law based on Charles Rice's *50 Questions on the Natural Law* (1993).[1] This discussion is then followed by the ethical personalism of Philip Turner based on his *Sex, Money & Power* (1985).[2] The third version of human sex and sexuality to be discussed is the pragmatic naturalist; I sketch out some of its philosophical implications put forward in my *Pragmatic Theology* (1998) and *Creative Exchange* (2008).[3] To be very clear, these three versions of human sexual ethics are used as heuristic devices for how we might think about Christian sexual ethics, its nature, and its goods and ends. My aim is to free up our languages regarding human sexual experience in relation to a generous pluralism, as articulated by the philosopher Nelson Goodman.

Ways of World Making

My talking about Christian versions of sexual ethics immediately flags
the philosophical problem of realism. In its most basic form, realism
suggests that reality is the world that is experienced outside of our
heads. Reality is the given background against which, or the foundation on which, we produce our thoughts and actions. For the realist,
reality is an existing set of things or the properties of things that make
up things existing independently of the mental. Stones, water, air, trees,
and animals are independent both of each other and of us. In relation
to our minds, they might be said to be "freestanding" entities. For the
realist, planetary *stuff* has existed prior to human thought and action
and will continue to exist when we are long gone from the planet. This
version of realism is taken by most people these days as the staging on
which we humans think and act. But it has not fared very well in the
history of Western thought and action, even as the languages of *the real*
remain embedded in our conceptions of the nature, the good, and the
morality of sex.

Nelson Goodman cuts through the problems of realism versus its
philosophical other, idealism.[4] The most available version of idealism
proposes that reality is not external to human beings' thinking but the
effect of our mentally assigning properties to things perceived to be
external to us as thinking subjects. These mental properties, called con-
cepts and ideas, are what are really real. The problem with idealism is
that the existence of things is predicated on their having been thought.
The world is constituted by ideas. Like realism, idealism too has deep
roots in our thinking about the morality of human sexuality. However,
between the positivist and idealist ways of thinking about reality stands
our conception of the "world." Goodman asks that we not slide whatever we mean by reality (externally or mentally) into what we mean by
the "world." Rather, Goodman frees up our talk about reality by propos-
ing a generosity of pluralism toward the word "world" so that we speak
instead of "worlds."

Such a generous pluralism regards our various philosophical and
moral thinking about things and human acts as versions of "world making." Human beings are engaged in acts of "world making," and our various accounts of human experience and actions are best understood as

complementary, contrasting, and occasionally contradictory "versions." However, the specter of epistemic relativism immediately raises its ugly head—the worry that we have no basis for affirming one version as being any more correct than another. However, Goodman does not see epistemic relativism as a necessary consequence of his proposal. "Doesn't a right version differ from a wrong one just in applying to the world, so that rightness itself depends upon and implies a world?" he asks. "We might better say that 'the world depends upon rightness.'"[5] Supposing that there are no "undescribed, undepicted, and unperceived" worlds available for comparison, having the right version becomes simply a matter of favoring one or another version as being right or more right than another.

Goodman's response to relativism is circular but not viciously so. Every version of reality, including human sexual experience, is mediated by acts of depiction, description, and perceptions. In this chapter I discuss three versions of Christian sexual ethics that I call the physicalist, ethical personalist, and pragmatist naturalist, but my purpose is not to single one out as alone valid. My approach is framed by the following passage from Goodman:

> I think that many different world-versions are of independent interest and importance, without any requirement or presumption of reducibility to a single base. The pluralist, far from being anti-scientific, accepts the sciences at full value. . . . To demand full and sole reducibility to physics or any one version is to forego nearly all other versions.[6]

On Goodman's account of versions in world making, our moral thinking about Christian sexuality might operate within any number of ways of framing our sexual practices and experience. Within a generous pluralism of ways of world making, sex and sexuality may actually exhibit this generous pluralism of worlds.

The Natural Law in the Physicalist Version of Christian Sexual Ethics

My discussion of the natural law is very brief, but I do not mean to trivialize its importance. Some versions of natural law are at the very center of some of our contemporary debates over human sexual life and practices. Moreover, in their fights for justice—as revolutionaries against brutal regimes and unjust sanctions—many have appealed to a higher law and a high morality in order to justify and establish the worth and dignity of all persons because they insist that human laws must be in agreement with the natural law and the eternal law.

It is within this enduring legacy of natural law that Charles Rice discusses the world made by the natural law and his defense of the Catholic position of abortion, euthanasia, and sexuality. He asks: "So does anybody care about natural law? Lots of people do, on both side of the aisle. Natural law is more than just a theory. Whether you accept it can determine whether you will accept or reject the legalized killing of innocent human beings. On abortion and other issues, jurisprudence kills people. Anyone who cares about life and death issues has to care about natural law, one way or another."[7]

Rice defines natural law as "a rule of reason, promulgated by God in man's nature, whereby man can discern how he should act." He cites Thomas Aquinas's definition: "The natural law is promulgated by the very fact that God instilled it into man's mind so as to be known by him naturally."[8] However, we need to note that "natural" here does not mean instinctive, for there is nothing instinctive about the natural law. Instincts belong to our bodily inclinations, but the natural law is a discovery that is derived from human reasoning about the natural order of things. One immediately recognizes circularity here, since what is reasoned about naturally is in fact what is already reasonably ordered naturally. Figure out the reasonable natural ordering of things, and you get the natural law. Rice explains it this way: "Just as the maker of an automobile builds into it a certain nature (it drives, it does not fly) and gives directions for its use so that it will achieve its end—that is, to be dependable transportation—so God has built a certain, knowable nature into man to follow if he is to achieve his final end, which is eternal happiness with God in heaven."[9] The nature of a thing is what a thing is wired to be and thus do.

Rice's point is that our bodies are machines that are driven by a rational intellect in need of directions. Those directions are needed if the machine is to perform to its maximal design, behavior, and handling. This is why we need the natural law. As Rice sees it, "The natural law provides a guide through which we can safely and rightly choose to love

God by acting in accord with our nature and by helping others to do the same."[10] Moreover, the natural law is "an objective standard of right and wrong" that is not justified by the subjectivity of actors, since the presence or absence of subjective culpability" is not ours to judge.[11] On the natural law version of human sex and sexuality, we "cannot change the objective rightness or wrongness of the act. The act either is or is not in keeping with the Manufacturer's directions written in our nature. The distinction between yes and no, true and false, good and evil cannot be given up unless men want to give up being human."[12]

Given Rice's physicalist version of reality, good is a species of the act. Rice again cites Aquinas: "All those things, to which a man has a natural inclination, are naturally apprehended by reason as being good, and consequently as objects of pursuit, and their contraries as evil, and objects of avoidance."[13] Rice solicits five natural inclinations to fill out his version of natural law for human moral perfection:

1. To seek the good, including his highest good, which is eternal happiness with God;
2. to preserve one's existence;
3. to preserve the species—that is, to unite sexually;
4. to live in community with others;
5. and to make use of the intellect and will—that is, to know the truth and to make one's own decisions.[14]

These precepts are hierarchical and perfectly satisfying of human natural goods and ends. Chief in the perfection of human good is that happiness found in blessed union with God; to this, all other precepts are intermediate. However, the problem, as Augustine stipulates, is that people do not always act in ways that fulfill these precepts because of lust, inordinate passions, perverse culture, and perverse habits. According to the physicalist version of the good in natural law, having a good or well-disposed heart does not determine the good within the natural law version of reality, for the good is not subjectively determined but objectively given in human acts.

Moral judgments are based on the objectivity, that is, the physicality of acts, and so-called unnatural acts are acts that are not in harmony with the precepts of natural law. Rice again cites Aquinas:

In matters of action it is most grave and shameful to act against things as determined by nature. Therefore, since it is by the unnatural vices that man transgresses that which has been determined by nature with regard to the use of venereal action, it follows that in this matter this sin is gravest of all. After it incest, which is contrary to the natural respect we owe to a person related to us. . . . Just as the ordering of right reason proceeds from man, so the order of nature is from God himself. Wherefore it is contrary to nature, whereby the very order of nature is violated, an injury is done to God, the Author of nature.[15]

It is evident from the preceding passage that on Rice's physicalist version of the natural law, sex acts, which are not in harmony with the natural order of things, insofar as all things are rationally ordered toward human perfection or completeness in the divine law, are thus considered "most egregious." Same-gender sex is among the "gravest" of human sexual acts; such sex acts stand higher in the order of sex sins, even above incest. If follows, then, that good sex acts will perfectly satisfy the precepts of the natural law and the rationally ordered good of human sex and sexuality.

In the physicalist Christian ethical version, the good of sex, within the natural law, counts against a generously pluralistic version of sex. On the physicalist version of sex, good sex is reducible to the objectivity of sexual act(s). With the physicalist version of Christian sexual ethics based on the natural law, subjective sexual satisfaction, and all that is involved, is of secondary importance to sex acts, and the whole person is divided between body and soul.

The Ethical Personalist Version of Real Sex

Philip Turner represents what I shall call an ethical personalist version of Christian sexuality. This stands in contrast to Turner's own rather pejorative descriptions of modern revisionist versions of sex, which he call libertarian, self-actualizationist, and personalist.[16] In the libertarian version, sex becomes a matter of interpersonal contracts between partners not to coerce, injure, exploit, or do harm to themselves.[17] With the self-actualizationist version of Christian sexuality, the good and end of sex is what it contributes to the personal growth or maximalization of "genuine potentiality" derived from sex of all sorts.[18] Turner then describes personalist versions of sex as holding that "sexual intercourse, though it need not in all cases be limited to married couples, ought always to express and strengthen personal relations, contribute to the well-being of both partners, and be governed by a high degree of mutual respect and care."[19]

Common to these three Christian versions of sexuality is that they are nonrestrictive regarding the gender and numbers of partners that may be engaged in sexual intercourse.[20] They are purely subject-centered versions of sexuality and are usually identified as egoist or hedonist. Even if rejecting the libertarian and self-actualizationist versions described earlier, Turner's own proposal comes very close to what he describes as personalist sex just so far as he actually evokes a relational conception of real sex marked by mutuality, gift giving, and reciprocity. For Turner, these three versions of Christian sexuality are regarded as "counterfeits."

In their stead, Turner offers a version of sexuality based on economic structures and laws that mimic the Trinitarian life of God. For Turner, the doctrine of creation implicitly connects the internal structure of the church, as a divine community, and the world, as a social order, to divine actions. And this connection has its analogue in economic life, which has three structural laws: corporation, exchange or gift giving, and reciprocity. Turner then connects these economic laws with Christian faith in the creation, divine governance, and the Trinity in which a system of mutual exchange rather than the commoditization of markets constitute his ethical version of "real sex."

One connection holds Turner's argument together, namely, that the economic structure of human relations is the same for all, Christians and non-Christians alike. Human economic life is characterized by social exchange, reciprocity, and mutuality. According to Turner, Christians learn most "truly" and "faithfully" what the structure and law of life require from within the life of the church. However, they are also taught how these laws apply not only among Christians but in all social relations. "Knowledge of this structure and law comes through participation in the common life of the church, and can give Christians a vision of the sort of common life God intends not merely for the church but for society as a whole."[21] When Christians understand what God intends in all human relations, they can then promote transformative practices that will "bring about a pattern of social relations which more closely approximates the form and quality of life that will be obtained in God's kingdom."[22]

Yet these requirements are not particular to the church. They are structurally embedded in social life in general and knowable by others without a necessary appeal to Christian doctrine, vocabulary, or theological arguments, because they are revealed in the deep structures of economic life. Thus, in commending his version of the Christian form of life to the world, direct appeal to religious beliefs and practices is not necessary, although they may provide "good reasons" for why one who is not a Christian should entertain the moral vision that he commends. Still, these reasons will make sense only if they are shown to be properties of exchange, reciprocity, and mutuality in the whole of human social life. Although differing from the version of sexuality based on the natural law, Turner nevertheless inscribes a weaker version of physicalism into his own version of sexuality.

For Turner, the doctrine of the Trinity suggests a model of mutually affective reciprocity that grounds the vision of the kingdom of God and human relationships. And the subjective inner life of the Trinity is one of giving, receiving, returning in and through the spirit, and occurs among persons, in this case, the Father, Son, and Spirit. This is what I described as an ethical personalism. The Trinity involves total presence and exchange, giving and bestowal. By analogy, then, Turner suggests that such an inner structure of the divine life also represents the structure of human life as it is created in the image of God. This means that "presence, reciprocity, giving, receiving and returning" all define the deep structure of both divine and human life.[23] This Trinitarian structure of the divine life and human life is presented through narratives of the life, death, and resurrection of Jesus Christ.

Within Turner's version of the good of sex and its nature, Christians are regarded as the New Adam, constituted by men and women, males and females, who are called to imitate God, walk in love, and become one. They are summoned to participate in the divine life of the Trinity and to express in all of their relations the structures of divine love, which are exchange, reciprocity, and mutuality. For Turner, this kind of love is in the very structure and intentions of human social exchange and ought to be commended for both Christians and non-Christians alike.

Turner argues that theological revisionists or theological liberals have undermined the Christian meaning of sex by rendering sexual relations a matter of private interests, self-realization of genuine human potentials, and dualism insofar as they think of persons as independent of bodies.[24] He calls this position "personalist," but it is better understood as egoist because the egoist "point of view is rooted in the notion that 'human beings' are to be pictured or understood first as autonomous, individual 'persons' whose sex is accidental to their nature and whose social relations are displayed as an individually based set of 'rights' and 'duties' which protect and promote private benefit."[25] Moreover, on this view, sex is most successful when it results in mutual satisfaction through sexual communication or contracts.[26]

In opposition to egoist sex, which Turner describes as counterfeit sex, is what he calls "real sex," which involves sexual relations between males and females. The theological sources of real sex are rooted biblically in a faithful reading of Genesis 1–3, which entails the creation narratives, and Ephesians 5:21–33, which qualifies heterosexual marriage. In Turner's version, sexual relations constitute real sex if they are sex exchanges between males and females. What is it about these texts that are so appealing for Turner? They present Christians with substantive teachings about human origins and purposes and point in the direction of a primordial structure of human relations.[27] They place human relations in reference to God's actions. And they imply that the intentions and purposes of God in human sexuality are ordained and socially mandated by divine will. Therefore, if God ordains the structure of human sexuality, the structure will exhibit permanence and not change. In other words, the structure is its nature; the good of sex, exchange, reciprocity, and mutuality, is its nature, even as the will and purposes of God are one and eternal.[28]

Although I appreciate Turner's version of the good of sex and its nature, his desire to connect sexual subjectivity with sex, which is bodily, within the Trinitarian life is not without problems. Neither Turner's conception of the New Adam nor his vision of the Trinity unambiguously supports the claims that he wants to make for real sex. Christian narratives can be just as easily read to support the revisionist or egoist claims that Turner criticizes and rejects, and the inner life of the Trinity suggests many other forms of intimacy more strongly than it does coupled heterosexuality. In the end, Turner may have offered a theologically persuasive account of the Trinitarian life of God, a life that is characterized by exchange, reciprocity, and mutuality. But the real issue is whether the Trinity can be commended to all as an unambiguous version of Christian sexual ethics.

Pragmatic Naturalism and a Generous Pluralism

Pragmatic naturalist and theologian Tyron Inbody reminds us that "experience is never 'pure experience' (individualistic, subjective, original, underived, autonomous, and foundational)."[29] It is "always derived from, shaped, and interpreted in a social context, both a natural environment of interrelationships and interdependence (nature) and a cultural environment of language, symbol, and myth (tradition)."[30] As Goodman suggests, experience is described, depicted, and perceived. This means that nature, like culture, operates on a field of relationality that is interdependent and interactive, simultaneously open and limited. In the pragmatic naturalist version of world making, our perceptions, depictions, and descriptions of human experience characterize the world shared by all as dynamically organic, open to change, flux, adaptations, adjustments, and accommodation to the environing whole. And this environing whole opens us to our pluralistic universe.

In the pragmatic naturalist version, sexual experience is irreducible yet complexly integrates profiles of human experience: the physical, temporal, spatial, social, and basic human senses or affectivities. Moreover, just as experience opens to the widest ranges of our *experiencing* the world in and through experiential complexes, so sexual experience also is expansive and opens to novelties. This means that what is natural should be understood as what we can count on as an organism with capacities for openness, expansion, and novelty.

Whatever our versions of sex may be and however we value our sexualities, we should not think of sex as fixed by a really real beyond the apparent, or as being metaphysically derived from nature, or from primordial economic laws and structure, not even divine laws that are eternal. Rather, such descriptions or pictures can be understood with

Goodman as alternative versions of a plurality of worlds of our own construction and are based on our sexual experience and experiencing of the world shared by our fellow human organisms. No version of human sexuality, whether favoring descriptions internal to faith, doctrine, and Christian practices, can endow sexual experience with a fixed point of reality based on the natural law or a primordial structure immanent in the social world of economic exchange, or divine sanctions and restrictions. As the late Richard Rorty well asserted, these fixed worlds are well lost to the pragmatic naturalist.

Like our organic life and experience, sexual experience is organic and not immune from change, growth, diversity, indeterminacy, and novelty. Sex is good not because it is natural or because it has a surplus of value. Rather, sex is good because it is good for human purposes as wide as human creative exchange. The pragmatic naturalist proposes a generous pluralism of versions of sexual experience that satisfy the requirements of creative human exchange. Creative exchange fulfills both the sexual enjoyment of our human bodies and our erotic subjectivities. At their best, queer Christianities become emblematic of this epistemic demand for a generous pluralism in our Christian versions of human sexuality.

NOTES

1. Charles Rice, *50 Questions on the Natural Law: What It Is and Why We Need It* (San Francisco, CA: Ignatius Press, 1993).
2. Philip Turner, *Sex, Money & Power: An Essay in Christian Social Ethics* (Cambridge, MA: Cowley, 1985).
3. Victor Anderson, *Pragmatic Theology: Negotiating the Intersections of an American Philosophy of Religion and Public Theology* (Albany: State University of New York Press, 1998); Anderson, *Creative Exchange: A Constructive Theology of African American Religious Experience* (Minneapolis, MN: Fortress Press, 2008).
4. Nelson Goodman, *Ways of World Making* (Indianapolis, IN: Hackett, 1978).
5. Ibid., 4.
6. Ibid., 4–5.
7. Rice, *50 Questions on the Natural Law*, 23–24.
8. Thomas Aquinas, *Summa Theologica* Ia.IIae, Q. 90, A. 4 ad 1.
9. Rice, *50 Questions on the Natural Law*, 45.
10. Ibid.
11. Ibid.
12. Ibid., 29.

13. Aquinas, *Summa* Ia.IIae, Q. 94, A. 2.
14. Rice, *50 Questions on the Natural Law*, 45.
15. Aquinas, *Summa* IIa.IIae, Q. 154, A. 12.
16. Turner, *Sex, Money, & Power*, 34.
17. Ibid.
18. Ibid., 35.
19. Ibid., 37.
20. Ibid., 41.
21. Ibid., 8.
22. Ibid., 9.
23. Ibid., 10.
24. Ibid., 14.
25. Ibid., 15.
26. Ibid., 16.
27. Ibid., 18.
28. Ibid., 19.
29. Tyron Inbody, *The Constructive Theology of Bernard Meland: Postliberal Empirical Realism* (Atlanta, GA: Scholars Press, 1995), 232; for a fuller account, see my *Creative Exchange*, 1–23.
30. Inbody, *Constructive Theology of Bernard Meland*, 232.

14

Disrupting the Theory-Practice Binary

KATHLEEN T. TALVACCHIA

While I was in graduate school, I was asked to participate in a worship service at Union Theological Seminary in New York sponsored by the seminary's LGBTIQ caucus on the theme of coming out. We were asked to bring to the service a symbol related to our personal experience of coming out and to speak for a few minutes on the symbol and its connection to our personal history. The chapel's main altar was full of various artifacts that the organizers had collected from all of us. When it was my time to speak, I walked to the altar and picked up the symbol that I had brought—a book on the Spiritual Exercises of Saint Ignatius Loyola with a large image of Saint Ignatius on the cover. I held the book up and explained to the community the meaning of the symbol: "I came out through the Ignatian Spiritual Exercises of the Catholic Church." A collective gasp erupted in the chapel when I made that statement. I understood the reason for their surprise—yet my experience had been different than most: for me Christianity had aided my awareness and acceptance of my sexuality, rather than repressing its expression. As I spoke my short reflection, I continued to see conflicted amazement on the faces of many in the group at this very liberal and progressive seminary.

The fact of the matter is that I came out as a lesbian through engaging a traditional spiritual practice of the Roman Catholic Church. While this fact seemed perfectly reasonable and natural to me, it was at the time and continues to be a source of surprise and consternation among both religious and secular persons with whom I share this aspect of my life experience.

How is it possible that a religious practice from the Christian tradition became a source of insight, clarity, empowerment, and—most surprisingly—transgressive action? In what ways did theological and scriptural tradition, analytical thinking and personal experience come together to fuel a transformation? Reflection on such experiences as this lives in the intersection of queer theologizing, queer theorizing, and queer living. This is the place from which practical theology from a queer perspective seeks to understand and to construct theological expression.

This chapter explores the possibilities of practical theology from a queer perspective in queer theologizing. Its focus on the practices of religious individuals and communities as well as its theory-practice methods of inquiry hold the potential to disrupt binaries in which practice disengages theorizing and theory disengages experience. In this place of intersection where theoretical reflection and the practices of religious persons live, theological interpretation and construction occur. Practical theologizing queers the split between what we think about and how we act, allowing an alternative view into the ways in which queer persons are constructing and sustaining lives both within and outside religious traditions. In this way it can be an important contributor to the articulation of queer theology.

The chapter first seeks to establish the theological context of my thinking, along with a short explanation of the method of inquiry used—theological reflection. From there I engage the theological reflection process as an example of lived theological analysis from a queer perspective. I conclude with my reflections on the potential usefulness of disrupting theory-practice binaries as a way to theologize from a queer perspective.

Theological Context and Method

A major assumption lies at the heart of my thinking: I question the helpfulness of a theory-practice divide when analyzing religious and theological experiences that are specifically centered in the lived experience of religious persons and the faith communities to which they belong. In considering the religious experience of queer persons, both theorizing and practical reflection have a place in investigation; however, holding these two separate, as parallel lines of inquiry, might tell only a partial story. Theories can provide new ways of understanding and articulating a religious tradition and the practices within it, but in what ways is that theologizing experienced and lived in queer religious persons and communities? Is the theology genuinely freeing, or does it perpetuate discourses that discipline those outside of it? Theorizing alone cannot discover this nuance. Engaging practices, both individual and communal, provides another way of discovering the lived experience of queer religious communities as they test out theological meaning that is constructed in theorizing. But these practices can become rigid and disconnected from larger meta-understandings, sinking down to the level of "we have always done it this way." Theorizing challenges those rigidities and creates an analytic perspective that can break calcified practices.

In order to understand religious experience as it is lived in the lives of queer persons and the communities in which they belong, it would be useful to have a place of inquiry in which the integration of theory and practice can flourish. Practical theology done from a queer perspective can be such a place. It has the potential to intentionally disrupt the binary of theory and practice in order to create an integrated approach in which the practices of queer religious communities and the theorizing about those practices can be more deeply in conversation with each other.

In this chapter the method of theological reflection serves as one way to engage theology as it is lived in communities. This method provides an action-reflection basis for engaging faith experience from an analytic perspective.[1] There are many different articulations of how to engage in theological reflection,[2] but Patricia O'Connell Killen outlines the basic steps that ground this type of theological thinking:

1. nonjudgmental narrating of experience,
2. identifying the "heart of the matter"—the key issue or question that the reflection engages,
3. structuring a correlation between the key question or issue and an aspect of the religious tradition (scripture, theology, or philosophy)—forming a single analytic question used to probe the matter at hand,
4. identifying new learnings and new actions for living.[3]

Like all contextual theologies, practical theology begins with experiences of religious communities and persons. However, it engages those experiences in depth, articulates the key elements existing in those experiences for intensive analysis, seeks to understand them, and then develops theological construction from those insights. Theological reflection makes space for the engagement of a faith practice with theology, philosophy, and the doctrinal articulations of a religious tradition.

Specifically, I will focus the theological reflection on my own experience of coming out as a way of exploring practical theology from a queer perspective. Let me clarify at the outset a few important contextualizing factors.

It is important to mention that queer theory contests the notion of coming out as a perpetuation of a binary that creates the false assumption that there exist essential categories of a marginalized "in" of false identity and a liberated "out" of a "true" or "real" identity.[4] I do not understand coming out as a binary either-or reality. Rather, in the course of living our lives we understand our sexual selves in varying ways that ground us in specific moments. The fluidity of sexual identification and erotic desire shapes the way we live in the world with others. From this standpoint, then, I understand coming out as a reality that helped me to articulate a sexual awareness of self that created a grounded identification as a woman who loves women erotically. This articulation proved useful, perhaps even necessary, to define a sexual self that transgressed heteronormativity. Rather than as a sharing of a personal faith experience, examining my coming-out experience provides a way to analyze the movement toward a greater awareness of my sexual identification in the context of religious practices.

Queer Theological Reflection in Practice

The Spiritual Exercises of Saint Ignatius Loyola, the religious practice at the heart of my coming-out experience, are a series of meditations and contemplations on the life of Jesus that form the basis of the spiritual energy and commitment of the Jesuits (the Society of Jesus) and of Ignatian spirituality. These exercises are widely used as a spiritual practice in the lives of Christian persons both lay and in vowed religious vocations, helping them discover a sense of self-identification that roots

Naturally

Queer

itself both in God and in freedom. In that self-awareness, a person freely and actively seeks an awareness of God's desire for the meaning of his or her life.[5] I went through the "retreat" as a part of daily life: rather than going away for one month to complete these prayer exercises, I did them as an integral part of my daily routine, combining one hour each day of individual prayer, reflection, and writing. This allowed for a deep integration of the religious experience with the workings of events that were naturally occurring in my life. Thus, I came out in a moment when the prayers I was praying and the activities of my life outside of the retreat experience coalesced in a way that created radical insight.

Narrating Experience

When I began the Spiritual Exercises in the early 1980s, I was in my midtwenties and worked full-time as a religious educator of college students in a social justice education program in a Jesuit university. My personal experience growing up was deeply rooted in Catholic culture, schools, and church communities. With eighteen years of Catholic schooling, including an undergraduate minor in theology and a master's degree in religious education, both from Jesuit universities, as well as an active participation in Roman Catholic faith communities, I had a grounded and rigorous understanding of the tradition, its teachings, and its institutional culture.

While I was firmly rooted in that work and in my professional identity as a religious educator, I struggled emotionally with a restless sense of disjointedness. I sought to find a way in which my desire to live an authentic justice-oriented faith could be integrated with my intellectual curiosity about Christian theologies and with a larger sense of life direction. I was engaging these questions with a Jesuit spiritual director, who suggested to me the discipline of the Spiritual Exercises as a way to wrestle with my questions. This discipline involved setting aside significant time each day for the religious practice of prayer and meditation as instructed by my spiritual director. The process can be done over four weeks contiguously in a retreat setting or as a daily practice integrated in one's everyday life. I chose to engage the Exercises as a part of my daily life both for practical reasons and as a personal preference—I was seeking precisely a process of integrating spirit, intellect, and life.

As I engaged the process over a period of several months, the social justice research and teaching I was doing in my job, the topics of the prayers and meditations in the Spiritual Exercises, and my personal relationships all became part of the insight that I was gaining. As I opened myself up to the process of personal reflection and a deeper awareness of my feelings and desires, I began to first come to understand and then fully embrace the passionate desires of my life. Embracing my queer sexuality was a natural step in this process of self-understanding and relational action. Concretely, how did this happen? There were two significant steps for me: first, I began to look back at the friendships in my life, both male and female, and tried to understand the emotional and sexual dynamics within them, and second, I fell in love with a woman.

My self-awareness emerged gradually as I progressed through the various reflections and meditations. Significantly, though, I came to see at the completion of each "week" or stage of the Spiritual Exercises that I was clearer and more accepting of my queer erotic orientation. Most important, in that acceptance I understood that this orientation was not disordered or unnatural but rather an instinctive part of my sexual engagement with others. In the process of deep spiritual connection with God, I understood that this way of being in the world was affirmed, and therefore I felt free, empowered, and passionately engaged with life. With this energy, I slowly began to live as an openly queer and openly religious person.

Key Issues and Analytic Correlation

How did this transformation occur? As I reflect upon this experience from the vantage point of almost thirty years as an out queer person, I am struck by several significant questions. Through a very traditional religious practice I came to understand and accept my queerness in a way that radically and transgressively challenged what the Catholic religious tradition understood to be normative beliefs about the morality of homosexuality. What aspect of that religious practice and of the Ignatian tradition allowed that queering to occur? What allowed for the disrupting of the binaries of gay and straight, moral and immoral, and sacred and secular, so that I might be able to live openly and freely as a queer person who participated in a religious community? For the purposes of this analysis, Saint Ignatius's understanding of the Principle and Foundation in the Spiritual Exercises will function as a lens through which to examine my coming-out experience toward the goal of understanding how this religious tradition made space for my queer identification.

The Spiritual Exercises are grounded in a specific goal, which Saint Ignatius refers to as the Principle and Foundation. It is a primary stance from which to approach the process and its goal. It stipulates the spiritual intention of the Exercises, and all of the meditations and contemplations are focused on this goal: (1) to understand God's plan, which is for human beings to discover God's unconditional love and grace in their lives; (2) to participate in that plan for creation through embracing that which leads one toward that end and avoiding that which leads away from it; and (3) to become indifferent to all that one desires with the intention to open the self to embrace what God desires more than what one desires for oneself.

John Reilly provides a useful contemporary translation of Ignatius's statement of the Principle and Foundation:

As Christians we believe we come from a loving God who freely creates us to discover the mystery of God's love in our lives.

We believe God creates all things that we may find in them God's presence and energy by learning to share our lives with other people and care for our kinship with all that wonderfully shares and supports our lives.

We find the beauty and mystery of our human lives, therefore, only by choosing, insofar as it is left to our free choice, what helps to share our lives in love, not what hinders this.

For the freedom to love we need to hold ourselves open to all things—wealth or poverty, fame or disgrace, health or sickness, a long life or a short one, and to all else.

We need to let God grace us into a spiritual freedom, gratefully responsive to God's prior love in our lives, to desire and choose what better helps us live the love for which God made us.[6]

Reilly's translation gives a clear sense of the goal of the Exercises. In the meditations and contemplations on the life of Jesus that constitute the Spiritual Exercises, all is directed toward the end of understanding God's unconditional love and grace and finding God in all that we experience in our lives toward the goal of living in the love for which humanity is created and which is humanity's salvation. This journey is sustained and renewed through actions that allow a fuller embrace of love and a disregard for actions that become obstacles to authentic loving.

From this understanding it is apparent that participation in these Exercises can lead a person toward a major reorientation in life. As Jesuit theologian Roger Haight points out, the process can produce a "decisive commitment" and focus in one's life: "All elements of the Exercises are marshaled toward breaking the attachment to things that constrict human freedom, allowing reflection on values and feeling for ideals to attract freedom in a new direction, and then finally taking hold of the self in a decision that changes, reorients, or rededicates a person's trajectory."[7]

Learning

What was that emotional breakthrough and reorientation in my life? Through the practices of meditative and contemplative prayer in the Exercises, I came to have a firm conviction of God's unconditional love and acceptance of me in my humanity as I was created, and that the goodness of my created self was in part as a woman who loved women erotically. As noted earlier, these spiritual insights from my religious practice came to light at the same time in my life experience that I was falling in love with a woman. Through the discernment process I came to understand the positive, life-giving reality of my queer sexuality. Thus, for me, this religious practice removed any sense of shame about my sexual identification and disqualified the idea of being disordered in any way. In coming out as a lesbian I understood a fundamental truth for my life: the way that I loved in the world was part of the goodness from which I was created by God as a human being, and for which my life needed to be oriented. There was nothing immoral for me in my queer sexuality. Rather, it was part of the self that was (and is) radically and unconditionally loved and accepted, and thus deeply connected to my human freedom.

Most significantly, it became clear that a refusal to accept and embrace this part of me would constitute a profound restriction of God's grace in my life, and thus would be in itself something disordered. Thus, my queerness itself was not disordered; it would only be so if I denied that understanding.

Once I understood myself as a woman who loves queerly, I had a very clear conviction that it required agency on my part, and that I needed to live this reality in a way that allowed me to embrace the things that connected me to God and avoid the things that would hinder that connection. The decision was a clear sense that I must live my life as out as possible. To hide and be ashamed of my queer self would be something that kept me from freedom, from God's love. Even if it meant personal and professional cost—and for many queer persons there is certainly a cost—I reoriented my life to be as out as possible in as many situations as possible. It meant being spiritually aware of where the energies of healthy relationships, moral loving, and generous inclusivity lay.

Lived Theology in Queer Perspective

In my particular case a spiritual practice of Catholicism knit together disparate elements of my life into greater coherence and led to a transgressive sexual self-identification. Through further reflection on that experience, I suggest in this last section ways in which practical theology that considers queer themes and questions can serve to disrupt theory-practice binaries and, in doing so, contribute to constructive queer Christian theologizing.

Coming out as a queer person in this way revealed for me the power and importance of a fully realized and embraced queer passion. From this awareness I came to understand that in my deeply realized sexual and gendered self, I could be most connected to the reality of God and God's grace *through queer desire*. Rather than disconnecting me from God, embracing my erotic passion and acting upon it created a possibility for connecting deeply to God and having that energy become part of how I lived as a religious person in the world. Rather than questioning the morality of queer sexual acts, the question became more one of how to live with moral integrity as an embodied sexual person. Thus, practical theology from a queer perspective might ask: In what ways does the religious tradition allow members of the community to reflect upon theologically or study the activity of erotic desire? What practices, traditions, or theologies open up dialogue between erotic passion and faithful religious living?

It is striking to me that the experience of doing the Spiritual Exercises created an experience of both *consolidation* of boundaries and *queering* of boundaries. The consolidation of boundaries occurred through the clarification of sexual identification and an awareness of its variety: that there are many ways to love erotically and that these need not necessarily be in the category of immoral. But the disrupting of the boundaries of moral and immoral occurred as a result of orientation clarity received from a Catholic spiritual practice. In taking me in a direction that transgressed the tradition, the religious practice forced me to understand traditional Christianity in a new way. In a certain sense, my sexuality construction was in dialogue with my religious construction, seeking a way in which these two seemingly incompatible movements might create an integrated self in the world. When considering sexual and gender boundaries, practical theology from a queer perspective might ask: What practices of a religious community work to both consolidate and queer the boundaries of gender and doctrine? In what ways does it sustain or destroy an articulation of oneself as a gendered and sexual religious person?

Through a traditional spiritual practice of the Roman Catholic community I experienced the opposite of what most queer person experience from the practice of religion. Instead of being judged as deficient and immoral, *my integrated sense of being religious and being queer was affirmed*, giving me a sense of happiness, peace, and vocational direction. Obviously, one person's experience must be taken in perspective; however, if it is true to say that it is the intention of the Spiritual Exercises as a religious practice to connect a person more deeply to God in order to understand something truthful about the self, then this religious practice might provide similar freedoms for others. Thus, practical theology from a queer perspective might ask: What practices of a religious community foster the development of an integrated sense of queerness and religiousness? What aspects of a religious tradition allow gendered, sexual persons the freedom to live openly in lives of freedom and responsibility, and what aspects of the religious tradition prevent this freedom?

In its capacity to reveal the ways in which queer Christians live and thrive with the aid of religious practices, practical theology from a queer perspective makes an important contribution to the development of queer theology. It allows us to see what might be the queerest statement of all: the tradition itself holds the power of transgression and transformation within its own practices.

NOTES

1. For a full discussion of the multiple methodological approaches to the discipline of practical theology, see Bonnie J. Miller-McLemore, ed., *The Wiley-Blackwell Companion to Practical Theology* (Hoboken, NJ: Wiley-Blackwell, 2011), 89–265.

2. See, e.g., Kathleen McAlpin and Mary Jo Leddy, *Ministry That Transforms: A Contemplative Process of Theological Reflection* (Collegeville, MN: Liturgical Press, 2009); Robert L. Kinast, *Making Faith-Sense: Theological Reflection in Everyday Life* (Collegeville, MN: Liturgical Press, 1999); James D. Whitehead and Evelyn Eaton Whitehead, *Method in Ministry*, rev. ed. (Kansas City, MO: Sheed and Ward, 1995); Patricia O'Connell Killen and John de Beer, *The Art of Theological Reflection* (New York: Crossroad, 1994).

3. Patricia O'Connell Killen, "Assisting Adults to Think Theologically," in *Method in Ministry*, rev. ed., ed. James D. Whitehead and Evelyn Eaton Whitehead (Kansas City, MO: Sheed and Ward, 1995), 103–11.

4. See Michel Foucault, *The History of Sexuality, Volume 1: An Introduction* (New York: Vintage, 1990), 69–70; Judith Butler, "Imitation and Gender Insubordination," in *The Lesbian and Gay Studies Reader*, ed. Henry Abelove, Michele Aina Barale, and David M. Halperin (New York: Routledge, 1993), 307–20; Eve Kosofsky Sedgwick, *Epistemology of the Closet* (Berkeley: University of California Press, 1990), 71–72.

5. For a helpful overview of the Spiritual Exercises, see Roger Haight, *Christian Spirituality for Seekers: Reflections on the Spiritual Exercises of Ignatius Loyola* (Maryknoll, NY: Orbis, 2012), and the website http://www.ignatianspirituality.com/ignatian-prayer/the-spiritual-exercises/.

6. John Reilly, SJ, "Principle and Foundation: A Contemporary Version," at the website Ignatian Spirituality.com, http://jesuits.ca/orientations/pandf_reilly.html. For a more classic articulation, see David L. Fleming, SJ, *The Spiritual Exercises: A Literal Translation and a Contemporary Reading* (St. Louis, MO: Institute of Jesuit Sources, 1978), 23.

7. Haight, *Christian Spirituality for Seekers*, 49–50.

15

Everything Queer?

KATHRYN LOFTON

After reading about early Christian celibates, medieval spiritual marriages, and contemporary theologies of sadomasochism, it seems obvious that the history and present of Christianity are filled with queer possibilities. These possibilities seem so abundant that a strange new question arises. Is anything Christian *not* queer?

Voluntary Gay, Involuntarily Queered

We cannot answer this inquiry without marveling first at how far we have come. In 1997, promotional language for the edited collection *Que(e)rying Religion* dramatized the newness of this conjunction, asking, "Is it possible to be religious and to be gay, lesbian, or queer? Until recently, many persons—gay or straight—would have said no."[1] The question ("Is it possible . . .") presumes differentiable identities: that one can be religious or not, that one can be gay or not. The answer ("Until recently . . .") assumes a collective sensibility toward these identities and their relation. The possibility had seemed impossible.

  Both this assumption and that presumption possess history and historiography. The terms "gay" and "lesbian" and "queer" are relatively new categories, as are social replies to them. And during the short history of these designations, an equation developed in which it seemed impossible to be both religious and homosexual. *Que(e)rying Religion* replied to this seeming impossibility with a documentary certainty, collecting an array of historical analyses and personal testimonies that proved gay-identified individuals existed within religious communities *and* that religious cultures included source material for its queer participants.

These are two separate proofs: the proof of gay-identified subjects within religious sects, and the proof of queer life within religious sects. Let us call the former "voluntary gays," and the latter "involuntarily queered." Whereas voluntary gays elect to examine themselves as demographic and sociological subjects, the involuntarily queered receive the analysis of scholars seeking to find the sexual complexity within ecclesiastical structure or orthodox doctrine. In *Que(e)rying Religion*, documentation of the former included a testimony by Andrew Sullivan, a professed gay Catholic; documentation of the latter included a close reading of Leviticus to discern the permissibility of same-sex coupling. Within conference panels, classrooms, and edited volumes, these documents have been collected. This volume does more, suggesting in its content as well as its structure that these two genres of expression have much to say to one another—and have, in fact, long been in conversation in some Christian lives.

Let us take them up independently, first, in order to understand their commiseration. In the collection *Gay Religion* (2004), sociologist Wendy Cadge offered a strong example of the voluntary gay demographic in her essay on lesbian, gay, and bisexual Buddhists in the United States. By evaluating the available participant data, as well as conducting fieldwork in the Cambridge Insight Meditation Center, Cadge observed how some gay Buddhists chose to align themselves with specifically gay fellowships, whereas others were involved in mixed organizations for straight and gay Buddhists. She concluded that the vast majority of gay Buddhists in America are comfortable in every Buddhist organization, since "Buddhist texts are generally read in the United States as being neutral about homosexuality," and American Buddhist communities are, by and large, gay-friendly.[2] Even as such an account may suggest a largely affirming view of gay life within U.S. congregations, however, the majority of voluntary gays attested to significant struggle within their particular sects. Indeed, surviving the judgmental scars of religious authority might be understood as a rite of passage for gay Americans. Analysts of the voluntary gay then account for the new enclaves of spiritual acceptance and religious community that homosexuals might find, whether within promotionally gay sects like the Metropolitan Community Church (MCC) or within more heteronormative orders like the Roman Catholic Church. To offer a queer analysis is, in part, to resist promotions and prescriptions: to seek out what is normative in the MCC and what is queer in the Roman Catholic Church.

While sociologists and historians have tracked the experience of identifiably gay subjects, scholars informed by queer theory have observed the more ambiguous dynamics within religious communities lacking an articulate gay demographic. "Queer" has become an increasingly generic term for anyone who seeks to differentiate themselves from socially normative heterosexual experience. Literary studies scholar Marilee Lindemann has discouraged such vague applications of queer, recommending instead that it is "most productive as a mode of action rather than a way of being."[3] Within studies of religious material, such a mode of action, or "queering," has become a scholarly habit in which the researcher exhumes the sexual hermeneutics within and surrounding religious structures. In contrast to Cadge's work, Robert Shore-Goss has supplied an analysis of the queer aspects of Buddhist life. In particular, Shore-Goss searched for historical reports of sodomy within Buddhist monasteries, while also considering the struggle of contemporary Asian and American immigrant Buddhists to reconcile social homophobia with "queer sex" like sodomy.[4] If Cadge sought to locate the institutional involvement of gay Buddhists, Shore-Goss explained the hermeneutics of sexuality within the diverse religious tradition. The former has largely been labeled the work of LGBT studies; the latter has been described as queer analysis.

The work of Cadge and Shore-Goss demonstrates that scholarship on LGBT and queer subjects within religion has expanded considerably in the years since the publication of *Que(e)rying Religion*. It would now be impossible to deny the existence of gay Catholics, gay Muslims, gay Seventh-Day Adventists, gay Latter-day Saints, or practitioners of Santeria who self-identify as gay. Likewise, thanks in part to projects like *The Queer Bible Commentary* (2006) and *Torah Queeries* (2009), scriptural texts seem up to unending queer grab, as does every religious tradition. Within studies of modern Judaism, queer analysis is nearly inescapable.[5] Over the past two decades, researchers have demonstrated the inextricable histories of Christian nationalism, homosexuality as a medical diagnosis, and anti-Semitism as a social phenomenon. "Anti-semitism was driven by religious and ethnic hatred with an admixture of sexual threat," Steven Lapidus has argued. "With the advent of modernity and the putative espousal of rationality, medical theories began to foster a biologically based antisemitism that paralleled a biologized homophobia."[6] Beyond the actual numbers of self-identified gay or lesbian Jews in Conservative or Reconstructionist synagogues, the Jewish experience in modernity has been queered as a result of its iconic relationship to the normative cultures of Christianity alongside which it has struggled and survived.

The foregoing may suggest that there is a divide between the voluntary gay subject and the involuntarily queered community. In reality, the narrative experience of the two is intertwined; often, the story of the voluntary gay subject includes immersion in a religious community that is retrospectively queer. For instance, in *Recruiting Young Love* (2011), theologian Mark D. Jordan provided this analytical summary of the novel *Better Angel* (1934). Jordan argued that the protagonist, Kurt Gray, was a stand-in for the author, Forman Brown, and that Gray—like Brown—had a story prototypical of "a certain class of American male homosexual":

> Kurt Gray . . . has a boyhood marked by solitude, bookish seriousness, gender dislocation, and religion. He dislikes sports and delights in staging plays (especially when he can perform a princess). Then Kurt undergoes a perplexing Christian conversion. It turns, by the end of high school, into a faith in music and poetry. Kurt attends the University of Michigan, where he begins a sexual relationship with another young man and perfects his aesthetic philosophy. Then to a scholarship in France and the artsy circles of Manhattan. The pattern of Gray's life—of Brown's own—will become standard for a certain class of American male homosexual. Indeed, it will become something like the standard myth: escape from the religious and sexual oppression of a small town through (self-) education to an art-filled and sexually gratifying cosmopolitanism.[7]

Jordan described the character of Kurt Gray not only as moving *through* Christianity to become homosexual but also as finding *within*

Christianity certain experiences of worship that offer proxy forms of intensity to a young gay man hungry for erotic intimacy and social intensity. In this account, Christianity was something to graduate from in order to become sexually free.[8] But Christianity itself was also queer: a tradition simultaneously averse to expressions of homosexuality while also offering multiple scriptural, ritual, and social experiences of self-understanding, self-formation, and revelation as a dissenting subject.

The increasing repository of work grappling with the intersection between queer life and religion—especially queer experience and Christianity—may suggest that the course is clear for ongoing excellence in the subject. Yet sociologist of religion Melissa M. Wilcox has expressed concern about the overarching disciplinary and institutional support for such work. Describing the state of the field, she wrote:

> We have a queer studies that is largely cynical about religion, though willing to consider it in studies countering fundamentalism or studies of identity undertaken by literature scholars; a religious studies wary enough of things queer to occasionally deny tenure to and sometimes refuse to hire scholars who work in the area; queer studies scholars untrained in the study of religion; and religious studies scholars untrained in queer studies—the latter two as a result of the former. This, at least, must change. Religious studies scholars must show how our work can contribute to the development of queer theory—in its fullest, most justice-oriented sense, and not in the guise of Christian supremacism—and queer theorists must consider whether a serious look at religion might not be in the interest of their ultimate goals.[9]

The arguments and engagements of this volume might make Wilcox more optimistic about the present relationship between queer studies and religious studies. There is no wariness here, and every scholar is committed to the "justice-oriented" labors of queer theory. *Que(e)rying Religion* responded affirmatively to the question: "Is it possible to be religious and to be gay, lesbian, or queer?" This volume begs an inquiry into the inverse: "Is it possible to be Christian *without* being queer?" And the evidence it gathers suggests that the answer to this question might be no.

What If Christianity Is Oz?

These are just some of the things we read about in this volume: theological midwives, golden showers, natural law, polyandrous monogamists, mixed-orientation marriages, sacramental holy unions, condoms, oppression sickness, reception and contraception, undue and underdeveloped cooperation, double love, pride parades, boy-girl haircuts, Adam, Eve, Augustine, Foucault, Butler, Calvin, Goodman, Eusebius, Fosdick, Orsi, Aquinas, Cheng, Wyoming, Yonkers, Nebraska, San Francisco, Iowa, Clement and Weeks, Eloise and Abelard, Troy Perry and Tyler Perry, friendship and sex, sin and grace, desert mothers, Metho-Bapti-Costals, the Presbyterian Directory for Worship, and the scene of Calvary. We visited monasteries, private dungeons, and worship halls and considered civil law and canon law. And along the way we encountered ambivalent legacies, erotic celibacies, promiscuous privilege, eschatological repetition, hermeneutics of suspicion, and the Spiritual Exercises of Ignatius Loyola. And, most movingly perhaps, a woman named Evalyn.

This range bespeaks a rebellious confidence. In the chapters of this book, the authors have done something that once would have seemed heretical: they have presumed that Christianity itself can be queer. As the editors remarked in the introduction, "Christianity has not only always had queer members, has not only always had the potential to be queered, but has from the start been a site of radical queerness." There is no Christianity (no sect or proposition or person) that is not asking us to conceive the body; no Christianity that is not, in that very gaze upon the body at Calvary, looking into something strange.

This is the ironic pinch of contemporary political debates asking voters to coordinate Christianity with certain family values and with a certain heterosexual norm. The irony of such propositions—the irony to those of us within this volume—is that they are made by Christians seemingly unconscious of *their* strange, of their participation in a long genealogy of propositions in which voluntary monogamous marriage is just one of many formats of relational devotion. They do not know (as we learn through the chapters in this volume) that there was always a question mark over the very concept of family, over the concept of procreation, over the presumption of monogamy. There is no concept of marriage that is not itself a very strange proposition, as an attempt to manage our bodies as social artifacts, as ontological problems, as desiring sight and desiring to be seen.

Christianity did that time and again, from its origins. Christianity said, "You have a body." Christianity then asked, "How will you manage it?" This was an insurrectionist question at its origins and has remained one always, however diverse and at times domineering the answers have been. This volume has come to apply the term "queer" so broadly because the lived history of Christianity offers an overflowing repository of passionate, constrained, prescribed, and rebellious embodiment. Theologians and historians have always known this, yet it has only been in the last decades of scholarship that it has been made central to the interpretation of that theologizing and those histories. This is a very recent turn in the historiography, motivated by the pioneering strength of works like John Boswell's *Christianity, Social Tolerance and Homosexuality* (1980), Leo Steinberg's *Sexuality of Christ in Renaissance Art and in Modern Oblivion* (1983), and Marcella Althaus-Reid's *Indecent Theology* (2001), each of which combined technical expertise with profound revisions to the standard shibboleths of Christian normativity. If this volume is any testimony, the rebellion inaugurated in those works has become presumptive fact: if we look for the queer in Christianity, we will find it.

What if this presumption is wrong? After reading these chapters, it seems impossible to imagine any facet or epoch of Christian history that cannot usefully be read as relevant to or supportive of queer identity. Yet the marker "queer" was meant to distinguish something from the norm, not to describe a norm. As a concept, queer "is unruly and undermines attempts at fixation or containment."[10] Have we divested the queer of its essence if we contain it in our readings? If everything is queered, can anything still *be* queer?

Maybe the problem is not religion but academics studying religion. What if we are pulling cards out, over and over, from the base of the thing that is already trembling with its total queerness? Perhaps Wilcox is right to stare down the academy's reticence toward Christianity. Maybe Christianity has become the place for sexual creativity, and the academy is just the place of sexual parsing. What if *Christianity* has become the colorful world of Oz and the academy is the black-and-white cinematic state of Kansas?

The Gospel of the Queer

As the history of LGBT politics and voluntary gays within denominations proceeds apace, we may find that we need to recalibrate our identification of queer in our anthropological, biographical, historical, scriptural, and theological subjects. Once upon a time, invoking the queer
meant placing a spotlight on subtext, on crevices, on the periphery.
Doing queer analysis felt exciting because it brought to the center stage
something that had survived in hidden places. Through the first generation of queer studies, we learned a lot about that place—about the
periphery and its productivity. We learned that occupying the periphery was an opportunity (even though it seemed like, felt like, and could
be exclusion). The periphery was a gift (even though it seemed like, felt
like, and could be a punishment). To be sure, the gifts of the periphery
were often missed, but this overlooking was exactly the kind of obstacle
that made the periphery necessary to begin with. Being shoved to the
side was something to endure but also something to survive. And in
that grimy survival was the gospel of the queer.

Michael Warner recently described the originating points of departure for queer theory as including:

> a broadening of minority politics to question the framework of the say-
> able; attention to the hierarchies of respectability that saturate the world;
> movement across overlapping but widely disparate structures of violence
> and power in order to conjure a series of margins that have no iden-
> tity core; an oddly melancholy utopianism; a speculative and prophetic
> stance outside politics—not to mention an ability to do much of that—
> through the play of its own style.[11]

It cannot be the case that we believe queer theory has finished its
work—that hierarchies have been upended, that violence has been
eased and power relented, that a new politics of antipolitics has begun,
or that there is any less reason for melancholy or utopian dreaming. The
world is still far too steroidal in its gender play, and still too precious
with its perpetuation to believe that a few essays on queer religion represent the world's revision. They merely represent the critical beginning
of that revision and the inspiring possibility of its next turning.

A church of the queer may or may not be possible. As we continue, let us agree on what is not queer. Or rather: let us try to say more often what it is not, and fight over and for *that*, for what is not meeting the standard of strange that we have set for Christianity. Let us do this, rather than merely seek to include everyone in the tent, everyone inside the ubiquitous queer conceit. This would be my bid: that what is not queer is deciding in favor of tradition. That what is not queer is any recourse to the natural. What is not queer is any argumentative recourse to safety. What is not queer is living a life without fear. What is not queer is imagining that sex is not awkward, is not lonely, is not always a challenge of the highest epistemological, theological, and experiential order. What is not queer is thinking that self-identifying *as* queer makes you bracketed from critique about your normative suppositions. What is not queer is thinking something is worth saving when you can't stomach what it is to lose. What is not queer is thinking that you may ever dominate, pervade, or rule. What is not queer is trying to have everything, when from the beginning, it was always and ever about a protest on behalf of those who don't, who can't, who struggle from margins unnamed, to be seen by you. Christianity could be queer, but only and ever if it is a protest and not the rule.

NOTES

1. Gary David Comstock and Susan E. Henking, eds., *Que(e)rying Religion: A Critical Anthology* (New York: Continuum, 1997), back cover.
2. Wendy Cadge, "Lesbian, Gay, and Bisexual Buddhist Practitioners," in *Gay Religion*, ed. Edward R. Gray and Scott Thumma (Walnut Creek, CA: AltaMira Press, 2004), 149.
3. Marilee Lindemann, "Who's Afraid of the Big Bad Witch? Queer Studies in American Literature," *American Literary History* 12 (2000): 767.
4. Robert Shore-Goss, "Queer Buddhists: Re-visiting Sexual Gender Fluidity," in *Queer Religion*, vol. 1, *Homosexuality in Modern Religious History*, ed. Donald L. Boisvert and Jay Emerson Johnson (Santa Barbara, CA: Praeger, 2012), 25–50.
5. Daniel Boyarin, Daniel Iskovitz, and Ann Pellegrini, eds., *Queer Theory and the Jewish Question* (New York: Columbia University Press, 2003).
6. Steven Lapidus, "Bottoming for the Queen: Queering the Jews in Protestant Europe at the *Fin de Siècle*," in *Queer Religion*, vol. 1, *Homosexuality in Modern Religious History*, ed. Donald L. Boisvert and Jay Emerson Johnson (Santa Barbara, CA: Praeger, 2012), 147.

7. Mark D. Jordan, *Recruiting Young Love: How Christians Talk about Homosexuality* (Chicago: University of Chicago Press, 2011), 22.

8. This mythic plot for a certain young homosexual man can be found, too, in literary scholar Sam See's examination of the 1933 novel *The Young and Evil* by Charles Henri Ford and Parker Tyler. Yet there See takes up the gay subject where Jordan leaves off, finding in the literary depiction of Manhattan gay enclaves a certain "queer mythology" at work. See described *The Young and Evil* as "a folkloric document composed in the style of the mythical method," especially in the ways the novel shuttles "between the historical particularity of Greenwich Village and the mythic universality of the sexual-aesthetic." Like *Better Angel, The Young and Evil* depicted queer community as a mythic construction—as a narrative end point and a new experiential beginning for those who are in exile from other provincial, ethnic, and denominational enclaves. Sam See, "Making Modernism New: Queer Mythology in *The Young and Evil*," *ELH* 76 (2009): 1098, 1096.

9. Melissa M. Wilcox, "Queer Theory and the Study of Religion," *Queer Religion*, vol. 2, *LGBT Movements and Queering Religion*, ed. Donald L. Boisvert and Jay Emerson Johnson (Santa Barbara, CA: Praeger, 2012), 245.

10. Robert McRuer, *The Queer Renaissance: Contemporary American Literature and the Reinvention of Lesbian and Gay Identities* (New York: NYU Press, 1997), 22.

11. Michael Warner, "Queer and Then?," *Chronicle Review*, January 1, 2012, http://chronicle.com/article/QueerThen-/130161/.

A. B. T. "Bold New Church Welcomes Gay." *Advocate*, February 1968, 2–3.

"An Advocate Interpretive: Gay Marriage 'Boom': Suddenly, It's News." *Advocate*, June 10–23, 1970, 6.

Akamatsu, Norma. "Teaching White Students about Racism and Its Implications in Practice." In *Re-visioning Family Therapy: Race, Culture, and Gender in Clinical Practice*, 2nd ed., ed. Monica McGoldrick and Kenneth V. Hardy, 413–24. New York: Guilford Press, 2008.

Alison, James. *Faith beyond Resentment: Fragments Catholic and Gay*. New York: Crossroad, 2001.

Allen, Woody. *Without Feathers*. New York: Random House, 1972.

Althaus-Reid, Marcella. *Indecent Theology: Theological Perversions in Sex, Gender, and Politics*. London: Routledge, 2000.

Anderson, Victor. *Creative Exchange: A Constructive Theology of African American Religious Experience*. Minneapolis, MN: Fortress Press, 2008.

———. *Pragmatic Theology: Negotiating the Intersections of an American Philosophy of Religion and Public Theology*. Albany: State University of New York Press, 1998.

Augustine of Hippo. *The City of God against the Pagans*. Ed. and trans. R. W. Dyson. Cambridge: Cambridge University Press, 1998.

———. *Confessions*. Trans. Henry Chadwick. Oxford: Oxford University Press, 1992.

———. "The *Confessions* of Saint Augustine: An Electronic Edition." Ed. O'Donnell. James. www.stoa.org/hippo/comm3.html#CB3C8S15.

———. *De Bono Coniugali: De Sancta Virginitate*. Trans. P. G. Walsh. Oxford: Clarendon Press, 2001.

———. *On Christian Teaching*. Trans. R. P. H. Green. Oxford: Oxford University Press, 1997.

———. *The Works of Saint Augustine: A Translation for the 21st Century*. Ed. John E. Rotelle. Brooklyn, NY: New City Press, 1990–.

Baldwin, James. *The Fire Next Time*. New York: Vintage, 1962.

Berkowitz, Richard. *Stayin' Alive: The Invention of Safe Sex*. New York: Basic Books, 2003.

Berlant, Lauren, and Michael Warner. "Sex in Public." In Michael Warner, *Publics and Counterpublics*, 187–208. Brooklyn, NY: Zone Books, 2005.

Bevans, Steven B. *Models of Contextual Theology*. Rev. ed. Maryknoll, NY: Orbis, 2002.

Bevans, Steven B., and Katalina Tahaafe-Williams, eds. *Contextual Theology for the Twenty-First Century*. Eugene, OR: Wipf and Stock, 2011.

Boisvert, Donald L., and Jay Emerson Johnson, eds. *Queer Religion*. 2 vols. Santa Barbara, CA: Praeger, 2012.

Boswell, John. *Christianity, Social Tolerance, and Homosexuality: Gay People in Western Europe from the Beginning of the Christian Era to the Fourteenth Century*. Chicago: University of Chicago Press, 1980.

———. *Same-Sex Unions in Premodern Europe*. New York: Villard, 1994.

Boyarin, Daniel, Daniel Iskovitz, and Ann Pellegrini, eds. *Queer Theory and the Jewish Question*. New York: Columbia University Press, 2003.

Brier, Jennifer. *Infectious Ideas: U.S. Political Responses to the AIDS Crisis*. Chapel Hill: University of North Carolina Press, 2009.

Brown, Lea D. "Dancing in the *Eros* of Domination and Submission within SM." In *Dancing Theology in Fetish Boots: Essays in Honor of Marcella Althaus-Reid*, ed. Lisa Isherwood and Mark D. Jordan, 141–52. London: SCM Press, 2010.

Brown, Peter. *The Body and Society: Men, Women, and Sexual Renunciation in Early Christianity*. New York: Columbia University Press, 1988.

Brundage, James A. *Law, Sex, and Christian Society in Medieval Europe*. Chicago: University of Chicago Press, 1987.

Bugge, John. *Virginitatis: An Essay in the History of a Medieval Ideal*. The Hague: Martinus Nijhoff, 1975.

Burke, Peter. *Popular Culture in Early Modern Europe*. London: Temple Smith, 1978.

Bussell, Donna Alfano. *Heloise Redressed: A Re-examination of Letter V*. San Francisco: San Francisco State University Press, 1996.

Butler, Judith. "Imitation and Gender Insubordination." In *The Lesbian and Gay Studies Reader*, ed. Henry Abelove, Michele Aina Barale, and David M. Halperin, 307–20. New York: Routledge, 1993.

———. *Undoing Gender*. New York: Routledge, 2004.

Cade, John B. "Out of the Mouths of Ex-Slaves." *Journal of Negro History* 20 (1935): 294–337.

Cadge, Wendy. "Lesbian, Gay, and Bisexual Buddhist Practitioners." In *Gay Religion*, ed. Edward R. Gray and Scott Thumma, 139–52. Walnut Creek, CA: AltaMira Press, 2004.

Califia, Pat. *Public Sex: The Culture of Radical Sex*. San Francisco: Cleis, 1994.

Carroll, Joseph. "Americans: 2.5 Children Is 'Ideal' Family Size." Gallup News Service, June 26, 2007.

"Celibate Homosexuality or Victorious Singleness?" New Hope blog. December 31, 2012. www.newhope123.org/new-hope-blog/.

Cervantes, Vincent. "Loving Promiscuously: A Queer Theology of Doing It." http://blog.vincentcervantes.com/2011/08/loving-promiscuously-queer-theology-of.html#more.

Chauncey, George. *Why Marriage? The History Shaping Today's Debate over Gay Equality*. New York: Basic Books, 2004.

Cheng, Patrick S. *Radical Love: An Introduction to Queer Theology*. New York: Seabury, 2011.

Chinula, Donald M. *Building King's Beloved Community: Foundations for Pastoral Care and Counseling with the Oppressed*. Cleveland, OH: United Church Press, 1997.

Clanchy, M. T. *Abelard: A Medieval Life*. Oxford: Blackwell, 1999.

Cloke, Gillian. *This Female Man of God: Women and Spiritual Power in the Patristic Age, 350–450 AD*. London: Routledge, 1995.

Cohen, Cathy. "Punks, Bulldaggers, and Welfare Queens: The Radical Potential of Queer Politics?" *GLQ* 3 (1997): 437–65.

Cole, Rob. "Two Men Ask Minnesota License for First Legal U.S. Gay Marriage." *Advocate*, June 10–23, 1970. 1.

Comiskey, Andrew. "Telling the Haggard Truth." http://desertstream.org/ Groups/1000040183/Desert_Stream_Ministries/Looking_For_Help/Free_ Resources/Articles_and_Newsletters/Articles_and_Newsletters.aspx.

Comstock, Gary David. *Gay Theology without Apology*. Cleveland: Pilgrim Press, 1993.

———. *Unrepentant, Self-Affirming, Practicing: Lesbian/Bisexual/Gay People within Organized Religion*. New York: Continuum Publishing, 1992.

Comstock, Gary David, and Susan E. Henking, eds. *Que(e)rying Religion: A Critical Anthology*. New York: Continuum, 1997.

Cone, James. *The Cross and the Lynching Tree*. Maryknoll, NY: Orbis, 2011.

Copeland, M. Shawn. "Wading through Many Sorrows." In *A Troubling in My Soul: Womanist Perspectives on Evil and Suffering*, ed. Emilie Townes, 109–29. Maryknoll, NY: Orbis, 1993.

Coriden, James A. "The Canonical Doctrine of Reception." *Jurist* 50 (1990): 58–82.

———. "The Canonical Doctrine of Reception." Association for the Rights of Catholics in the Church (ARCC). www.arcc-catholic-rights.net/doctrine_of_reception.htm.

Cornwall, Susannah. *Controversies in Queer Theology*. Louisville, KY: Westminster John Knox Press, 2011.

Crimp, Douglas. "How to Have Promiscuity in an Epidemic." *October*, Winter 1987, 237–71.

———. *Melancholia and Moralism: Essays on AIDS and Queer Politics*. Cambridge, MA: MIT Press, 2002.

Dart, John. "A Church for Homosexuals." *Los Angeles Times*, December 8, 1969.

Davies, Bob. *Portraits of Freedom: 14 People Who Came Out of Homosexuality*. Downers Grove, IL: InterVarsity Press, 2001.

Davies, Bob, and Lori Rentzel. *Coming Out of Homosexuality: New Freedom for Men and Women*. Downers Grove, IL: InterVarsity Press, 1993.

Davis, Rebecca. *More Perfect Unions: The American Search for Marital Bliss*. Cambridge, MA: Harvard University Press, 2010.

Davis, Stephen J. *The Cult of Saint Thecla: A Tradition of Women's Piety in Late Antiquity*. Oxford: Oxford University Press, 2001.

Delgado, Teresa. "Dead in the Water . . . Again." In *Reinterpreting Virtues and Values in the U.S. Public Sphere: Life, Liberty, and the Pursuit of Happiness in Twenty-First*

Century United States, ed. Mary McClintock Fulkerson, Rosemary Carbine, and Ada Maria Isasi-Diaz. Forthcoming.

Eastman, Susan. "Commentary on Philippians 2:1–13." Working Preacher. www.workingpreacher.org/preaching.aspx?lect_date=9/25/2011&tab=3.

Elliott, Dyan. *The Bride of Christ Goes to Hell: Metaphor and Embodiment in the Lives of Pious Women, 200–1500*. Philadelphia: University of Pennsylvania Press, 2011.

Erzen, Tanya. *Straight to Jesus: Sexual and Christian Conversions in the Ex-Gay Movement*. Berkeley: University of California Press, 2006.

Eusebius of Caesarea. *The Proof of the Gospel*. Vol. 1. Trans. W. J. Ferrar. London: SPCK, 1920.

Exodus International newsletter. December 2012. http://exodusinternational.org/wp-content/uploads/2009/12/December-2012.pdf.

Fanous, Samuel. "Christina of Markyate and the Double Crown." In *Christina of Markyate*, ed. Samuel Fanous and Henrietta Leyser, 53–78. New York: Routledge, 2005.

Fanous, Samuel, Henrietta Leyser, and C. H. Talbot, eds. *The Life of Christina of Markyate*. New York: Oxford University Press, 2010.

Farajaje-Jones, Elias. "Breaking Silence: Toward an In-the-Life Theology." In *Black Theology: A Documentary History*. Vol. 2, *1980–1992*, ed. James H. Cone and Gayraud S. Wilmore, 139–59. Maryknoll, NY: Orbis, 1993.

Farley, Margaret A. *Just Love: A Framework for Christian Sexual Ethics*. New York: Continuum, 2006.

Fernandez, Eleazar S. *Reimagining the Human: Theological Anthropology in Response to Systemic Evil*. St. Louis, MO: Chalice Press, 2004.

Fisher, Pete. "Gay Couples Celebrate Engagement at Marriage Licensing Bureau." *Gay* 2, no. 54 (July 5, 1971).

Fleming, David L., SJ. *The Spiritual Exercises: A Literal Translation and a Contemporary Reading*. St. Louis, MO: Institute of Jesuit Sources, 1978.

Foucault, Michel. *Ethics: Subjectivity and Truth*. New York: New Press, 1998.

———. *The History of Sexuality, Volume 1: An Introduction*. New York: Vintage, 1990.

Freeman, Elizabeth. *Time Binds: Queer Temporalities, Queer Histories*. Durham, NC: Duke University Press, 2010.

———. *The Wedding Complex: Forms of Belonging in Modern American Culture*. Durham, NC: Duke University Press, 2002.

Friedman, Jaclyn, ed. *Yes Means Yes: Visions of Female Sexual Power and a World without Rape*. Seattle, WA: Seal Press, 2008.

Furey, Constance. "Sexuality." In *The Cambridge Companion to Christian Mysticism*, ed. Amy Hollywood and Patricia Z. Beckman, 328–40. Cambridge: Cambridge University Press, 2012.

Gardiner, Christine J. *Making Chastity Sexy: The Rhetoric of Evangelical Abstinence Campaigns*. Berkeley: University of California Press, 2011.

Georgianna, Linda. "Any Corner of Heaven." *Mediaeval Studies* 49 (1987): 221–53.

Gerber, Lynne. "The Opposite of Gay: Nature, Creation and Queerish Ex-Gay Experi-
ments." *Nova Religio* 11, no. 4 (2008): 8–30.
———. *Seeking the Straight and Narrow: Weight Loss and Sexual Reorientation in Evan-
gelical America.* Chicago: University of Chicago Press, 2011.
Gold, Penny S. "The Marriage of Mary and Joseph." In *Sexual Practices and the Medi-
eval Church*, ed. James Brundage and Vern Bullough, 102–17. Buffalo, NY: Pro-
metheus Books, 1982.
Gomes, Peter J. *The Good Book: Reading the Bible with Mind and Heart.* New York:
William Morrow, 1996.
Goodman, Nelson. *Ways of World Making.* Indianapolis, IN: Hackett, 1978.
Grenz, Stanley J. *Welcoming but Not Affirming: An Evangelical Response to Homosexu-
ality.* Louisville, KY: Westminster John Knox Press, 1998.
Gritter, Wendy. "Mixed-Orientation Marriage: A Case Study for the Now and the Not
Yet." Bridging the Gap blog. March 29, 2012. http://btgproject.blogspot.com/search/
label/mixed%20orientation%20marriage.
Gritz, Jennie Rothenberg. "Sexual Healing: Evangelicals Update Their Message to Gays.
Interview with Alan Chambers." *Atlantic*, June 20, 2012.
Guttmacher Institute. "Supplemental Tables on Religion and Contraceptive Use." www.
guttmacher.org/media/resources/Religion-FP-tables.html.
Haight, Roger. *Christian Spirituality for Seekers: Reflections on the Spiritual Exercises of
Ignatius Loyola.* Maryknoll, NY: Orbis, 2012.
Haley, Mike. *101 Frequently Asked Questions about Homosexuality.* Eugene, OR: Harvest
House, 2004.
Halperin, David. *Saint Foucault: Towards a Gay Hagiography.* Oxford: Oxford Univer-
sity Press, 1997.
Hart, David Bentley. *The Doors of the Sea: Where Was God in the Tsunami?* Grand
Rapids, MI: Eerdmans, 2005.
Harvey, Jennifer. "Both/And Thinking on Same-Sex Marriage." huffingtonpost.com.
March 28, 2013.
———. "Waiting One More Day (on DOMA)." huffingtonpost.com. June 25, 2013.
Harvey, Jennifer, Karin A. Case, and Robin Hawley Gorsline, eds. *Disrupting White
Supremacy from Within: White People on What We Need to Do.* Cleveland, OH:
Pilgrim Press, 2004.
Head, Thomas. "The Marriages of Christina of Markyate." *Viator* 21 (1990): 75–102.
Hicks, Stephen. *Lesbian, Gay and Queer Parenting: Families, Intimacies, Genealogies.*
Houndsmills, Basingstoke: Palgrave Macmillan, 2011.
Highley, Ron, and Joanne Highley. "Our Objections to a Current Exodus Policy." In
The Best Words of L.I.F.E.: Celebrating 20 Years of L.I.F.E. Ministries, 226–29. New
York: L.I.F.E., 2002.
Hintz, Marcy. "Choosing Celibacy: How to Stop Thinking of Singleness as a Problem."
Christianity Today. September 12, 2008. www.christianitytoday.com/ct/2008/sep-
tember/20.47.html.

Howell, Tom, Jr. "White House Urges Supreme Court to Reject Nuns' Appeal for Birth Control Exemption." *Washington Times*, January 3, 2014.

Hugh of Saint Victor. *Hugh of Saint Victor on the Sacraments*. Trans. Roy J. Deferrari. Eugene, OR: Wipf and Stock, 2007.

Hunt, Mary E. *Fierce Tenderness: A Feminist Theology of Friendship*. New York: Crossroad, 1991.

———. "Just Good Sex." In *Good Sex*, ed. Patricia Beattie Jung, Mary E. Hunt, and Radhika Balakrishnan, 158–173. New Brunswick, NJ: Rutgers University Press, 2001.

———. "Same-Sex Marriage and Relational Justice," part of "Roundtable Discussion: Same-Sex Marriage," *Journal of Feminist Studies in Religion* 20 (2004): 83–117.

———. "Will Francis' Statements on Women and Gays 'Make a Mess' inside the Church?" July 29, 2013. religiondispatches.org.

Hunter, David G. "Augustine and the Making of Marriage in Roman North Africa." *Journal of Early Christian Studies* 11 (2003): 63–85.

———. *Marriage, Celibacy, and Heresy in Ancient Christianity: The Jovinianist Controversy*. Oxford: Oxford University Press, 2007.

Hunter, David G., and Susan Ashbrook Harvey, eds. *The Oxford Handbook of Early Christian Studies*. Oxford: Oxford University Press, 2008.

Inbody, Tyron. *The Constructive Theology of Bernard Meland: Postliberal Empirical Realism*. Atlanta, GA: Scholars Press, 1995.

Isherwood, Lisa, and Mark D. Jordan, eds. *Dancing Theology in Fetish Boots: Essays in Honor of Marcella Althaus-Reid*. London: SCM Press, 2010.

Jaeger, C. Stephen. *Ennobling Love: In Search of a Lost Sensibility*. Philadelphia: University of Pennsylvania Press, 1999.

———. "The Loves of Christina of Markyate." In *Christina of Markyate*, ed. Samuel Fanous and Henrietta Leyser, 99–115. New York: Routledge, 2005.

John Chrysostom. *On Virginity, against Remarriage*. Trans. Elizabeth A. Clark and Sally R. Shore. New York: Edwin Mellen Press, 1983.

Jordan, Mark D. *The Ethics of Sex*. Oxford: Blackwell, 2002.

———. *The Invention of Sodomy in Christian Theology*. Chicago: University of Chicago Press, 1998.

———. *Recruiting Young Love: How Christians Talk about Homosexuality*. Chicago: University of Chicago Press, 2011.

Kamitsuka, Margaret D., ed. *The Embrace of Eros: Bodies, Desires, and Sexuality in Christianity*. Minneapolis, MN: Fortress Press, 2010.

———. *Feminist Theology and the Challenge of Difference*. Oxford: Oxford University Press, 2007.

Kater, John L. *Christians on the Right: The Moral Majority in Perspective*. New York: Seabury, 1982.

Kinast, Robert L. *Making Faith-Sense: Theological Reflection in Everyday Life*. Collegeville, MN: Liturgical Press, 1999.

Kramer, Larry. *The Normal Heart* and *Destiny of Me*. New York: Grove Press, 2000.

Lapidus, Steven. "Bottoming for the Queen: Queering the Jews in Protestant Europe at the *Fin de Siècle*." In *Queer Religion*. Vol. 1, *Homosexuality in Modern Religious History*, ed. Donald L. Boisvert and Jay Emerson Johnson, 147–68. Santa Barbara, CA: Praeger, 2012.

Lehr, Valerie. *Queer Family Values: Rethinking the Myth of the Nuclear Family*. Philadelphia: Temple University Press, 1999.

Lindemann, Marilee. "Who's Afraid of the Big Bad Witch? Queer Studies in American Literature." *American Literary History* 12 (2000): 757–70.

Linden, Robin Ruth, Darlene R. Pagano, Diana E. H. Russell, and Susan Leigh Star, eds. *Against Sadomasochism: A Radical Feminist Analysis*. East Palo Alto, CA: Frog in the Well, 1982.

Lochrie, Karma. *Heterosyncrasies: Female Sexuality When Normal Wasn't*. Minneapolis: University of Minnesota Press, 2005.

———. "Mystical Acts, Queer Tendencies." In *Constructing Medieval Sexuality*, ed. Karma Lochrie, Peggy McCracken, and James A. Schultz, 180–200. Minneapolis: University of Minneapolis Press, 1997.

Loughlin, Gerard, ed. *Queer Theology: Rethinking the Western Body*. Malden, MA: Blackwell, 2007.

MacKendrick, Karmen. *Counterpleasures*. Albany: State University of New York Press, 1999.

McAlpin, Kathleen, and Mary Jo Leddy. *Ministry That Transforms: A Contemplative Process of Theological Reflection*. Collegeville, MN: Liturgical Press, 2009.

McBrien, Richard P. "*Humanae Vitae* after 40 Years." *Tidings*, July 25, 2008. https://www3.nd.edu/~newsinfo/pdf/2008_07_25_pdf/Humanae%20Vitae%20After%20 40%20years.pdf.

McClory, Robert. *Turning Point: The Inside Story of the Papal Birth Control Commission*. New York: Crossroad, 1995.

McCormick, Richard A. "'Humanae Vitae' 25 Years Later." *America*, July 17, 1993. http://americamagazine.org/node/148840.

McGuire, Meredith B. *Lived Religion: Faith and Practice in Everyday Life*. New York: Oxford University Press, 2008.

McLaughlin, Mary Martin. "Heloise the Abbess." In *Listening to Heloise: The Voice of a Twelfth-Century Woman*, ed. Bonnie Wheeler, 1–17. New York: St. Martin's Press, 2000.

McNamer, Sarah. *Affective Meditation and the Invention of Medieval Compassion*. Philadelphia: University of Pennsylvania Press, 2000.

McRuer, Robert. *The Queer Renaissance: Contemporary American Literature and the Reinvention of Lesbian and Gay Identities*. New York: NYU Press, 1997.

Medinger, Alan. "God Healed My Marriage." 1985. www.exodusglobalalliance.org/godhealedmymarriagep2.php.

Mehta, Samira K., and Anthony Petro. "Big Vampire Love: What's So Mormon about *Twilight*?" religiondispatches.org. December 4, 2009.

Mercado, Leonardo N. *Elements of Filipino Theology*. Tacloban, Philippines: Divine Word University, 1975.

———. "Notes on Christ and Local Community in Philippine Context." *Verbum SVD* 21 (1980): 303–15.

Miller-McLemore, Bonnie J., ed. *The Wiley-Blackwell Companion to Practical Theology*. Hoboken, NJ: Wiley-Blackwell, 2011.

Moore, Mignon R. *Invisible Families: Gay Identities, Relationships, and Motherhood among Black Women*. Berkeley: University of California Press, 2011.

Moore, Stephen D. *God's Beauty Parlor: And Other Queer Spaces in and around the Bible*. Stanford, CA: Stanford University Press, 2001.

National Center for Health Statistics. "Contraceptive Utilization, United States (Data from the National Survey of Family Growth)." Vital and Health Statistics, Series 23, No. 2 (1979). www.cdc.gov/nchs/data/series/sr_23/sr23_002.pdf.

Newman, Barbara. *From Virile Woman to WomanChrist: Studies in Medieval Religion*. Philadelphia: University of Pennsylvania Press, 1995.

Nicolosi, Joseph. *Healing Homosexuality: Case Stories of Reparative Therapy*. Lanham, MD: Rowman and Littlefield, 2004.

O'Connell Killen, Patricia. "Assisting Adults to Think Theologically." In *Method in Ministry*, rev. ed., ed. James D. Whitehead and Evelyn Eaton Whitehead, 103–11. Kansas City, MO: Sheed and Ward, 1995.

O'Connell Killen, Patricia, and John de Beer. *The Art of Theological Reflection*. New York: Crossroad, 1994.

Origen. *Fragmenta ex commentariis in 1 Cor*. Ed. C. Jenkins. *Journal of Theological Studies* 8–9 (1908): 370–71.

Orsi, Robert A. *Between Heaven and Earth: The Religious Worlds People Make and the Scholars Who Study Them*. Princeton, NJ: Princeton University Press, 2006.

———, ed. *The Cambridge Companion to Religious Studies*. Cambridge: Cambridge University Press, 2012.

———. "Is the Study of Lived Religion Irrelevant to the World We Live In?" *Journal for the Scientific Study of Religion* 42 (2003): 169–74.

Otnes, Cele, and Elizabeth Hafkin Pleck. *Cinderella Dreams: The Allure of the Lavish Wedding*. Berkeley: University of California Press, 2003.

Pagels, Elaine. *Adam, Eve, and the Serpent: Sex and Politics in Early Christianity*. New York: Vintage, 1989.

Patton, Cindy. *Fatal Advice: How Safe-Sex Education Went Wrong*. Durham, NC: Duke University Press, 1996.

Paulinus of Nola. *Poems of St. Paulinus of Nola*. Trans. P. G. Walsh. New York: Paulist Press, 1975.

Pennington, Edgard Legare. *Thomas Bray's Associates and Their Work among the Negros*. Worcester, MA: American Antiquarian Society, 1939.

Petro, Anthony M. *After the Wrath of God: AIDS, Sexuality, and American Religion*. Oxford: Oxford University Press, forthcoming.

Pope John Paul II. *Man and Woman He Created Them: A Theology of the Body*. Trans. and intro. Michael Waldstein. Boston: Pauline Books and Media, 2006.

Pope Paul VI. *Humanae Vitae*. July 25, 1968. www.vatican.va/holy_father/paul_vi/encyclicals/documents/hf_p-vi_enc_25071968_humanae-vitae_en.html.

Powell, Morgan. "Listening to Heloise at the Paraclete: Of Scholarly Diversion and a Woman's 'Conversion.'" In *Listening to Heloise: The Voice of a Twelfth-Century Woman*, ed. Bonnie Wheeler, 255–86. New York: St. Martin's Press, 2000.

Radice, Betty, trans. *The Letters of Abelard and Heloise*. Rev. ed. London: Penguin, 2003.

Réage, Pauline. *Story of O*. Trans. Sabine d'Estrée. New York: Ballantine, 1965.

Reynolds, Philip Lyndon. *Marriage in the Western Church: The Christianization of Marriage during the Patristic and Early Medieval Periods*. Leiden: E. J. Brill, 2001.

Rice, Charles. *50 Questions on the Natural Law: What It Is and Why We Need It*. San Francisco: Ignatius Press, 1993.

Robinson, V. Gene. "Keep on Dancing." Sermon preached at the First Presbyterian Church in the City of New York, June 28, 2009. Privately published.

Salih, Sarah. *Versions of Virginity*. Cambridge: D. S. Brewer, 2001.

Samois, ed. *Coming to Power: Writings and Graphics on Lesbian S/M*. Boston: Alyson Publications, 1981.

Schneider, Laurel C. "Promiscuous Incarnation." In *The Embrace of Eros: Bodies, Desire and Sexuality in Christianity*, ed. Margaret D. Kamitsuka, 231–46. Minneapolis, MN: Fortres Press, 2010.

Sedgwick, Eve Kosofsky. *Epistemology of the Closet*. Berkeley: University of California Press, 1990.

See, Sam. "Making Modernism New: Queer Mythology in *The Young and Evil*." *ELH* 76 (2009): 1073–1105.

Sharf, Robert. "Experience." In *Critical Terms for Religious Studies*, ed. Mark C. Taylor, 94–116. Chicago: University of Chicago Press, 1998.

Shaw, Jane. "Reformed and Enlightened Church." In *Queer Theology: Rethinking the Western Body*, ed. Gerard Loughlin, 215–29. Malden, MA: Blackwell, 2007.

Shively, Elizabeth. "Commentary on Philippians 2:5–11." Working Preacher. www.workingpreacher.org/preaching.aspx?lect_date=3/24/2013&tab=3.

Shore-Goss, Robert. "Queer Buddhists: Re-visiting Sexual Gender Fluidity." In *Queer Religion*. Vol. 1, *Homosexuality in Modern Religious History*, ed. Donald L. Boisvert and Jay Emerson Johnson, 35–50. Santa Barbara, CA: Praeger, 2012.

Silverstein, Charles, and Felice Picano. *The New Joy of Gay Sex*. San Francisco: Harper-Collins, 1992.

Silverstein, Charles, and Edmund White. *The Joy of Gay Sex: An Intimate Guide for Gay Men to the Pleasures of a Gay Lifestyle*. San Francisco: Outlet, 1977.

Sinnard, Elaine. "Finding Joy as a Woman." http://exodus.to/content/view/255/148/.

Smid, John. *Ex'd Out: How I Fired the Shame Committee*. Charlotte, NC: Create Space Independent Publishing Platform, 2012.

Smith, William E., III. "Anne Wentworth's Apocalyptic Marriages: Bigamy, Subjectivity, and Religious Conflict." In *Marriage in Premodern Europe: Italy and Beyond*, ed. Jacqueline Murray, 357–75. Toronto: Centre for Renaissance and Reformation Studies, 2012.

"The Spiritual Exercises." www.ignatianspirituality.com/ignatian-prayer/the-spiritual-exercises/.

Steinberg, Leo. *The Sexuality of Christ in Renaissance Art and in Modern Oblivion*. New York: Pantheon, 1983.

Stuart, Elizabeth. *Gay and Lesbian Theologies: Repetitions with Critical Difference*. Farnham, UK: Ashgate, 2003.

———. *Just Good Friends: Towards a Lesbian and Gay Theology of Relationships*. London: Mowbray, 1995.

———. "Making No Sense: Liturgy as Queer Space." In *Dancing Theology in Fetish Boots: Essays in Honor of Marcella Althaus-Reid*, ed. Lisa Isherwood and Mark D. Jordan, 113–23. London: SCM Press, 2010.

Sullivan, Maureen. *The Family of Woman: Lesbian Mothers, Their Children, and the Undoing of Gender*. Berkeley: University of California Press, 2004.

Trecker, Barbara. "Gay 'Marriages' Catching On." *New York Post*, April 14, 1971, 3, 53.

———. "Two Women Are Joined in 'Holy Union' at Church." *New York Post*, April 19, 1971, 3, 47.

Turner, Philip. *Sex, Money & Power: An Essay in Christian Social Ethics*. Cambridge, MA: Cowley, 1985.

"Two L.A. Girls Attempt First Legal Gay Marriage." *Los Angeles Advocate*, July 8–21, 1970, 1.

U.S. Department of Health and Human Services. *Understanding AIDS*. Publication No. (CDC) HHS-88-8404. Washington, DC: U.S. Government Printing Office, 1988.

Wadell, Paul J. *Becoming Friends: Worship, Justice, and the Practice of Christian Friendship*. Grand Rapids, MI: Brazos Press, 2002.

Ward, Benedicta. *The Sayings of the Desert Fathers: The Alphabetical Collection*. Kalamazoo, MI: Cistercian Publications, 1975.

Warner, Michael. *Publics and Counterpublics*. Brooklyn, NY: Zone Books, 2005.

———. "Queer and Then?" *Chronicle Review*, January 1, 2012. http://chronicle.com/article/QueerThen-/130161/.

———. *The Trouble with Normal*. Cambridge, MA: Harvard University Press, 1999.

Weinandy, Thomas G. *Does God Suffer?* South Bend, IN: University of Notre Dame Press, 2000.

Weiss, Margot. *Techniques of Pleasure: BDSM and the Circuits of Sexuality*. Durham. NC: Duke University Press, 2011.

"Welcome to Restored Hope Network." www.restoredhopenetwork.org/.

White, Heather R. *American Churches and the Rise of Gay Rights*. Chapel Hill: University of North Carolina Press, forthcoming.

———. "Virgin Pride: Born Again Faith and Sexual Identity in the Faith-Based Abstinence Movement." In *Ashgate Research Companion to Contemporary Religion and Sexuality*, ed. Stephen J. Hunt and Andrew Yip, 241–54. London: Ashgate, 2012.

Whitehead, James D., and Evelyn Eaton Whitehead. *Method in Ministry*. Rev. ed. Kansas City, MO: Sheed and Ward, 1995.

Wilcox, Melissa M. "Queer Theory and the Study of Religion." In *Queer Religion*. Vol. 2, *LGBT Movements and Queering Religion*, ed. Donald L. Boisvert and Jay Emerson Johnson, 227–52. Santa Barbara, CA: Praeger, 2012.

———. *Queer Women and Religious Individualism*. Bloomington: Indiana University Press, 2009.

Wilde, Oscar. *The Picture of Dorian Gray and Other Writings*. Ed. Richard Ellmann. New York: Bantam Classics, 2005.

Wiley, Tatha. "Humanae Vitae, Sexual Ethics and the Roman Catholic Church." In *The Embrace of Eros: Bodies, Desire and Sexuality in Christianity*, ed. Margaret D. Kamitsuka, 99–114. Minneapolis, MN: Fortress Press, 2010.

Williams, Delores S. *Sisters in the Wilderness: The Challenge of Womanist God-Talk*. Maryknoll, NY: Orbis, 1993.

Williams, Rowan. "The Body's Grace." In *Sexuality and Theology: Classic and Contemporary Readings*, ed. Eugene F. Rogers, 309–21. Oxford: Blackwell, 2002.

Wilson, Nancy. *Our Tribe: Queer Folks, God, Jesus, and the Bible*. New York: HarperCollins, 1995.

Victor Anderson is the Oberlin Theology School Professor of Ethics and Society at Vanderbilt University. He is the author of *Beyond Ontological Blackness: An Essay in African American Religious Cultural Criticism* (1995), *Pragmatic Theology: Negotiating the Intersection of an American Philosophy of Religion and Public Theology* (1999), and *Creative Exchange: A Constructive Theology of African American Religious Experience* (2008).

Sister Carol Bernice, CHS, is a member of the Community of the Holy Spirit, a monastic community for women (so far!) in the Episcopal Church. She lives and works at the community's primary work/ministry, Bluestone Farm and Living Arts Center in Brewster, New York. (www.chssisters.org)

Teresa Delgado directs the Peace and Justice Studies Program and is Associate Professor of Religious Studies at Iona College in New Rochelle, New York. Her publications include "This Is My Body: Theological Anthropology Latina/mente," in *Frontiers of Catholic Feminist Theology: Shoulder to Shoulder* (2009); and "Dead in the Water . . . Again," in *Reinterpreting Virtues and Values in the U.S. Public Sphere: Life, Liberty, and the Pursuit of Happiness in Twenty-First Century United States* (forthcoming).

Yvette Flunder is the founder and bishop of the City of Refuge UCC in Oakland (www.sfrefuge.org). She is an ordained minister in the United Church of Christ, an internationally recognized preacher, and the author of *Where the Edge Gathers: Building a Community of Radical Inclusion* (2005).

Lynne Gerber is a postdoctoral scholar at the Religion, Politics, and Globalization Program at the University of California, Berkeley. She is the author of *Seeking the Straight and Narrow: Weight Loss and Sexual Reorientation in Evangelical America* (2011).

Jennifer Harvey is Associate Professor of Religion at Drake University in Des Moines, Iowa. She is the author of *Whiteness and Morality: Pursuing Racial Justice through Reparations and Sovereignty* (2007) and a coeditor of *Disrupting White Supremacy: White People on What* We *Need to Do* (2004).

Mary E. Hunt is cofounder and codirector of the Women's Alliance for Theology, Ethics and Ritual (WATER) in Silver Spring, Maryland. She is the editor of *A Guide for Women in Religion: Making Your Way from A to Z* (2004) and coeditor with Diann L. Neu of *New Feminist Christianity: Many Voices, Many Views* (2010).

David G. Hunter is the Cottrill-Rolfes Chair of Catholic Studies at the University of Kentucky. He has published widely in early Christian Studies, most notably *Marriage, Celibacy, and Heresy in Ancient Christianity: The Jovinianist Controversy* (2007) and the *Oxford Handbook of Early Christian Studies* (2008), coedited with Susan Ashbrook Harvey.

Nicholas Laccetti is studying for the Master of Divinity in theology at Union Theological Seminary in New York. His writing has appeared in publications such as *Killing the Buddha*.

Mark Larrimore is Associate Professor of Religious Studies at Eugene Lang College The New School for Liberal Arts. He is the editor of *The Problem of Evil: A Reader* (2001) and *The German Invention of Race* (with Sara Eigen, 2006) and author of *The Book of Job: A Biography* (2013).

Kathryn Lofton is Professor of Religious Studies, American Studies, History, and Divinity at Yale University. She is the author of *Oprah: Gospel of an Icon* (2011).

Elijah C. Nealy, MDiv, LCSW, is a licensed social worker with a clinical practice specializing in LGBT concerns. He is also a faculty member at the Columbia University School of Social Work. He provides frequent trainings on topics of gender identity/expression and has published numerous articles and book chapters.

Anthony M. Petro is Assistant Professor of modern Christianity at Boston University. He is the author of the forthcoming book *After the Wrath of God: AIDS, Sexuality, and American Religion*.

Michael F. Pettinger is Assistant Professor of Literary and Religious Studies at Eugene Lang College The New School for Liberal Arts. His research is focused on sexuality in the patristic period.

William E. Smith III holds a PhD in religious studies from Indiana University. He has published several articles and has a book chapter in *Marriage in Premodern Europe: Italy and Beyond* (2012).

Kathleen T. Talvacchia is Associate Dean for Academic and Student Affairs at New York University Graduate School of Arts and Science. Formerly, she was Associate Professor of Theology and Ministry at Union Theological Seminary in New York. She is the author of *Critical Minds and Discerning Hearts: A Spirituality of Multicultural Teaching* (2003).

Jon M. Walton is Senior Pastor of the First Presbyterian Church in the City of New York. He is the author of *Imperfect Peace: Teaching Sermons on Troubling Texts* (1999), as well as of numerous articles and sermons published in professional journals.

Heather R. White holds a PhD in religion and has written extensively on race and sexuality in the history of American religion. She is the author of the forthcoming book *American Churches and the Rise of Gay Rights*.